REFORMING THE WORLD BANK

In the many studies of the World Bank, a critical issue has been missed. While writers have looked at the Bank's political economy, lending, conditions, advice, ownership, and accounting for issues such as the environment, this study looks at the Bank as an *organization* – whether it is set up to do the job it is supposed to do and, if not, what should be done about it. This book is about the problems of organization and reorganization as much as it is about the problems of assisting third-world development, and it is a case study in flawed organizational reform as much as a critique of the way development assistance is managed. It covers the period that starts at the time of the first major reorganization, in 1987 under President Barber Conable, and ends at the time of the resignation of Paul Wolfowitz, in 2007, but it focuses especially on what happened during the tenure of James Wolfensohn.

David A. Phillips has spent many years in developing countries, especially in Africa. He is an economist who, after starting his career in multinational companies, turned his attention to the field of development, spending fourteen years at the World Bank Group and in recent years working as director of a private consulting firm based in the UK and United States. Dr. Phillips held a lectureship at the University of Bradford Development Center in the UK and was an official at the Commonwealth Secretariat in London. He has also lived and worked on an extended basis in Tanzania, Nepal, and Belarus, and especially in Africa and the former Soviet Union. Dr. Phillips has published journal papers on small business development and cost-benefit analysis.

Reforming the World Bank

Twenty Years of Trial – and Error

DAVID A. PHILLIPS

CAMBRIDGE
UNIVERSITY PRESS

CAMBRIDGE UNIVERSITY PRESS
Cambridge, New York, Melbourne, Madrid, Cape Town, Singapore, São Paulo, Delhi

Cambridge University Press
32 Avenue of the Americas, New York, NY 10013-2473, USA

www.cambridge.org
Information on this title: www.cambridge.org/9780521883054

First published 2009

Printed in the United States of America

A catalog record for this publication is available from the British Library.

Library of Congress Cataloging in Publication Data

Phillips, David A., 1946–
Reforming the World Bank : twenty years of trial and error / David A. Phillips
p. cm.
Includes bibliographical references and index.
ISBN 978-0-521-88035-4 (hardback)
1. World Bank. 2. Development banks. 3. Economic assistance. I. Title.

HG3881.5.W57P45   2008
332.1'532–dc22   2008045314

ISBN 978-0-521-88305-4 hardback

Contents

Preface

The Search for Effectiveness in the World's Premier Development Institution

Why write another book about the World Bank?

Many studies have been conducted and books have been written over the past few decades about the World Bank, which I refer to from here on as 'the Bank'.[1] But what has been written about up to now has largely missed a critical issue. Writers have been concerned mainly, and justifiably, with the Bank's external role within world development, that is, its political economy, its place within the process of globalization, the character of its lending, to whom it lends, what conditions it imposes, how far it accounts for socioeconomic concerns such as the natural environment, the kind of advice it gives, and, most recently, who should own it. This study, without ignoring the wealth of wider issues, looks at the Bank as an *organization*. That is, is it configured organizationally to

---

[1] Some major recent works focusing on the Bank include: Kapur, Devesh, J. Lewis, and R. Webb, *The World Bank: Its First Half Century*, Brookings, 1997; Gilbert, Christopher L. and David Vines, *The World Bank: Structure and Policies*, Cambridge University Press, 2000; Pincus, Jonathan R., and Jeffery A. Winters, *Reinventing the World Bank*, Cornell University Press, 2002; Easterly, William, *The Elusive Quest for Growth: An Economist's Adventures and Misadventures in the Tropics*, MIT, 2001; Easterly, William, *The White Man's Burden: Why the West's Efforts to Aid the Rest Have Done So Much Ill and So Little Good*, Penguin, 2006; Mallaby, Sebastian, *The World's Banker: A Story of Failed States, Financial Crises, and the Wealth and Poverty of Nations*, Penguin, 2004; Ritzen, Josef, *A Chance for the World Bank*, Anthem, 2005; Buira, Axel, ed., *Reforming the Governance of the IMF and the World Bank*, Anthem, 2005; Woods, Ngaire, *The Globalizers: The IMF, the World Bank and Their Borrowers*, Cornell Studies in Money, Cornell University Press, March 2006; Birdsall, Nancy, ed., *Rescuing the World Bank: A CGD Working Group Report and Selected Essays'*, Center for Global Development, 2006; and Wolfensohn, James, *A Global Life: My Journey among Rich and Poor, from Wall Street to the World Bank*, Public Affairs Press, 2008 (forthcoming).

do the job it is supposed to do and, if not, what should be done about it? In particular, the question is whether the *reorganizations* that have taken place over about the past twenty years have made the Bank more capable of doing the job it is supposed to do, as they have each laid claim. This book is thus about the problems of organization and reorganization as much as it is about the problems of assisting third-world development, and perhaps it would serve as a case study in organizational reform as much as a critique of the way development assistance is conceived and managed. The period that the story covers starts at about the time of the first major reorganization, which took place in 1987 under President Barber Conable, and ends at about the time of the resignation of Paul Wolfowitz, the tenth president, in 2007.

During fourteen years working in the operations side of the Bank from 1987 to 2001, I, like many others, often had questions about the way the organization was being run, but I was not in the right place, nor did I have the time or the understanding, to answer them. I was managing Bank projects and studies in Africa and the former Soviet Republics, mainly in Tanzania, Mozambique, Belarus, and Armenia, with occasional sorties outside. It was a demanding task to navigate continuously through the conflicting and sometimes counterintuitive internal organizational and external pressures and requirements, to try to arrive at an effective solution for matters on the ground. Generally, I spent my time heavily engaged in what I was supposed to do rather than in questioning how or why I did it. Yet answers were needed more and more, especially as the organization went though increasingly complicated changes, and so I finally decided, when I left, to see if I could tell a story that I thought needed to be told and arrive at some answers that needed to be arrived at. Perhaps the answers I come to will inform other organizations similar to the Bank.

To try to find these answers I particularly focus on the reorganization that took place under James D. Wolfensohn, who was appointed to the Bank's presidency by President Bill Clinton in 1995 and who departed in 2005. The reorganization that he presided over is now in the past, but its effects live on. Paul Wolfowitz, during his short tenure from 2005 to 2007, did not have time to effect substantive additional changes to the organization, but those steps he did take built largely on foundations already established by Wolfensohn. Robert Zoellick, who succeeded to the office in 2007, has been developing an agenda as this is written.

Why is it important to ask this question about 'organization'? The answer is that the World Bank is a key global institution, and it is the prototype of all the other public international financial institutions, which, although smaller, have similar organizational features and similar capital and governance structures and do similar kinds of financing and advising. The efficient organization of the World Bank is important in the efficient delivery of foreign assistance and also in how effective that assistance is on the ground, which is the ultimate objective of delivering it. Effective development assistance also requires good organization within international financial institutions as a whole. The lack of effectively organized, as well as broadly owned and controlled, financial institutions will increase the probability of a splintering of world economic governance into geopolitical blocs as wealth increases outside the Organization of Economic Cooperation and Development (OECD) countries as a result of Eastern economic strength and high oil prices.

The Bank was a child of America's postwar foreign policy and a testament to the internationalist attitudes of the time. It is located in the capital city of the United States, Washington, DC, and has been a leader in, and a lightning rod for, criticism of the place of foreign economic aid in the world. In a world where globalization is a fait accompli, through the cross-border diffusion of products, capital, labor, and technology, there are still not enough truly global organizations that are mandated to, or capable of, dealing with multinational economic challenges, that is, those that cannot or will not be dealt with by private interests or national governments, and those that exist need to work properly. After years of costly and time-consuming reforms, is there any reason to believe that it now does?

This study is critical of what the reforms achieved. It is an on-the-ground examination of things that were generally not done right. Sometimes it is dismissive, but it does not question the existence of the institution. On the contrary, it is because, as a global institution, its role is probably now more important than ever, that defects in its makeup, and some of the history behind them, are worth understanding. Nor do I critique the actions of individuals per se, because that is not relevant. I try to maintain a balance, but my focus is on explaining the things that went wrong and why they went wrong, the problems that need to be fixed, not those that do not. Perhaps there is no need to pile on more pressure. But the more fully the issues are set out, the more chance there is that someone will be motivated constructively to take up the challenge of creating an effective organization that might serve as a better model for others as well.

Since the 1940s, the industrialized world has accepted that it has a responsibility to try to share the benefits of economic development with economies that have for various reasons not made much progress on the development ladder, in its own interests as well as those of the poorer countries themselves. But accepting such a responsibility, I believe, has not meant that industrialized countries are actually in a good position to assist them. In the past, some more extreme development pessimists even held that the rich countries by their very existence could not help poor countries because they preempted economic progress in those poor countries. There was a tendency, they thought, whereby rich countries increasingly monopolized worldwide resources and trade and entrenched a widening technological gap, which in turn increased their lead and the dependence of poorer countries on supplying materials to them and buying goods from them, making catch-up ever more difficult.[2] But the facts of the past few years suggest that at least in major parts of the once-very-poor world, like East Asia and now parts of China and India, this is not so, and the most pessimistic view does not hold true, except, at least up to now, in some of the most marginalized economies of the world, for example, in regions of Africa. Thus the most serious pessimism about development has proved wrong.

Nevertheless, while worldwide economic development is possible, this does not mean that effective aid for development is possible. After sixty years it is still not clear that rich countries actually know how best to assist poor countries. If there is doubt about whether economic assistance can be effective at all, then there is not much point in dwelling on the possibility of improving the effectiveness of economic assistance organizations,

---

[2] For an example of this view see Frank, Andre Gundar, 'Capitalism and Underdevelopment in Latin America,' *Monthly Review Press*, 1968.

whether they be the Bank or any other international financial institution. It might be better to close them down. So I want to start by considering this point further before moving ahead.

On recent projections, made before the 2008 food price increases, the number of people living in the worst poverty (less than $1 per day) will fall from 1.2 billion (28% of the world's population) in 1990 to about 620 million (10%) in 2015.[3] This is largely due to the awakening of the Indian and Chinese economies. But in Africa, in other parts of South Asia, in Central Asia, and in Latin America things have not generally improved. For forty countries, in which 900 million people live, poverty has continued to increase.[4] Infant mortality rates and primary school enrollment have improved everywhere, but they still remain bad in sub-Saharan Africa, where less than 60% of children complete primary school and nearly one in five still dies in early childhood. The situation has worsened with the world food shortages of 2008. Poverty is also based on an arbitrary measure. If the poverty line threshold was raised from $1 a day to $2 a day, then 1.9 billion people in Asia alone are in poverty, 30 percent of humanity, so there obviously remains a huge problem, and it is not certain whether development assistance can provide the solution.[5]

Former Bank economist Bill Easterly[6] wrote that economists are no closer than they were fifty years ago to figuring out how to accomplish the basic mission of making a poor economy grow. 'The genuine success stories, where poor countries have achieved long-term growth, have been pitifully few', he said. 'And in some of these it's far from clear that Bank

---

[3] Although this claim has been challenged as underestimating poverty and overestimating its rate of decline. Reddy, Sanjay G. and Pogge, Thomas, 'Shooting the Messenger of Good News: A Critical Look at the World Bank's Success Story of Effective Aid', *Third World Economics*, No. 287 (16–31 August 2002).

[4] A discussion of who are the poorest and why is in Collier, Paul, *The Bottom Billion – Why the Poorest Countries Are Failing and What Can Be Done About It*, Oxford University Press, 2007. Collier proposes that foreign aid should be concentrated in countries facing defined 'poverty traps'.

[5] In fact the World Bank reported in August 2008 that, as of 2005, 1.4 billion people were living under a revised poverty line of $1.25 a day.

[6] In *The Elusive Quest for Growth*, op cit, Easterly argued that many of the assumptions of the Bank and other donors about effective aid are fallacious – e.g., the relationship between growth and investment; the relationship between growth and education; and the relationship between growth and reform lending.

aid was a major factor, or even any factor at all'. Despite 'sixty years of countless reform schemes and dozens of different plans, the aid industry is still failing to reach the beautiful goal (of making poverty history)'. [7]

At an important Conference on Finance and Development in Monterrey in 2002, the Bank argued for the doubling of aid to $100 billion a year.[8] It cited success stories that included, for example, China, India, Poland, Uganda, Vietnam, and Mozambique.[9] But total aid to China, one of the greatest success stories, had only been 0.4% of its gross domestic product (GDP) (2 to 3% of investment) and it had paid little attention to the policy reform prescriptions of the Bank and the International Monetary Fund (IMF). So it cannot be claimed that external aid had anything to do with China's economic growth. Similarly, India received only 0.7% of its GDP in aid and has also been growing successfully, as has Poland, which got 1.5%. On the other hand, there were several other former socialist economies, like Moldova and Kyrgyzstan, which got more aid, and their economies declined. Mozambique and Uganda did well, but they were exceptions among fifty-four low-income countries that averaged zero per capita growth. Zambia received large inflows of aid and had minus 2% growth in the 1990s. Aid to African countries has been quite a large proportion of their economies, and in general they have followed the Bank and IMF prescriptions more closely but have grown very slowly, stagnated, or declined.

Revisiting this negative correlation between aid and economic growth, researchers found that aid is still effective in countries with good institutions and good policies, including macroeconomic stability, fiscal discipline, trade openness, private property rights, and the rule of law – that is, mainly in relatively well-organized economies. It has had a poor record in countries with poor institutions and policies.[10] Further research then showed that, within the

---

[7] Easterly, William, *The White Man's Burden*, op cit.
[8] 'The Role and Effectiveness of Development Assistance', World Bank, March 2002.
[9] Easterly, William, *Washington Post*, March 14, 2002.
[10] For example Collier, Paul and David Dollar, 'Can the World Cut Poverty by Half? How Policy Reform and Effective Aid Can Meet International Development Goals', *World Development* 29(11), 2001; Dollar, David and Aart Kray, 'Growth Is Good for the Poor', World Bank discussion paper, February 2000.

good-policy category, high-aid-to-GDP economies grew faster than low-aid-to-GDP economies,[11] which would provide the justification for continuing to provide aid. However, the finding that there was a high correlation between aid and growth in 'good-policy' countries was itself challenged and then resurrected by other researchers. There was found to be a correlation between certain types of short-term directed assistance and growth, but this was also challenged and then resurrected.[12]

But whatever the merits of the see-sawing research findings, the suggestion that good-policy countries should be getting more foreign aid is odd. After all, strong-institution/good-policy countries do well because they tend to use *all* their resources more efficiently (e.g., capital, technology, skills, and natural resources), whether local or foreign, aid or investment. They are also more likely to have a culture and societal expectations that favor economic growth. Thus, many good-policy countries may tend not to face a foreign resource constraint. They may well be able to use foreign aid money in a beneficial way, but they may not need it. On the other hand, economies that have poor institutions and organizations tend to use all their resources poorly, not just foreign aid. These economies are the ones that, conservatives argue, become 'hooked' on aid, like welfare, to no useful effect, and should therefore not get it, except maybe as humanitarian assistance. Thus, countries with good institutions and policies do well with or without aid and they do not really need help, but they 'deserve it'; countries with poor institutions and policies do poorly with or without aid and they do really need help, but do not deserve it.

---

[11] *Assessing Aid*, World Bank, 1998, p. 14.

[12] Easterly provides a blow-by-blow account of the evolution of aid and growth research in *White Man's Burden*, op cit, pp. 38–57. Another problem facing foreign aid in the countries where it does play a major role is the so-called Dutch disease effect. As an illustration, in his farewell speech on October 31, 2001, one executive director, Valeriano Garcia, from Argentina, made the following statement: '[T]he Bank should take a new look at the effect of ODA (aid) on development. ... ODA has the effect of appreciating the exchange rate, reducing export capacity; is negatively correlated with the rate of growth and negatively correlated with the country's savings rate ... (what are we really financing in a World of fungible money?)'.

These points might well lead to a degree of aid-pessimism – that foreign aid really has little role to play in the grand scheme of things, that aid donors assisting good-policy, emerging economies really do little more than add to the general applause, while in low-income, poor-policy countries they may rush about energetically but for little purpose and at high cost. This is not a matter of pessimism about development, that is, the ability of the people of a country to help themselves with better social organization, political stability, institutions, and knowledge – not at all, because development has shown itself to be possible worldwide. It is pessimism only about the effect of subsidized outside assistance often based on outside initiatives and outside prescriptions.

But foreign aid has also shown some good results, at least on a more micro scale, for example, in areas like education and health. Australian aid doubled school enrollment in Papua New Guinea. Oral rehydration therapy provided by the United States reduced by 82% infant deaths from diarrhea in Egypt in the 1970s.[13] The elimination of river blindness in Niger was a significant achievement of the World Health Organization (WHO) and other agencies, helped by Bank money. There are numerous examples of cases where specific, well-targeted bits of advice or funding paid off through successful capacity changes or effective infrastructure in the recipient countries. Even the best-run business and the best-run economy can and does certainly gain from specific outside advice and specific investments and technology acquisition.[14]

The aid-optimistic view is represented by, among others, Jeffery Sachs,[15] who has written: '[T]he time to end poverty has arrived, although the hard work lies ahead. ... I have shown that the costs of action are small and indeed a tiny fraction of the costs of inaction. I have identified a timetable to 2025, including the Millennium

---

[13] Levine, Ruth and Molly Kinder, *Millions Saved: Proven Successes in Global Health*, Center for Global Development, 2005.

[14] Riddell, Roger, *Does Foreign Aid Really Work?* Oxford, 2007, is an exhaustive examination of the role of foreign aid, which concludes with reservations that it can be effective given changes in its delivery mechanism. For example, he recommends an international aid fund to circumvent the adverse effects of national interests on aid policy and allocation.

[15] Sachs, Jeffrey, *The End of Poverty – Economic Possibilities for Our Time*, Penguin, 2005.

Development Goals, as a mid-way station in 2015'. Further, he writes that the world community should commit to those goals and its leaders should adopt a specific global plan to meet them. Nicholas Stern, the Bank's former chief economist, is another aid-optimist. He believes that the understanding of how to deliver effective aid has improved in the past decade, especially as a result of the emphasis on capacity- and institution-building. '[W]hen we use what we have learned, aid works', he writes. 'The time is right for rich countries and developing countries to enter into a deep and lasting partnership to promote development and build a more inclusive world'.[16]

For our purposes here, we take a very cautious aid-optimist's view, that at least some foreign assistance can have a beneficial impact, if it is responding to the right needs in the right places, is conceived intelligently for additional benefit, and is implemented well. Thus, if we accept first that worldwide economic development is possible, and second that some form of assistance by rich countries to the poorest countries is needed to help them follow China and the other industrializing economies, then it is necessary to find ways to bring it about. This is likely to require global collective action, and global action requires effective global institutions. The Bank, and the other parallel public sector institutions, have to show that they can be cost-effective providers of 'public goods', and that they deal equitably with their client countries. The rest of this study thus concentrates on how the effectiveness of key existing assistance infrastructures can be improved rather than whether assistance should be given at all.

For sixty years, therefore, the Bank has been a key part of the infrastructure of assistance – a global financier, adviser, advocate, and, by intent, honest broker in international development. It has provided large amounts of loans and subsidized credit and now grants to its members, and each year it provides an additional $20 billion or more, an amount as large, or larger, than the gross national income of many small countries. Increasingly it has also acted as a provider of know-how.

---

[16] Stern, Nicholas, 'The Role and Effectiveness of Development Assistance,' in *A Case for Aid: Building Consensus for Development Assistance*, Ed. Stern, Nicholas and Wolfensohn, James D., United Nations International Conference on Financing for Development, World Bank, 2002.

It holds billions of dollars in assets and in debts to others, and it employs thousands of people. Its assets and its know-how are a resource that it holds in trust, and it is the world community's interest to hold accountable organizations that retain its trust, because of the money it manages, the advice that it gives, and the policies that it promotes on behalf of the world. This study is about the deployment of this capacity.

I have organized the study into three main parts. Part I contains two chapters that set out the role and achievements of the Bank since its founding, and the critique of it that developed. The second part contains seven chapters that form the bulk of the story. It starts with a brief review of the history of organizational reform within the Bank leading up to the 1990s reforms, and then it focuses on the reforms that took place in the late 1990s under James Wolfensohn and a little beyond, and the extent to which they succeeded or failed.

The story of these reforms covers the main changes – in organizational structure, culture, people, skills, development products, and their effectiveness; and it considers the financial underpinnings of the reforms. Part II concludes with a chapter examining reasons why most reforms did not succeed.

Part III looks ahead. In doing so, it focuses on two ingredients of reform that I believe are critical but which were essentially ignored in the reform process that actually took place, and which remain central parts of a continuing unmet agenda. They relate to governance. That is, the reform of the Bank's boards of governors and directors, and the reform of its leadership. Serious change in both these areas is the *sine qua non* for effective reform and the creation of a better organization in the future, in the Bank and perhaps in other international financial institutions.

Finally, this book went to press just as the 2008 financial crisis broke, but it might be worth saying a few words about its relevance. In fact, the World Bank is not a factor in the crisis, because of the nature of its assets – that is, long-term loans guaranteed by borrower goverments, and its liabilities, fully backed by its owner governments, as there will be occasion to discuss later. On the other hand, the crisis will tend to enhance the role of the Bank, in support of its partner institution, the IMF, as a source of investment funding and as an architect of a new international financial stabilization framework.

I want to thank many people for their help in writing this book. In particular I want to thank Alan Roe, a former Bank staff member and a senior faculty member at Warwick University, UK, whose comments were invaluable to the delivery of this study. I also want to thank Scott Parris of Cambridge University Press, who was the main editor; David Cook, Steve Denning, and Sri Ram Aiyer, former senior staff of the Bank, for reading and commenting on early drafts; and David Vines of Oxford University, who also commented at length. Other anonymous reviewers also provided me with useful guidance, and numerous others discussed particular topics or helped with clarifications on particular points along the way. None of these individuals is responsible in any way for my views or errors. Finally, I want to thank Nadya, without whose patience and support I could not have completed the long journey to finish this project; Joshua and Josephine, who helpfully distracted my attention at critical moments; and Caroline and Jacqui for their continuous moral support from afar.

REFORMING THE WORLD BANK

PART I

ORIGINS AND EVOLUTION

1

What Does the World Bank Do and
How Does It Do It?

BRIEF ORIGINS

The World Bank, in the form of the International Bank for Reconstruction and Development (IBRD), was founded at an international conference at Bretton Woods, New Hampshire, in 1944. Its purpose was to move toward the creation of a framework for world economic governance. The conference had been called, largely at the initiative of the United States, to work out a system for global economic stabilization following the depression of the 1930s and for reconstruction after the Second World War. Forty-four governments, including the USSR, attended.

The architects of the new system were, principally, Harry Dexter White, U.S. Treasury Secretary Morgenthau's chief economist, and legendary British economist John Maynard Keynes. At Bretton Woods, White took charge of the proposals for monetary stabilization. An outstanding intellect who authored the proposals that he hoped would help save the world from more wars, he was later brought before Senator McCarthy's Unamerican Activities Committee. Keynes, the leader of the UK delegation, had separately come up with his own ideas of a central bank for the world. However, he went along with the American plan, and he assumed responsibility, with reluctance, for running the discussions on the Bank.[1]

The initial focus at Bretton Woods was on the stabilization of the world economy, and the conference proposed the establishment of

---

[1] Keynes' many misgivings about the arrangements, invitees, and agenda for the conference are portrayed in Skidelsky, Robert, *John Maynard Keynes: Fighting for Freedom, 1937–1946*, Penguin Books, 2002, pp. 340, 347 et al.

the International Monetary Fund (IMF) as the center of the system. The World Bank, that is, the IBRD, was at the time the secondary concern and subject to less scrutiny. It was at the behest of the United States that it finally saw the light of day. This and its large financial contribution meant that the United States was allowed the main say in its design, including its location (the UK and others had pressed for it to be located outside the United States or else in New York), the role of its directors, the selection of its president, and the salary levels of its staff.[2] The British had wanted non-resident outside directors, while the United States wanted in-house executive directors to monitor the managers. Keynes thought the U.S.-proposed salaries were 'scandalous'; board directors were to get salaries of $17,000 a year, more than the U.S. vice president and more than five times as much as a British Member of Parliament. In terms of its governance, and staffing, it was a creature of U.S. design. The special status for its employees was deliberate and contrasted with its Washington neighbors in Congress and the federal government.

The Articles of Agreement, which were adopted at Bretton Woods, stated[3] that the IBRD's objectives were to provide assistance to governments. It was to assist in reconstruction and development by facilitating investment for productive purposes; to promote private foreign investment through guarantees or participations in loans and investments and to supplement private investment if unavailable at reasonable cost from the private sector; to promote the long-term balance and growth of international trade and payments; to coordinate priorities with other international lending agencies; and to assist in bringing about a smooth transition to a peacetime economy.

The IBRD started business in 1946, and its inaugural governors meeting was held in Savannah, Georgia, in March. There, its bylaws were adopted; its board of directors elected; and Washington, DC, confirmed as its location. Eugene Meyer, owner of the *Washington Post* and a Wall Street banker, took over as the first president in June. In September, at its first annual meeting, it had thirty-eight members and a staff of just seventy-two. It started slowly. Its first loan, for US$250 million, was to

---

[2] For a further account of these events see Mason, Edward S. and Robert E. Asher, *The World Bank Since Bretton Woods*, Brookings, 1973.

[3] IBRD Articles of Agreement, Article 1, pp. 1–2.

the French government in May 1947, a year after it formally started operations and when it was already into the term of its second president, John McCloy. The Bank became a specialized agency of the UN, which was itself founded in San Francisco in 1945, and its employees carry a UN laissez-passer. However, it has avoided close identification with the UN, distancing itself from the UN's ECOSOC, the committee of the UN General Assembly that should in principle oversee its work. By this and other means the Bank endeavored to maintain an independence of action and a special status as the leading agency in the financing of development.

Sixty years on, the Bank's membership has increased to 185, so that it now accounts for all but a handful of the world's nations. During its life, under the leadership of eleven presidents, it has managed the transfer of more than $500 billion of investment resources to the poor world, loans for development and for crisis assistance. Its lending steadily increased up to the late 1990s and broadened continually into new fields. It gained the confidence of and successfully raised a large amount of money from the private financial markets at low rates of interest, and it pioneered new financial instruments including derivatives. It has broadened its range of lending products and developed its advocacy platform. It also manages billions of dollars of Trust Fund money on behalf of other donor agencies.

The IBRD, which remains the major lending arm of the Bank Group, currently holds outstanding loans of about $100 billion. It has averaged more than US$1 billion per annum in profit since its foundation, which has allowed it to make grants to other organizations including the International Development Association (IDA), its soft loan partner that lends to the poorest countries (with national income per head of less than $865 a year, or $2.36 a day, at 2004 prices).[4] The IDA itself carries a similar level of assets, in the form of soft loans and grants.[5]

---

[4] The World Bank Group also consists of several other organizations. In addition to the IFC, these include the Multilateral Investment Guarantee Agency (MIGA), the International Center for Investment Disputes (ICSID), and the Center for International Agricultural Research (CGIAR).

[5] The value of the IDA's annual lending has been less, about two-thirds of that of the IBRD in recent years. However, its outstanding loans have recently grown to exceed those of the IBRD because of their longer average term (40 years as opposed to 16). Against this the IDA has recently started to forgive debt, resulting in a fall in the value of its outstanding loans.

Neither the IBRD nor the IDA has ever suffered from borrower defaults of any major significance, and, by its own account, the Bank has maintained a satisfactory project success rate, with steady improvement for the past twelve years.

These are impressive achievements, and equally impressive is the Bank's prize-winning, cathedral-like atrium entrance built in the 1990s, which reflects such achievements, with photographic displays of village children and energetic development activity, and the sculpture of a child leading an old man suffering from River Blindness, a scourge that Bank money helped to stamp out in large parts of West Africa. This atrium hosts every year a kind of bazaar called the Development Market Place, which for a few million dollars in prizes, successfully mobilizes thousands of small-scale development project ideas worldwide. In 2002, shortly after the Development Market Place was invented, the *Harvard Business Review* described it as 'nothing short of a miracle'.[6]

WHAT DOES THE BANK DO AND WHAT SHOULD IT DO?

The rationale for a public sector international financing institution like the Bank remains fundamentally a simple one. It has to meet a social (public goods) necessity that the private sector will not meet – that is, it has to address market failures, or market gaps, and it has to address them in relation to world development. The evolution of the market failures or gaps addressed by the Bank could be conceived as having gone through three stages. First, the problem was seen as a general capital deficiency. Second, it was seen as a structural one involving capital deficiency but with a related skill/know-how deficiency. Third, it came to be seen as largely a problem of indigenous capacity, know-how, and 'information', with capital scarcity only applicable to the more marginal, poorest economies, within a complex set of resource scarcities.

---

[6]   Robert Chapman Wood and Gary Hamel, in the *Harvard Business Review* of November 2002, wrote, '[T]he development marketplace has laid to rest the broadly held suspicion that large organizations are incapable of grass roots innovation'. The marketplace is being extended to some of the Bank's overseas offices.

As the rationale for public intervention in imperfect markets, or the provision of public goods, has broadened out, so has the realization that a specifically global development institution should be developing its long-term rationale not in the general category of public goods, but rather in global public goods, that is, in failing global markets.[7] Such goods include vaccines, food security, environmental protection, and global climate initiatives. The category also includes the creation of new worldwide markets such as for carbon trading. These are goods and services whose supply requires collective global action. In the long run, therefore, it might be expected that the Bank would increase its focus on these types of products.

During most of the past century, market failure was regarded as an inevitable constraining factor on economic development, and consequently the public sector was regarded as playing an important, if not a critical, role. For example, the experience of the 1930s depression, the loss of trust in the financial system, and the New Deal era in the United States lent considerable weight to arguments about the imperfections of financial markets. It was a time of central controls – fixed exchange rates, trade barriers, capital controls, and very little external private lending or investment in poorer countries. The tasks of reconstruction and development, and the stabilization of the world economy, were ones that par excellence were thought by mainstream economists to be impossible if left to private enterprise, because developing economy markets were thought to be beset by structural problems that discouraged the right type or quantity of private investment.[8] In 1956, the Nobel Laureate Gunnar Myrdal wrote that '[S]pecial advisers to underdeveloped countries who have taken the time and trouble to acquaint themselves with the problem . . . all recommend central planning as the first condition of progress'.[9] While the

---

[7] Global public goods are those that, once produced, provide net benefits to their consumers and users that are greater than could be gained by a private investor or an individual country, and so justify international public provision.

[8] This does not mean that there were no opponents of public intervention, even in the case of structural impediments. One of the most notable was Peter T. Bauer, a professor at the London School of Economics, in *Economic Analysis and Policy in Under-developed Countries*, Cambridge University Press, 1957; and *Dissent on Development: Studies and Debates in Development Economics*, Weidenfeld & Nicolson, 1971.

[9] Myrdal, Gunnar, *An International Economy: Problems and Prospects*, Harper & Bros, 1956.

need for central planning itself was hardly supported in the West, benign public intervention through market regulation was broadly accepted.[10]

How did the Bank's product menu evolve to meet the deficiencies in markets?

With its planned role in postwar reconstruction, the primary purpose of the Bank at the start was to provide finance or guarantees to a capital-constrained world economy. Initially it acted as a reconstruction financier in Europe. It soon moved on during the 1950s to assume a general infrastructure and industry financing role to governments in poorer economies. As it shifted its priorities to developing economies, the needs came to be perceived as beyond finance, incorporating wider problems of economic structure and growth. For this reason the IDA, the Bank's soft loan arm, was established. Nevertheless, the key factor was still regarded as finance, to fill savings and investment gaps, in accordance with then-conceived growth models. Capital went to large infrastructure projects such as telecommunications and power, and to industry.

The role of the Bank, the IBRD and the IDA, evolved to become considerably more complex over the next decades. It diversified into different sectors of lending outside infrastructure, including social sectors, support to economic reform, capacity, and institution-building lending. It incorporated technical assistance projects, advisory services, training, research, and advocacy.

The initial emphasis on large infrastructure projects shifted during the presidency of Robert McNamara (1968–1981) in response to the increasing belief that growth and large investments alone were not addressing the problem of poverty, and that direct, redistributional assistance to the rural and urban poor was needed, in terms of both finance and know-how.

The paradigm shifted further in the 1980s, which were dominated by the issues of debt and adjustment and restoration of private capital flows to developing countries. There was a move away from project lending to macroeconomic adjustment and program lending to

---

[10] Bauer, however, wrote for forty years about misconceptions of central planning and state interference in development.

accommodate this. This was the era of the so-called Washington Consensus on macroeconomic balance and growth.[11] While international debt was a dominant issue at this time, this no longer implied a pure capital constraint. Rather, indebtedness was seen as a function of a combination of excessive borrowing and inattention to macroeconomic management and capacity building. By now capital market imperfections were seen as applicable more narrowly. The Bank's offshoot, the International Finance Corporation (IFC), addressed one of the narrower needs, the development of emerging equity markets.

The resolution of the 1980s debt problems enabled the private banks to resume lending to the developing world, and World Bank lending per se became less important as the international capital market opened up. Bank lending was reduced to a very small component of international financing. While capital market cycles still created intermittent needs for international public institution financing, generally the international capital market was substantially different from what it was in 1945.

As the capital market constraints eased, concern with know-how and information market constraints emerged. Under President James Wolfensohn there was an overt shift with the 1996 announcement of the 'knowledge bank', toward capacity building and knowledge creation, and with it a shift from infrastructure and macroeconomic adjustment projects into institution building, market regulation, legal reform, and anti-corruption measures. At the turn of the millennium funding of investment per se remained a core rationale only in the more marginalized economies, and here increasingly it is in the form of grants linked to capacity building. Knowledge development came to be seen as a key role of the Bank, on a par with financing.

Thus, over the last quarter of the twentieth century, culminating in the collapse of the Soviet Union, the assumptions about the need for public investment were diluted or shifted, although the belief that the public sector still had an investment role in transitional economies was reflected in the establishment of the European Bank for Reconstruction

---

[11] The term 'the Washington Consensus' was originally coined in 1989 by John Williamson of the Institute for International Economics, to describe the basic elements of liberalization reform that were accepted by major donors.

and Development (EBRD), as late as 1991, to finance the rehabilitation of the former Eastern bloc states.

What about the provision of global public goods (GPGs)? The initial Bank focus on large infrastructure development provided such goods to the extent that the private sector and national governments would not have been prepared or able to finance waterways, dams, and power stations critical to international development. However, most of the work that the Bank has done up to now has not been for global interests, but for national governments, and the GPG rationale has been promoted rather late in the day. Work is now being stepped up in areas such as climate change, environmental degradation, and communicable diseases. It is also being carried out in knowledge-intensive areas such as the infrastructure for international financial stability and in the creation of completely new markets such as the carbon trade.

While the product menu has broadened considerably, the Bank's output can still be thought of, however, as consisting of two basic products – financing and information. In the first case it has diversified over time from the provision of loans at semi-commercial interest rates, into soft loans, and, more recently, into outright grants to finance development projects in poorer countries. In the second case it has provided advice, information, and analysis, supported by its relatively large research department, and this knowledge output has also evolved over time from a focus on technical project issues to country economic policy, and in more recent years to proactive advocacy on world economic problems. Its research and advice have provided a forum for development thinking and technical know-how, and provided training for many developing country professionals.

The allocation of the Bank's resources between financing and information or knowledge creating is a key determining factor in the Bank's role as a development assistance organization and is also a potentially critical factor in its financial sustainability because knowledge generation does not generally pay for itself. This has led to some recent reversion from knowledge creation back to large-scale lending. The split between money and knowledge is in fact quite complex, since, to a degree, money leverages knowledge by providing it with a transmission vehicle and a high profile in the eyes of the governments that approve projects. Thus the role of finance in the Bank's production line is likely to remain important regardless of how far knowledge generation is elevated to priority status.

HOW IMPORTANT IS THE BANK?

The Bank's diversification away from financing has reduced its importance in international finance. Even during its major lending expansion, under McNamara, its contribution to total international resource flows was not more than 5%. Private flows from banks, investors, suppliers, and migrant labor are dominant. The Bank Group was in the top ten of individual global financiers from its early days up into the 1970s. However, as the world recovered from the 1980s debt crisis there was a boom in private lending and investment, starting in 1992 and resuming after the Asian economic crisis, and it now accounts for about 85% of total capital flowing to developing countries, mainly in the form of direct investments in foreign enterprises and portfolio investments.[12] Private migrant labor remittances (to countries like Mexico, India, and the Philippines) are also now worth far more than official aid, well over $100 billion a year, and that is only the amount reported. The Bank has also fallen to nearer fiftieth place in the league of lending institutions.

Thus, the Bank is providing a reducing proportion of official funds, and a very small proportion of the developing world's investment. Only in Africa, which gets a tiny proportion of private investment, does official aid still play an important part, exceeding the amount of private finance. In Africa workers' remittances are also still a relatively small proportion of the total amount of money coming in. Countries like Mozambique remain aid-dependent.

Given its relatively small role in the financial market, the level of concern by the stakeholders with what the Bank does with its money can be somewhat excessive. More important has been the leverage it has exercised, and indeed expected, over its client country economic

---

[12] Source: 'Global Development Finance: Mobilizing Finance and Managing Vulnerability', World Bank, 2005.

policies and its expanding role as policy adviser, know-how provider, and advocate on poor country issues.

WHO GOVERNS THE BANK?

The design of the Bank (IBRD) governance structure derived from three important influences: the 1930s depression, the suspicion of Wall Street within the Roosevelt/Truman administration, and the paternalistic notions of late-stage colonialism. The experience of the depression resulted in the need to make its capital base extremely secure. The concept of a bank dedicated to lending to quasi-insolvent governments did not go down well on Wall Street in the 1940s, since the depression had been a time of frequent defaults on sovereign bonds of both developing and industrialized countries. Nevertheless, the administration's suspicion of Wall Street resulted in an attempt to distance the Bank from it geographically and to put governments rather than financiers in charge of it. A board voting structure was created that was heavily weighted toward the OECD countries, which initially received 70% of the voting shares. A further provision was that amendments to the Articles would require a supermajority of 80% of the vote. Thus 20% of the voting shares constituted a blocking percentage, and the United States was the only country to have this shareholding (initially 35%).

Initially, the IBRD had lent mainly to its own OECD members (France, The Netherlands, Luxembourg, and Denmark in 1947–1948). In this sense it acted as a type of cooperative savings association.[13] The expansion of its membership resulted in its transformation from a cooperative into an agency in which the small number of part 1 members (donors) lent money to the large number of part 2 members (the poorer economies). A recent movement toward a wider voting representation by the poorer is a sign of a return to the association model, and at the same time a possible move beyond the OECD domination of the institution.

The way the Bank is governed is most important to understanding the way it behaves. There are a number of groups, beyond government and

---

[13] See Birdsall, N., ed., *Rescuing the World Bank: A CGD Working Group Report and Selected Essays*, op cit., pp. 74–75. Birdsall describes the IBRD at this point as a 'global club'.

financiers, that have an interest in the Bank as their 'agent'. The spectrum of interested parties consists of lenders, shareholders, and informal activist groups. Each group can be divided into different interest subgroups. While in theory each shareholder subscribes to the objective of economic development and poverty reduction, each in practice might have different objectives. Compounding this problem of multiple interests are the uncertain development instruments, that is, the lack of clear understanding on how to assist development. This is very different from a commercial corporation making a product where the objectives are clear – produce with the least-cost technology, sell, and make a profit.

The multiple interests include borrower shareholders who might pursue the objective of reducing interest rates, loan conditions, and lender interference, and donor shareholders who might be trying to increase loan conditions and interference in order to satisfy their political constituencies back home. The Bank's creditors' main objective is that their bonds retain their value and get repaid on time, so they are concerned about financial profits and security. The United States can be singled out because it is the largest shareholder, it has the most active physical presence within and around the Bank, and it has treated it much more as a vehicle for its foreign policy objectives than the other members, and the U.S. positions are themselves affected by a wide assortment of interests inside and outside the U.S. Congress.

The shareholders are represented through the board of governors, 24 individuals representing the 185 countries, on which 5 (the G5) are permanently represented by their own governor. The governors make the ultimate policy decisions but only meet twice a year. They in turn delegate most of their powers to executive directors. The executive directors are in permanent residence and are somehow sandwiched between the governors and the Bank's top management, which can in turn talk directly to the governors. The multi-polar communications network compounds the problem of multiple objectives and uncertain means to meet those objectives.

The activists (for example, the non-government organizations) are an informal force that, especially during the presidency of James Wolfensohn, managed to gain a large voice in Bank decisions, especially on debt reduction and the environment. They represent varied interests, ranging from those of the rich country taxpayers who ultimately fund the Bank and guarantee its loans, to the poor country citizens whose escape from poverty and whose social and environmental well-being are supposed to be main concerns of the Bank. The activists, largely U.S.-based, are self-selected and the positions they represent can be biased toward special interests. Supporters of trade controls stand alongside supporters of reducing rich country trade barriers. Opponents of a system that treads on the sovereignty of poor nations stand with supporters of labor rights in rich nations.

The Bank's clients' interests and power also differ considerably, so that in some cases (e.g., Brazil and India) the Bank has been essentially a partner, while in others (e.g., Mozambique and Nepal) it retains power over the country's economic and political agenda. The multiple objectives of its various principals, its undefined product, and its heterogeneous member-clients create a complicated and indeterminate decision-making environment that it has to solve through negotiation, and it is thus particularly vulnerable to political interference even though it claims to be apolitical.

In 1946 a signal event occurred for the governance of the institution. The first president, Eugene Meyer, resigned after six months because of what he saw as excessive interference by the U.S. director, Emilio Collado. He advised John McCloy, the nominee to succeed him, to insist as a condition of taking the job that the board be excluded from close supervision of Bank activity. It was agreed that, from then on, loan proposals would be originated by management and that the Board would be limited to supervision and responding to management initiatives. The Bank's historians, Devesh Kapur and his colleagues, wrote:[14] '[T]he board, quite explicitly, was not strong. It was permitted no initiatives, and in response ... the quality of its membership declined markedly during the 1950s'. (The first board included major figures such as Pierre Mendes France and Sir John Grigg.) But, they continue; '[A]lthough the Board was not able to put forward new initiatives, management recognized that, without Board consensus, the negative power of the Board could become a problem. Consequently

---

[14] Kapur, Devesh, J. Lewis, and R. Webb, *The World Bank: Its First Half Century*, Brookings, 1997.

tradition arose that while the Board was kept on a short leash, it was treated with generous respect'.

In 1974 there was an attempt to create a more effective executive board with the establishment of a Development Committee of twenty-four ministers, usually from treasury or aid ministries. The Development Committee was originally intended as an interim arrangement to advise on the real effects of changes in the international monetary system, but it became a permanent feature and is supposed to develop policy on major development issues, and to advise governors on issues and assistance needs. Accordingly it has its own secretariat. The IMF version of the development committee (the Interim Committee) was revamped in 1998 with the setup of the ad hoc G22 group to discuss financial reform – in response to U.S. frustration with the original committee. However, the Development Committee format remains substantially the same, and its purpose largely formal, so it has not lived up to the hopes that it would take charge of the Bank's business.[15]

The Development Committee meets and issues its communiqués just prior to the World Bank annual meetings, twice a year. The fall meetings are the showpiece events, usually held in Washington, attended on average by about 10,000 people, including 3,500 from official delegations that the Bank pays for, 1,000 from the media, and more than 5,000 guests normally from private business, and they are enormously demanding in conference space, equipment, accommodation, food and drink, entertainment, international and local transport, and security arrangements. The lowest recent turnout was for the 2001 meeting following the 9/11 terrorist attacks, but it still ran to many thousands. The 2006 meetings, which were held in Singapore, attracted a record crowd of more than 20,000.

The Bank's executive board has expanded steadily over time as the number of country members has grown. More mixed constituencies

---

[15] Naim, Moises, 'From Supplicants to Shareholders: Developing Countries and the World Bank', in Helleiner, G. K., ed., *The International Monetary and Financial System: Developing-Country Perspectives*, Palgrave Macmillan, 11995. Naim describes the Development Committee meetings as 'highly formalized, ritualistic events where no incentives exist to depart from the pre-established routine'. 'Why', he asks 'is it so difficult to dismantle a body that, while perceived as necessary by some, is largely regarded as useless?'

Table 1. *Board voting power*

	1965	1975	1985	1995	2006
Countries	102	125	149	178	185
Board members	20	20	21	24	24
G7 votes	54.9%	51.3%	49.7%	43.3%	43.0%
OECD votes	67.6%	64.7%	63.6%	57.7%	55%
U.S. vote	26.3%	22.7%	19.7%	17.0%	16.4%

allowed more representative views. As shown in Table 1, the U.S. voting share has fallen steadily but has retained its veto as the supermajority for changing the constitution was raised in 1989 from 80% to 85%.

While the United States has guarded its constitutional power despite a steady reduction in its shareholding, the overall OECD vote has similarly been retained in a narrow majority, and as a result the donor nations retain control of the institution, a situation now under scrutiny as the under-representation of several rising Asian countries becomes more evident. The zealousness with which countries have guarded their stakes in the Bretton Woods institutions reflects its highly politically driven institutional context.

The complex environment of governance in a multi-stakeholder development agency makes it particularly important that the organs of governance are designed to be as effective as possible, so that, as far as possible, high-quality oversight, strategy, and policy can be maintained.

THE FINANCIAL EDIFICE

The constitution given to the IBRD at Bretton Woods required it to raise funds from the capital market, backed by member governments' equity. As mentioned, it was not easy to implement this model because a number of nations had defaulted on bond issues that had been arranged by Wall Street, and in 1945 the majority of sovereign bonds were in arrears.[16]

---

[16] See Kapur, Lewis, et al., op cit. They write: '[A]s of the end of 1945, 87 per cent of European bonds outstanding, 60 per cent of Latin American bonds, and 56 per cent of Far Eastern bonds were in default. Of the twenty European borrowers, only three (France, Finland and Ireland) were in full service', Chapter 14, p. 917.

Within Congress there was discomfort as well. There were suspicions that the new institution would be a giveaway program. Republican Senator Taft of Ohio famously warned that the Bretton Woods proposals would be 'pouring money down a rat-hole'.[17] Despite the desire of the U.S. administration to create an institution independent of Wall Street, in the end Wall Street had to get involved and the first years of the new institution were preoccupied with persuading private lenders to support it. Eugene Meyer, the first president, was chosen because of his Wall Street connections, as have been most subsequent presidents. Convincing Wall Street of the merits of lending to the Bank awaited the appointment of the second president (John McCloy) from Chase Bank, with even stronger Wall Street connections, along with Eugene Black, the new U.S. executive director, also from Chase Bank.[18]

Under its Articles of Agreement, the IBRD was initially expected to focus more on guarantees than loans, that is, to act as a facilitator rather than an investor. However, Wall Street felt more secure in lending money to the Bank with the guarantees of its wealthy member countries than in making loans directly to foreign governments under an untested guarantee from the Bank. Thus the IBRD became a market player rather than a market maker or facilitator. In fact, its entry as a competitor in the loan market raised fears of its monopolistic position and was one of the triggers for the formation of the Inter-American Development Bank (IADB) as a counterweight, in 1960.

To satisfy the financial markets the IBRD's finances had to be extremely secure. Nevertheless, the design of its capital structure allows members to actually pay in very small proportions of their required subscriptions.[19] This allows a very conservative *de iure* lending principle (total loan commitments limited to 100% of authorized capital plus reserves) to be

---

[17] From Gardner, Richard. N., *Sterling-Dollar Diplomacy in Current Perspective*, Columbia University Press, 1980, cited in Kapur et al., op cit., p. 913.

[18] Among the first hurdles was the need to amend regulations to establish the legality of the U.S. government guarantee on Bank bonds, while initially the IBRD was not allowed to lend unless potential borrowers had settled outstanding arrears on prewar bonds, giving it effectively a debt collector role. For an authoritative account of these events see Kapur et al., op cit.

[19] The initial authorized capital as set out in the Articles of Agreement (Schedule A) was US$ 9.1 billion, of which the United States itself was to contribute about 33%.

combined with an operating rule that is somewhat more aggressive. In recent years, paid-in capital alone has been about 8%, and total equity about 30% of total lending. Thus the IBRD is able to lend at multiples of its equity, similar in principle to a commercial lender, while at the same time it is, in effect, guaranteed by its shareholders against insolvency through its callable capital, the money promised but not yet paid.[20]

By the end of the 1950s the market was sufficiently sure of the IBRD's security and reassured that governments would stand by their capital commitments that, following the first capital increase in 1959 (which more than doubled the authorized capital from $10 billion to $21 billion), the rating agencies finally gave the Bank a AAA credit rating, which allowed it to borrow in the market at the lowest possible rates. It was this increased confidence that allowed it from the 1950s to start lending to higher risk, developing countries, notably India. At the same time, the awareness of the risks propelled the Bank to push for the setup in 1960 of the IDA as its soft loan arm, so as to keep the most potentially risky clients off the IBRD's balance sheet.[21]

While most of its funding has come from Wall Street, so that it has to maintain a rigorous and conservative posture with the financial market, there are also situations in which the IBRD is exposed to wider, political, scrutiny. These arise largely when it seeks more capital from its members. The same applies to the IDA during its three-year fund replenishment cycle. The IBRD goes to talk to the donor community when it is running out of funds, and these capital increases have become increasingly difficult over time. At the first increase in 1959 the United States wanted to nurture the institution it had largely created. The second one, which occurred in two stages, in 1976 and 1980, was more difficult and needed five years of persuasion and negotiation, as the United States wanted limits on lending and interest rate adjustments.

[20] This protective arrangement is de jure quite distinct from the 'bailout' arrangements applicable to some Wall Street banks in 2008, but there might be a de facto resemblance.
[21] Other motives for setting up the IDA were to use up politically sensitive accumulated profits through a 'charitable' channel, and to forestall the UN's own plans to set up a soft loan agency, a reflection of the IBRD's discomfort at its subordination to UN control. The UN had been working on the establishment of the S.U.N.F.E.D (Special United Nations Fund for Economic Development).

The third increase was even more of a problem, since the U.S. administration, now under Ronald Reagan, generally rejected the idea of expanding an organization that they suspected was a kind of socialist trojan horse. For three years the management struggled to convince the United States that increased demands for loans necessitated an increase in its capital, until in 1984 an interim increase of US$8 billion was agreed. Meanwhile, the IBRD almost ran out of money for lending; that is, it hit its allowed ceiling. For two years the management considered ways of raising funds while arduous negotiations continued.

The problem was finally resolved in 1988 as a reward for a major reorganization under President Barber Conable (1986–1991). The capital was increased by about 75% to US$184 billion. Only 3% of the new amount was paid in, allowing the United States and other major donors to retain control at lower cost. But no further capital increase has been needed since then. Indeed, outstanding IBRD loans are currently not far above their 1988 level after the last few years of lending decline.

The Bank has had to face other financial pressures. For example, rapidly rising borrowing costs after the second oil shock in 1981 caused losses due to the time lag between loan commitments and loan signing. The problem was solved through a front-end fee on new lending. But the decision took more than a year to make after first notification to the board, by which time stable or falling interest rates and high yields on loans had changed the financial picture, and soon afterward the new fee was cancelled. As in the case of the ten-year wait to achieve the AAA credit rating, and the arduously slow capital increases, the problem was one of a politicized organization unable to act in a flexible manner.

To an extent the rating and capital increase struggles could have been avoided if a government (e.g., the United States) had done a government's work (to come out and reassure the market about its support of the IBRD, and to take a more constructive view on capital requirements). In a similar vein, the funding cost problem could have been avoided if a business had been allowed to do a business's work (to adapt quickly to changing business conditions). However, these misalignments have been characteristic of the Bank's history. They are symptomatic of regular, often ill-informed pressure from the various outside stakeholder groups who understand that the Bank is a global public institution answerable to them, but who do not know how to deal effectively with the institution.

In addition to protection against insolvency through its capital structure the IBRD has several other layers of protection. The most important is a government's guarantee of loan repayment.[22] Largely as a result of this the percentage of non-payments (called 'non-accruals') is at a very low level (around 1%). Another important safeguard under the general loan conditions is the 'negative pledge agreement' whereby government and public sector borrowers agree not to pledge assets as security to any other lender without first obtaining the IBRD's agreement and/or providing it equal security. A senior status for the Bank's loans has also been accepted by other official donors, who have at times forgiven their own borrowers' debts to protect the Bank's loan recovery record. Soft IDA money has also been used to pay off harder IBRD loans, thus allowing IBRD loans funded by the private sector seniority over IDA loans funded by donors. From 1996 IDA loans were forgiven under the Heavily Indebted Poor Countries (HIPC) initiatives, followed by the 2005 Multilateral Debt Reduction Initiative (MDRI). But the IBRD has not allowed any rescheduling or writing off of its own loans

Operational independence is also enhanced through the IBRD's large cash holdings. The build-up of cash in the initial years, helped by a special levy on operational income, reached a level of three years' lending by 1965, but there was a reluctance to reduce them for fear of adverse financial market reactions. Instead, in 1964 President George Woods (1963–1968) decided to make various annual grants out of net income, of which the main one was to the IDA. Under McNamara cash holdings were further built up, to reduce dependence on the United States and other countries as both shareholders and major financiers.[23]

---

[22] Article 3, Section 4 states that all borrowings by non-government sources will be guaranteed by the government or acceptable agency, and that otherwise borrowings are through the government, which by implication gives its guarantee.

[23] The Bank needed the permission of country governments before it could raise money on their national capital markets (the 'consent rule'), and this made it vulnerable to political and economic events in those countries. The diversification of borrowings helped to circumvent U.S. capital export controls when the dollar weakened over 1968 to 1974.

The cash level reached 30% of outstanding loans by the end of the reorganization period, boosted by prepayments on Asian crisis loans and by reduced lending. With its cash holdings the IBRD could operate for a long time like a foundation or a think tank, spending the income from an endowment.

These various forms of formal protection have still probably been less significant than informal power over borrowers, either through the IBRD's influence on the market or through the effects of loan conditionality. A relationship with the Bank, as with the IMF, has often been sought because of its powerful influence over finance from all sources. Many poorer governments might balance the costs of dealing with the Bank with the benefits of having its seal of approval. They often see their relationship as a political one, and will accept the high transaction costs because of the political benefits.

The reorganizations of the last twenty years may well have been impossible without these various types of financial insulations. The gold-plated financial structure explains how the organization was able to operate for a long time to some extent independent of outside criticism, and it also explains to some extent how the organization's shareholders were able to burden it with expensive organizational changes without serious financial risk, an issue that we will return to later.

THE IBRD AND ITS SISTERS

The IBRD was the first in a system of international financial institutions designed to assist world development, and has influenced all those that followed. The World Bank Group as a whole consists of several organizations. The IFC was set up as an offshoot of the IBRD in 1956, ten years after the establishment of the IBRD, in response to a growing demand for more commercial finance for the private sector in developing countries, while, as I mentioned earlier, the IDA was set up as a second offshoot of the IBRD in 1960 (though integrated with the IBRD) in response to a growing demand for less commercial, more concessional, guaranteed finance for the poorest countries.

Four regional multilateral development banks (MDBs) have been established on the model of the IBRD, financing developing, and transitional economies[24] – the Inter-American Development Bank in 1959, the African Development Bank in 1964, the Asian Development Bank in 1966, and the European Bank for Reconstruction and Development in 1991. There are also subregional institutions like the Caribbean Development Bank. The regional MDBs were set up with majority capital subscriptions from the United States, the UK, Germany, France, and Japan, amounting on average to about 70% of the shares. Together with the World Bank Group, they have been responsible for about US$40 to $50 billion a year of gross lending and guarantees over the past few years, of which the Bank Group has accounted for about half; between them they incur $3 billion of running expenses and have more than 12,000 permanent employees (as much as 17,000 on average at any one time if consultants are included).

Like the IBRD, the other MDBs' capital is either paid-in or guaranteed by member governments, and the paid-in part of it is very small. Thus, even though the other MDBs' loans are conservatively backed at least 100% by subscribed (on-call) capital and accumulated reserves, the equity based on paid-up capital and reserves is much less. This financial edifice is built on the assumption that principal government shareholders will without fail meet their commitments in the event of a capital call (e.g., to offset a major borrower default). The member governments are in turn prepared to make this commitment because they believe that government guarantees plus the Bank's financial and political leverage on its clients are such that major defaults are extremely unlikely.

While there are some differences, the rules for lending ceilings, reserve ratios, liquidity, lending terms, provisioning, and problem loans are generally of the same order. Paid-in capital is a similar proportion to assets as that of the IBRD in the case of the ADB and the IADB, at 6 to 7%, and somewhat higher in the AfDB and the EBRD. Reserve ratios for the other banks as a whole are somewhat higher. This general structure both provides comfort to the financial markets that are impressed by the 100% capital backing of loans, and suits the member

---

[24] A difference is that the regional banks concentrate most of the Bank Group's functions (developmental and commercial lending) into a unified agency. The European Investment Bank also makes loans to developing countries, but this is a small proportion of its activity.

governments that only have to go to their parliaments to get permission for a very small proportion of their committed subscription.

The Bank and the regional development banks differ operationally, if not constitutionally. The regional banks are politically less conspicuous than the World Bank because they cater to a narrower group of active 'principals', with less interest in pursuing individual agendas. They do not work at the macroeconomic policy level to the extent that the World Bank does, and therefore their loan conditions have less chance of being perceived as infringing on national sovereignty. Their client countries are more homogeneous and the regional nature of their staffing and their business means that country focus is better, and finally, their range of activities is narrower, leading to fewer openings to question their effectiveness. In effect they can do business in a relatively uninterrupted manner compared to the Bank.[25]

However, the organizational system of the Bank has been the model for the others, which is why it is important. What happens to the organization of the Bank could be applicable to these other organizations as well, since they have similar objectives, functions, structures, and governance. Consequently, reforms of one have implications for the whole system.

---

[25] Nevertheless, they have still been subject to criticism, as regularly depicted on activist Web sites such as 'Bankwatch'.

2

Critique and Response

EMERGING ISSUES

EMERGING ISSUES

A complex financial institution emerged over sixty years, which has continued to operate throughout without any major threats to its survival, providing a model to other international financial institutions. The IBRD has had a continuous, apparently successful, record of evolving lending and knowledge services, delivered with a reasonable profit that has enabled it to provide subsidies to other agencies while expanding its expertise and maintaining a position as the world's premier development institution.

But the Bank's successes have also been built behind a protective wall and its low funding costs have allowed it to remain profitable even with large overheads and an annual payroll that would be enough to lift a small country out of the worst poverty.[1] The layers of protection and a resulting perception of inadequate transparency have also tended to attract extra scrutiny of the Bank's work, and the level of success it has achieved with the resources it has at its disposal has been widely debated. For example, in June 2003, at the end of a period of major reform involving unprecedented outreach to its member countries, a poll of 2,600 'opinion leaders' from around

---

[1] In 2005, some 1.2 billion or 20% were living at or below the threshold of US$1.00 per day (in 1985 prices). Poverty reduction targets were defined in the Millennium Development Declaration to be achieved by 2015. The first of these goals is to close the poverty gap, reducing from 30% to 15% the percentage of the world's population living on less than $1 per day.

the world by Princeton Survey Research Associates found that large numbers of those surveyed had quite a dim view of the institution. Less than half of Africa's opinion leaders were happy with its work, and about 60% of South Asians and Middle Easterners. Somewhat better, over 70% of East Asians including Chinese thought it was doing well. But about a third of those interviewed in Nigeria, Mexico, and Pakistan actually thought that the Bank was a negative factor in the world. Most of the respondents thought that the Bank's economic reform proposals hurt more than they helped while only a minority believed that it was doing a good job of reducing poverty. This was in an organization that had been making special efforts over the previous few years to reach out and explain its raison d'etre in assisting world development, that is, poverty reduction.

Dissatisfaction with the Bank arose following the presidency of its strongest advocate, Robert McNamara. During the 1980s opponents began to emerge from, on the one hand, a coalition of liberal/left interests and, on the other, from the free marketeers of the right represented by a number of conservative U.S. foundations and, later on, famously by the Republican-sponsored Meltzer Commission. There has also been a long-running, more functional critique of the Bank's organizational effectiveness – did it deliver the results that it claimed to deliver, did it do so in a cost-effective way, and did it approach its work with the right attitude?

Liberal/left opposition groups wanted to curb the power of a crypto-capitalist institution and neo-conservative groups wanted to limit the power of a crypto-socialist institution. The liberal groups mounted their opposition on two principal grounds – the Bank's claimed inadequate attention to environmental issues, especially in large infrastructure projects, and its increasing focus on macro-economic reform through structural adjustment programs that, opponents claimed, undermined the interests of the recipient economies. The neo-conservative interests, opposing public sector interventions in markets, emerged during the Reagan presidency but gained ascendancy with the Republican takeover of Congress in 1994.

THE ENVIRONMENTAL LOBBY

The environmental movement's critique gathered momentum in the early 1980s when a coalition of U.S. environmental groups took their case against the Bank to Congress.[2] Some of the most famous examples of environmentally harmful projects, all approved in the 1980s, were the Sardar Sarovar (Narmada) dam in India, the Polonoroeste integrated development project in northeastern Brazil, and the population trans-migration project in Indonesia. These projects were beset by problems of unplanned displacement of populations, inundation of land, and destruction of rainforests by road development and resettlement. The Bank only funded a small minority of the huge costs of these projects, which were initiated by the governments concerned, but it was seen nevertheless in effect to be giving its seal of approval to the displacement of populations, inundation of land, and destruction of rainforests.

In the case of Polonoroeste, the chaotic resettlement of displaced Southern Brazilian small farmers on poor soils in the Amazon resulted in the leveling of 50,000 square miles of rainforest (an area the size of Britain) and decimation of the indigenous population. The Indonesian project involved the resettlement of millions of Javans to the outer islands, but, as in the case of Brazil, the soils were unsuitable in the deforested areas, the facilities not ready, the indigenous population uprooted, and the settlers unable to make a living, with many drifting to the cities.

In the case of the Sardar Sarovar dam, which required the demolition of dozens of villages and the resettlement of more than 200,000 farmers, the Bank was finally obliged to set up an independent review (the Morse commission), which turned out to be a precursor of the Bank's Inspection Panel, which was itself formed in 1993. A 1994 book by Bruce Rich of the Environmental Defense Fund – *Mortgaging the Earth* – reflected the challenge to what was seen as the environmental blindness of the Bank.[3]

---

[2] See Caufield, Catherine, *Masters of Illusion – The World Bank and the Poverty of Nations*, Henry Holt, 1996, p. 170.
[3] Rich, Bruce, *Mortgaging the Earth; the World Bank, Environmental Impoverishment and the Crisis of Development*, Beacon, 1994.

In an attempt to turn the tide, one of the first significant actions taken by James Wolfensohn on joining as president was to cancel a controversial investment in a large dam in Nepal, the so-called Arun lll project. The Bank also refused to finance China's giant Three Gorges dam, and with these and other actions, including the establishment of a Global Environmental Fund, the Bank went some way to defuse the opposition by the late 1990s.

OPPOSITION TO STRUCTURAL ADJUSTMENT

More intractable was the issue of whether to maintain what was known as structural adjustment lending. The Bank and IMF adjustment operations started in 1980, and grew to claim a significant proportion of the Bank's lending, well above the 25% target originally set. The concept of adjustment was consistent with the market liberalization certainties of the Reagan era. The idea was to find a way for poor, vulnerable economies to survive the shock of the 1979–1980 oil and associated price increases by recycling the surplus of petrodollars back to them in low-cost loans to shield them while they adjusted their economic structures. The first part of the cure was for the IMF to try to stabilize the affected economies through low-cost temporary financing while they cut public expenditure. The typical IMF package aimed to achieve fiscal balance, control the money supply, raise interest rates, and devalue the currency to improve the balance of payments. The Bank followed on, focusing on the 'switching' agenda to find ways of supporting longer term restructuring of the economy through market liberalization and easing the barriers to adjustment like state ownership, subsidies, price controls, inflexible wages, protective labor laws, and constraints to competition.[4]

This was the shape of adjustment lending in its pure and innocent form. But innocence was lost. The required reforms were highly demanding politically, and what was initially intended as about a three- to five-year interim regime to protect weak economies while they

---

[4] The case for macroeconomic reform as a precondition for viable lending projects was made in the important Bank report 'Accelerated Growth in Sub-Saharan Africa; an Agenda for Action', authored by Eliot Berg and others in 1981.

restructured to face market realities became a pretext for long-term outside intervention subject to difficult policy conditions. Furthermore, the loans unexpectedly concentrated on Africa.

Burke Knapp, a top adviser to the president for many years, was quoted in 1981, at the beginning of the adjustment phase:[5] 'I'm just not sure that we are wise enough' he said, 'I'm sure we are not *always* wise enough – to design these structural adjustment programs and to formulate conditions that are relevant and productive'. Nevertheless, structural adjustment became a quite unshakeable orthodoxy for many years. Among many commentators, Moises Naim, former executive director and now editor of the *Foreign Policy Journal*, wrote:[6] '[O]pponents of the concept were suspected of harboring anti-market ideologies, nationalism, anti-Americanism, and other forms of the modern day equivalent of obscurantism'. Government skepticism, he wrote, was denounced as evidence of a lack of political will, while 'the changing requirements coming from Washington and Wall St were presented as reasonable changes resulting from the incorporation of the 'lessons of experience'.

As it turned out, there were numerous problems with these programs. One unintended consequence of funding a country's budget was a reduced urgency for change and a tendency to delay the difficult adjustment decisions, while at the same time lenders were afraid to enforce the conditions because they might reduce the possibilities of repayment. Paul Collier, a leading Bank economist, wrote, '[I]n poor policy environments (when reform is being pushed from outside) aid-for-reform paradoxically tends to delay reform'.[7] Delay was exacerbated because losers from the reforms turned out to be the more vocal sections of the population (e.g., urban workers and civil servants) who faced the layoffs, rising prices, and reduced subsidies, while the gainers tended to be the silent rural population who would get higher prices for their crops, only later. Through

---

[5] Cited in Caufield, Catherine, *Masters of Illusion – The World Bank and the Poverty of Nations*, Henry Holt 1996, p. 145.

[6] Naim, Moises, 'Fads and Fashions in Economic Reforms: Washington Consensus or Washington Confusion', *Third World Quarterly*, 21(3), 2000.

[7] Collier, Paul, 'Consensus Building, Knowledge and Conditionality,' Paper for the Annual Conference on Development Economics, World Bank, April 2000, p. 11.

adjustment lending the Bank also became intrusive in national policy and politics, exposing it to charges of infringing on national sovereignty. The complexity of the programs themselves often contained difficult, politically sensitive actions that might well take many years to achieve even within the donor countries themselves.[8] A report in 1988[9] said that there were on average fifty-six policy conditions for each structural adjustment program, despite efforts to slim the programs down. The focus on reforms at the macro level itself crowded out the reforms at the micro level that were needed to change the economic structure.

While there were some successes, by the mid-1990s, eighty-eight countries had embarked on Bank-funded adjustment programs and few had kept to the Bank's original timetable of three to five years.[10] Easterly cites a number of examples.[11] Seven out of twelve African economies that were major recipients of structural adjustment loans over 1980–1999 experienced negative per capita economic growth. Only one (Uganda) experienced growth above 2%. Similarly, six out of the top ten structural adjustment program recipients from former communist bloc economies experienced negative per capita growth, while only three, Poland, Albania, and Georgia, experienced growth above 2%. Cote D'Ivoire was the extreme case. The Bank made twenty-six adjustment loans over 1979 to 1999 and by 1999 the Bank and IMF were responsible for three-quarters of new foreign lending in the country. Yet over the same period the average income fell by a half and 37% of Ivorians were in poverty in 1995, compared to 11% in 1985. For twenty years Bank loan conditions had repeatedly stressed the need to reduce budget deficits, free coffee and cocoa prices, and liberalize the foreign exchange rate.

---

[8] Some examples of major policy stalemates in high-income economies with strong institutions might include: the length of time needed to get changes to the EU Common Agricultural policy, to establish a consensus on how to reduce the U.S. fiscal deficit, and to stop the state bailout of failing Japanese banks.

[9] 'Review of Adjustment Lending ll', World Bank, 1988.

[10] Caufield, Catherine, *Masters of Illusion – The World Bank and the Poverty of Nations*, Henry Holt, 1996, p. 163.

[11] Easterly, William, *The Elusive Quest for Growth; an Economist's Adventures and Misadventures in the Tropics*, MIT Press, 2001, p. 133.

In a similar vein Paul Collier writes that '[T]he Government of Kenya sold the same agricultural reform to the Bank five times in fifteen years'.[12] 'Probably' he continued, 'the main reason why conditionality failed was that it underestimated the importance of the domestic political forces which determine policies in the long run'. 'Sustainable reform in the context in which the Government is opposed to it is radically more difficult than temporary reform'.

In a number of important areas the Bank and the Fund were obliged to amend policy and agree that there were no clear lessons of experience, just as Burke Knapp had predicted. There was no consensus on the pace and sequence of reform (gradualism or the big bang); whether exchange rates should be fixed or should float; whether the capital market should be liberalized or not (following the Asian financial crisis); whether adjustment should be accompanied by deflation or inflation; and what kinds of institutions were needed for recovery. Late in the process Joseph Stiglitz, the Bank's then chief economist, attacked the IMF over its approach and argued for gradualism.[13] When restrictive monetary policy, he wrote, 'is implemented without sufficient attention to the development of financial institutions oriented toward providing credit to small- and/or medium-sized domestic firms, it is almost impossible to create new jobs and enterprises. In country after country displaced workers went from low productivity jobs to zero productivity unemployment'.[14] Kenneth Rogoff, IMF chief economist, dismissed the critics, including Joseph Stiglitz.[15] Suggesting that countries expand out of a debt crisis was, Rogoff said, like arguing that debt

---

[12] Collier, Paul, 'Conditionality Dependence and Aid Coordination', in *The World Bank: Structure and Policies*, Gilbert, Christopher L. and Vines, David, Eds., Cambridge University Press, 2000 p. 304.

[13] Stiglitz, Joseph, *Globalization and Its Discontents*, W. W. Norton, June 2002, p. 188. Stiglitz, with the benefit of hindsight, dismissed the shock therapy approach. In Poland and Hungary, gradualist policies were more successful. 'In the race between the tortoise and the hare, it appears that the tortoise has won again', he wrote.

[14] Stiglitz, 'IMF's Missed Opportunity', www.Economictimes.com.

[15] Rogoff, Kenneth 'The IMF Strikes Back', *Foreign Policy*, January–February 2003. Stiglitz (2002) had attacked the IMF's attempt to deal with the 1997 to 1998 Asian crisis through contractionary fiscal policies in the midst of recession, reducing public expenditure, and raising interest rates. At the same time, the IMF also asked for the opening of capital markets, which, he argued, aggravated the crisis by encouraging capital flight.

problems should be solved by taking on more debt. Expenditure reduction (belt tightening) and resource reallocation were unavoidable given the serious economic imbalances in many poorer economies.

The opposition was arguing about fairness. The low level of starting employment and income meant that poor countries could not be expected to cut their expenditures and open up their economies to trade, risking more unemployment as they waited for the 'switch' to uncertain export markets subject to quotas, tariffs, subsidies, and patents. With such structural problems economic stagnation might be the normal state in many countries, and contractionary fiscal policies were beside the point. The IMF, on the other hand, was arguing about reality, that is, the need to face existing economic constraints. Both sides could be right.

Quotas tariffs and subsidies were finally given a hearing at the Monterrey Aid conference in 2002. Wolfensohn called on rich countries to 'build the pressure' for additional funds for development, and for a reduction in agricultural subsidies and other trade barriers to exports from developing nations.

FIFTY YEARS IS ENOUGH

The environmentalist and anti-adjustment lobbies developed into a broad opposition that also focused on the Bank's role in the build-up of global debt and loan conditionality. Later in the 1990s it embraced claims that the Bank had turned a blind eye to corruption.[16] This broad opposition announced itself in a riot in Seattle in November 1999, and then through unprecedented demonstrations in Washington, DC, in April 2000, and Prague in September 2000, organized by about 100 mainly U.S.-based activist groups, through the 'Mobilization for Global

---

[16] See Winters, Jeffrey A., 'Criminal Debt', in Jonathan R. Pincus and Jeffery A. Winters, *Reinventing the World Bank*, Cornell University Press, 2002, Chapter 5. In Indonesia it had been suggested that as much as 30%, or $10 billion of the Bank's total loans to that country, might have been misappropriated by the ruling elite, while the Bank kept quiet as long as its debts were being serviced and the relationship maintained with one of its most important clients. Here the relationship imperative was turned upside down – the Bank was dependent on the good will of one of its biggest borrowers.

Justice' and the 'Fifty Years is Enough' campaigns.[17] The activist groups
that were members of these coalitions were mainly small, focusing on a
wide variety of issues – the natural environment, human rights, women
and gay rights, labor conditions, fair trade, consumer protection, economic justice, anti-nuclear power, and peace. Some had no special
agenda. Their message was not always coherent and sometimes not
intended to be. The Ruckus Society was one of these groups. As one
activist monitoring Web sites put it,[18] 'whether the target *du jour* is
biotech foods, the World Bank, the World Trade Organization, or
globalization in general, (Ruckus) recruits, trains, transports, and
houses the army of militants needed to earn media coverage and make
life difficult for the rest of us'. The 100 groups did not include the
mainstream environmental or human rights groups that were regularly
talking to the Bank by this time. But they tended to represent the
message for all.

In 2001 an initiative demanding more information disclosure from
the Bank got 500 signatories, mainly from groups in the United States,
Brazil, and Mexico.[19] A coalition of the mainstream groups of activists,
notably the AFL-CIO, Catholic Relief Services, Environmental Defense
Fund, Friends of the Earth, National Resources Defense Fund, Oxfam,
World Vision, and twenty others, collaborated in a paper by the Civil
Society coalition calling for reform of the Bank, as a condition of the
U.S. replenishment of funds for the IDA.[20] They said 'Congress should
ensure that the hundreds of millions of taxpayer dollars that are provided to the World Bank this year do not fund more failure at the
institution'. The groups were concerned about numerous issues including improved transparency, debt cancellation, environmental
assessments, poverty, proper measurement of project results, user fees,
AIDS, privatization, trade and investment deregulation, and tobacco
projects.

---

[17] The 'Fifty Years is Enough' campaign was started in 1994, on the fiftieth anniversary
of the Bretton Woods conference.
[18] See www.Activistcash.com.
[19] The vice president was Joanne Salop.
[20] 'Responsible Reform of the World Bank; The Role of the US in Improving the
Development Effectiveness of World Bank Operations', U.S. Civil Society Coalition,
April 2002.

The shock of the terrorist attacks on the United States on September 11, 2001 led to a cooling off of activism as the more threatening implications of globalization made themselves felt. Nevertheless, the movement in 2002 claimed 'a coalition of over 200 U.S. grassroots, women's, solidarity, faith-based, policy, social – and economic – justice, youth, labor, and development organizations working with over 185 international partner organizations in more than 65 countries . . . committed to transforming the international financial institutions' policies and practices, to ending the outside imposition of neo-liberal economic programs, and to making the development process democratic and accountable'. Kevin Danaher, a Californian activist, wrote in 2001 of a 'secret global government being constructed behind the backs of the citizens of the planet'. The World Bank and the IMF, along with the World Trade Organization (WTO), he said 'are making policy for the entire bouquet of humanity but with only a mono-crop (the wealthy) sitting at the rule-making table'.[21] In contrast, this book is more concerned about the weakness of global governance

THE MELTZER COMMISSION

The Bank presidency of Robert McNamara that ended in 1981 had seen the organization's lending grow threefold as he tried to create a powerful global agency. With Ronald Reagan came an ideology that viewed the Bank as an organ of global welfare, suspected of advancing the interests of socialism, and of being itself a typically incompetent public sector institution, not one that needed to expand any further. Then, in 1998, the Republican Congress that launched the Contract with America set up the International Financial Institutions Advisory Commission (IFIAC) to investigate the Bank, chaired by Professor Alan Meltzer of Carnegie-Mellon University, although by that time the Bank's own organizational reforms were already under way.

The Meltzer Commission Report finally came out just prior to the Washington, DC, demonstration in 2000. It was a majority report,

[21] From Danaher, Kevin, *Ten Reasons to Abolish the IMF and World Bank* (Preface), Open Media Paperback, Dec 2001.

though with several dissenting opinions.[22] It proposed a radical reorganization and downsizing of the institution, intended to better meet its
key objective of reducing poverty, which, the report concluded, it had
so far failed to do. Among its recommendations was a switch from
lending to grants based on performance audits. The organization
should be downsized, its lending to investment grade middle income
countries should be phased out, and it should concentrate mainly on
Africa.[23] To the *Financial Times* in 2000 Meltzer wrote,[24] '[T]he World
Bank is an overstaffed, ineffective, bureaucratic institution . . . . By its
own admission, half of its projects are unsuccessful, and the failure rate
is even higher in the poorest countries . . . . The Bank's management
must stop its current public relations flimflam and start improving its
effectiveness in reducing poverty. If the demonstrators help to achieve
that their efforts will have been worthwhile'.[25]

The perception that the Bank was bloated and overstaffed was a
ritual reaction based on distrust of bureaucracy.[26] In fact, the 10,000

[22] Among the dissenters was notably Fred Bergsten of the Institute of International Economics.
[23] This recommendation and several others were in fact opposed by another commission, this time a 'blue ribbon' commission chaired by Paul Volcker and Angel Gurria
that reported in May 2001.
[24] Meltzer, Alan, *Financial Times*, April 28, 2000.
[25] Following this letter Meltzer wrote to *The Wall Street Journal* in 2001: 'The institution
does not welcome a career change from being an elegant banker dispensing large
volumes of largesse to being a gritty development agency with a demanding workload.
And it harbors a well-founded fear that, with grants, it must account for the effectiveness of programs'. In 2003 he wrote in the *Washington Times*: 'The bank claims that
poverty reduction is its overriding goal. Yet the most rapidly growing areas of World
Bank lending have been direct financial support for the private sector and large
"adjustment" loans that provide budget support in exchange for promises of economic reforms – operations with even less connection to helping the poor than the
more traditional project loans. IFIAC recommended instead that the bank exclusively
focus its scarce development resources on monitored grants . . . . The bank has, as
usual, paid lip service to these ideas but accomplished little'. Carnegie Endowment for
International Peace, 2001.
[26] Another colorful dissenter was Michael Irwin, a long-term UN employee and briefly
director of the Bank's health department. He gained brief notoriety by resigning,
holding a press conference, and writing an article for the Cato Institute: '[A]part
from its failure in really helping the many impoverished people in the World, I am
also concerned', he said, 'about the Bank's bloated, overpaid bureaucracy, its wasteful
practices, its generally poor management and its unjustified arrogance . . . . The institution is plagued by massive overstaffing, bureaucratic gridlock and staff preoccupation with further salary and benefit hikes' in 'Banking on Poverty: An Insider's Look
at the World Bank', *Cato Foreign Policy Briefing* 3(20), September 1990.

or so people dealing with 185 member countries, while attending to the enormous institutional demands, may well be far too few. As a casual comparison, Citicorp employs 270,000 and Barclays employs 150,000, worldwide. Lehman Brothers, Wall Street's fourth biggest specialized investment bank, entered bankruptcy proceedings in 2008 with 25,000 employees. The Bank's visibility in Washington earns a level of congressional indignation out of proportion to the extent of taxpayer money that is being used to support it. Brian Urquhart, otherwise also a Bank-pessimist, made a similar point about the UN: 'There is little realistic justification for describing this civil service as "a vast, sprawling bureaucracy". .... the entire UN system world-wide, serving the interests of some 5,500,000,000 people in 184 countries, employs no more workers than the civil service in the American state of Wyoming .... It is less than the staff of the District Health Services of the Principality of Wales in Britain'.[27]

The ritual nature of the opposition meant that it would continue regardless of such points. Professor Meltzer addressed a hearing of the U.S. Congress the following year (March 2001) in which he reinforced his proposals. He said that the Bank's initial reaction to his report had been 'hostile and obfuscating' And that 'the Bank's management has devoted much of its strategic effort to developing cliché-ridden, ambiguous statements such as the Comprehensive Development Program, and, more recently, the Strategic Framework Paper.... We must rid ourselves of a system that imposes changes that countries do not want and will not enforce, that brings demonstrators to the streets protesting real and imagined wrongs, and that is ineffective'.

INTERPRETING THE OUTSIDE CRITICS

In 2000 the Meltzer Commission and the Mobilization for Global Justice were unintentional bedfellows. They agreed on one thing – that the Bank was not doing its job properly and that it was fighting to preserve a flawed mission. But the commission thought that it was a quasi-socialist, welfare institution, fundamentally antagonistic to the objectives of global capitalism and free markets, while the Mobilization group

---

[27] Urquhart, Brian, 'Renewing the UN System', in Childers, Erskine B., and Urquhart, Sir Brain, *Renewing the United Nations System*, The Ford Foundation (New York), 1994.

thought that it was a capitalist institution fundamentally antagonistic to human welfare and the fight against poverty.

Some observers of the Bank talked about this disconnect. For example, Nancy Birdsall, a former senior Bank staff member, wrote,[28] 'The demonstrations this week in Washington are a reminder that the World Bank and its sister institutions are caught in a squeeze – between the champions of social justice on the left and the Meltzer Commission and *The Wall Street Journal* editors on the right. Those on the left say that the Bank is a vehicle for globalization that is run by finance and corporate insiders, imposing austerity and "conditionality" ... that hurts the poor. Those on the right say the Bank is crowding out private lending in middle income countries and using loans to grease the wheels of wasteful and corrupt Government practices'.

Ravi Kanbur, professor of economics at Cornell University and a former senior Bank employee, also tried to explain the disconnect. He wrote, '[I]n the year 2000 the Governors of the World Bank, whose mission it is to eradicate poverty, could meet only under police protection besieged by those who believe instead that the institution and the policies that it espouses cause poverty'.[29] Whereas the 'official' side, he said, saw the market as a force for improved resource use and rising incomes, the opposition saw the market as a source of monopolistic influence and an uneven distribution of power. But, he wrote, this was partly due to different interpretations of reality and statistics. For example, with population growth, the proportion below the poverty line could fall when the absolute numbers of those in poverty were still rising, and even with rising average incomes some parts of the population could get poorer. But such rational explanations did not make much difference to a conflict based on myths rather than facts.[30]

---

[28] Birdsall, Nancy, in 'Commentary', Overseas Development Council, Carnegie Endowment for International Peace, April 2000.

[29] Kanbur, Ravi, *Economic Policy, Distribution and Poverty; the Nature of Disagreements*, Cornell University Press, 2001. Kanbur resigned from the Bank when the management wanted to dilute the unorthodox anti-poverty message of the World Development Report in 2001, of which Kanbur was editorial director.

[30] The 'Fifty Years is Enough' Web site contains, for example, a section called 'Talkback', which provides talking points for Bank opponents when confronted with 'mainstream attitudes' on the World Bank and the IMF.

INTERNAL REFORM DRIVERS

The Bank was by no means oblivious to its own problems. Prior to Conable's arrival, in 1985 an internal report group, called 'Streamlining Bank Procedures', chaired by a manager in the Bank, Steve Denning, highlighted the need for corporate organizational reform. In 1992 a major internal task force report was issued, under the chairmanship of a vice president, Willi Wapenhans (known as the Wapenhans Report), which took a hard look at internal problems.[31] The problems, it reported, were partly externally created because of the economic difficulties that faced many poorer countries in the post-oil-shock 1980s. But they were also because of gaps in skills and the central problem of an 'approval culture' that put more emphasis on new loans than making sure the existing ones worked properly. The report stated that 'the Bank must be no less restrained in diagnosing and seeking to remedy its own shortcomings than it is in seeking to help member countries recognize and address theirs'.

The report found that project implementation was taking an excessively long time; designs were inflexible and financial covenants were not being adhered to, damaging the credibility of loan agreements; and lessons were not being learned. Despite lengthy preparation periods, there was a rush to closure, and in the end many agreements were entered into under pressure and policy conditions on loans were unrealistic and not taken seriously by the borrowers. The credibility of appraisals was weak and ex-post evaluation to see whether benefits really materialized was inadequate. The report set out five recommendations – sustainable development impact should be the indicator of performance; success required local ownership; the quality of the project design was critical to the project's outcome; a country focus was needed beyond project analysis; and portfolio performance must become a central concern of business.

The institution's internal conversation, however, encouraged further the chorus of outside disapproval, which continued through the short

---

[31] The Wapenhans Report, 'Effective Implementation: Key to Development Impact; Report of the World Bank's Portfolio Management Task Force', World Bank, 1992.

presidency of Lew Preston (1991–1995). There was double jeopardy; failure to honestly assess the Bank's deficiencies led to an uproar of criticism while an honest assessment of them was used as material by critics on the lines that 'even the Bank admits its failures'. After a decade of changes, and as the outside criticism was beginning to rise to its peak with the fifty-years-is-enough movement, James Wolfensohn arrived with a mandate to impose his version of reform on the organization.

THE 1990S REFORM AGENDA – THE 'STRATEGIC COMPACT'

While elements of the opposition, such as the Meltzer Commission, had yet to make their statement, by 1995 other problems were already well aired through both the concerns of outsiders regarding the Bank's assistance strategies and those of insiders regarding the Bank's processes and operational efficiency. By February 1997 Wolfensohn had refined the list of problems to one that he presented to the board of directors as part of a proposal for reforms known as the Strategic Compact.[32]

The main idea of the Strategic Compact, or the 'Compact', was that, in return for a short-term restructuring investment, the Bank would be reorganized in a way that would provide cost savings and improved output, to achieve greater effectiveness in its developmental goals. The Compact set a target of 100% satisfactory performance in portfolio management, lending services, and non-lending (advisory) services, and in the design quality of new projects. It also called for an increase in 'front-line' expenditure to 60% of the budget. Its benefits would be better development impact, improved service delivery, resource allocation and efficiency, stronger partnerships, and professional excellence.

The purpose of the Strategic Compact, as set down by Wolfensohn, was *inter alia* to '*invest now in order to deliver a fundamentally improved institution in the future – quicker, less bureaucratic, able to respond continuously to changing client demands and global development opportunities, and more effective in achieving its main mission: reducing poverty*' (p. 1).

---

[32] World Bank, 'The Strategic Compact; Renewing the Bank's Effectiveness to Fight Poverty'. The Strategic Compact was presented to the board in February 1997.

It continued: *'[A]ll of this will inevitably involve fundamental changes in the capabilities the Bank must build if it is to take its effectiveness to a higher level: more flexible organizational structures, which can empower and enable staff to be more responsive to our clients; higher professional standards and more investment in staff to acquire cutting edge skills, and a revitalized management cadre'.*

The Compact program divided itself into four sections, which were known as 1) refueling current business activity, 2) refocusing the development agenda, 3) retooling the Bank's knowledge base, and 4) revamping institutional capabilities.

The restructuring fund agreed to by the board was US$250 million over three years.[33] The fund was based on a gross cost of $420 million and a savings of $170 million, which amounted to about 11% of the current administrative budget. In addition, a supplementary amount was agreed to of $150 million over two years for an expected 500 to 700 employee redundancies. This latter fund was supposed to allow redundancies to be phased in in order to 'allow the Bank to move away from large, one-time redundancy exercises, which had caused serious disruption in the past', and to 'adjust its staffing smoothly, equitably and cost effectively'.[34] Following the conclusion of the Compact, in 2001, the administrative budget was to be reduced in real terms almost back to the level of 1997.[35]

Although the problems listed in the Compact were to some extent overlapping and needed similar kinds of remedies, they can be categorized into three main areas.

First were the problems of the Bank's corporate organization and internal processes. These were connected to the high transaction costs of delivering its output, failing product competitiveness, and failing

---

[33] Originally it had been budgeted over two years, but the board demurred on this, with the result that the up-front budget was reduced. The cuts in the projected restructuring programs were absorbed without opposition by management because there was an assumption that cost savings could be increased.

[34] About $400 million in redundancy payments were made over thirteen years (in 1987–1988, $149 million; in 1989–1994, $40 million; in 1995–1997, $120 million; and in 1998–2000, $120 million) and more than $75 million spent on leasing, outfitting, and moving out of office space.

[35] The original proposal was that by 2001 the real budget would be 3% above the 1997 level, but the board wanted a zero real increase in the 1997 budget.

project quality. There was an excessive *cost of doing business*, and *slow-ness* and *bureaucracy*. Information was not shared across the organization and instead confined to 'silos' and 'cylinders', while lengthy and demanding project processing schedules coincided with inflexibility in design and inability, and an excessive distance from the market, blunting the response to evolving county needs. These problems we look at in more detail in Chapter 4.

Second, there were problems connected with the Bank's inputs – in particular its human resources – that is, the appropriateness and level of its employee skills. This was thought to include a lack of *systematic knowledge building* and a decline in knowledge generation, a *lack of expertise*, and an under-investment in training. These problems are dealt with mainly in Chapter 5.

Third, there were *inappropriate projects* that were designed with insufficient relevance to the needs of client economies. There was a *decline in the Bank's project lending* despite low interest rates, partly due to the inappropriate projects, but also due to the high transaction costs and increasing competition from other sources of finance. There were the problems associated with *inappropriate project conditionality*, largely but not exclusively with the structural adjustment loans, as we have seen, which added to the transaction costs. There were *unsatisfactory project outcomes* whose measured quality had been declining for several years according to the Bank's own Operations Evaluation Department, and there was a static menu of *financial products*. This final set of problems we look at in more detail in Chapters 6, 7, and 8.

The reforms of the 1990s thus set out to address this combination of problems, which can be summarized as: a) ineffective business process, b) inadequate human resources, and c) unsatisfactory product type and quality.

In March 2001, at the conclusion of the Strategic Compact, Wolfensohn wrote a letter to the board accompanying an internal assessment of the Compact. He wrote:[36] *'We knew that the Strategic*

---

[36] Wolfensohn, James, 'Memorandum to the Executive Directors on the Assessment of the Strategic Compact', World Bank, March 13, 2001.

Compact was an ambitious undertaking, that required a certain degree of risk-taking and openness to learning from experience. In part because of the investments made through the Compact, and with the support of the Board and Management and the hard work of staff, the Bank today is a far more effective organization, with a richer capability to meet the complex development challenges of the 21st century'.

How far the reforms actually succeeded as a response to the critique is the concern of the rest of this book. The questions are: What changed? At what cost? Was the cost justified? Did the changes really improve the institution's ability to deliver on its mandate, the fight against poverty? And, if not, what should it do? What kind of process and organization should the Bank have to make it effective in producing these services? Part II considers these problems and the effectiveness of the measures taken to deal with them.

PART II

THE SEARCH FOR EFFECTIVENESS

3

Fifty Years of Bank Reforms

EARLY CHANGES

While the 1990s reforms are the major interest here, they were not the first. The Bank has gone through a number of reorganizations, from top management reshuffles and shifts in organizational emphasis to root-and-branch restructuring and re-engineering.

The first reorganization, of the IBRD, was in 1952. As the institution expanded, President Eugene Black found it necessary to regionalize operations, supported by a central projects department. In 1972 there was a more thoroughgoing reorganization. Using his experience at the Ford Motor Company, Robert McNamara introduced planning and financial control, an audit committee of the directors and an internal auditor. He set up an operational evaluation unit that was later, in 1973, renamed the Operations Evaluation Department (OED) reporting directly to the board of directors. He decentralized further to the regions, and country program plans were introduced as a focus for lending. The purpose of decentralization in McNamara's conception was to develop a 'creative tension' between country programs (oriented toward country monitoring and macroeconomic support) and country projects (oriented toward specific operations on the ground). This was an idea that foreshadowed much more complicated later initiatives. McNamara aggressively expanded the institution's role and capacity within this framework, and the subsequent history of the Bank has in some sense been a reaction to his initiatives.

After McNamara left the post the Bank entered a period starting with President Tom Clausen (1981–1986) during which it was less closely managed and became increasingly vulnerable to outside criticism and increasingly subject to a confrontational economic orthodoxy, discussed later. U.S. concern about overexpansion resulted in Clausen commissioning a report in 1983 by consultants Bowman Cutter,[1] which concluded that loan expansion had been at the expense of quality. The Bowman Cutter report broke new ground by proposing that the Bank should have a strategic plan. It put more emphasis on the quality of implementation, decentralization, and country focus, themes that have recurred ever since.

Shareholder pressure, mainly from the United States, started to develop on administrative costs, salaries, and effectiveness. In 1986, at the prodding of the United States, the board rejected the proposed staff expansion and administrative budget, and this triggered a third, much deeper, reorganization. The consistent U.S. refrain was now of an overpaid, bloated 'pin-stripe bureaucracy' that needed to be reined in. The Bank's location in Washington (originally at U.S. insistence and against the wishes of other shareholders) gave it a visibility and vulnerability that it would probably not have had if it had been based in New York, where the comparators might have included Wall Street. Congress now decided that World Bank staff should be subject to similar constraints as the increasingly impoverished federal civil service.

Barber Conable, who had had to be almost coerced into taking the job of president in 1986,[2] found himself having to cope with demands for a major reorganization. With no experience of world development assistance, or of running a large organization, he was obliged to initiate steps to change the way development assistance was organized. While growth had decelerated since the McNamara presidency ended, there had still been a steady increase in lending. The Bank, according to Conable, was now being perceived as 'an organization out of control'.[3]

---

[1] 'Resource Allocation and Control Study', Bowman Cutter, 1983.
[2] James Baker, then Treasury Secretary, was the main persuader.
[3] Interview with Barber Conable cited in Kapur, Devesh, J. Lewis, and R. Webb, *The World Bank: Its First Half Century*, Brookings, 1997, p. 1199.

The task was to rationalize and focus its lending activities, streamline its administration, and restructure its skills to address changed needs. He hired the consulting firm of Cresap, McCormick and Paget to recommend changes. The result was the 1987 reorganization – an event that changed the basic culture of the Bank like no other, and disposed of the growth-based optimism and to some extent the idealism of the McNamara era. The drive for institutional redefinition that started in 1987 now heralded an era of increasingly aggressive reform efforts.

THE 1980S: THE CONABLE REORGANIZATION

The 1987 reorganization focused, like previous reforms, on organizational structure, but it also sought to reorganize and reduce the workforce. The process produced redundancies that amounted in the end to about 5% of the total employment. The reorganization further developed the focus on countries by creating unified country-group departments supported by specialist units, this time at both the central and regional levels. Four senior vice presidents were created compared to the two previously, creating a complete extra top management layer. Technical specialists and engineers (especially in agriculture) were squeezed out, reducing the Bank's technical capacity, because it was expected that economic policy reform rather than technical projects would become increasingly the Bank's business. The organization was now redesigned to create skill pools to service country-based operational units and allow yet more focus on countries. The formal aim was to integrate more of the Bank's operations at the client level, thus following the path that the Bank has been on since Eugene Black.[4]

The objectives of the 1987 reorganization were not particularly controversial. There was widely perceived to be a need for change, in

---

[4] A more covert agenda was to reorganize top management, reducing the power of Ernie Stern, an American who had effectively been running the Bank. Stern became the finance chief while Moeen Qreshi became the operations chief.

particular less 'bureaucracy' and more responsiveness to country needs. The problem was the way it was done. In order to identify weak performers and excess management layers, all professional staff were nominally fired on a certain date in early 1987 and had to re-apply for newly created positions. Vice presidents selected senior managers, senior managers selected middle managers, and middle managers selected junior managers and staff over a period of several weeks, or, in some cases, months.

Despite the intention, the process was not likely to lead to a more effective workforce. This kind of hiring procedure was, for example, open to cronyism. The leader of the project, Kim Jaycox, reassured the *New York Times* on July 7, 1987, that 'the staff is in an uproar ... but the Bank will be stronger, less bureaucratic and more responsive to its debtor country clients'. But one employee said that 'people have been afraid to travel because they didn't know whether they would have a desk when they came back'. The Staff Association filed a complaint with the Bank's internal Administrative Tribunal charging arbitrary and subjective selection. However, William Stanton (former U.S. Congressman and Counsel to Barber Conable) said 'Barber bit the bullet; I don't know of any organization that's ever done anything this big, voluntarily, to make itself more efficient and to bring it in line with its future responsibilities'.[5]

Following the reforms, to his credit, Conable, who knew little about managing a large organization but who had been an effective chairman of the powerful U.S. House of Representatives Ways and Means Committee, skillfully managed to restore some morale. But, despite the sweeping nature of the reform process and the comfortable predictions of those responsible for it, the expected improvements in efficiency did not materialize. On the contrary, its legacy was a weakened sense of institutional worth and a damaged psychological contract between the employees and the institution. The reforms did not effectively match skills to requirements, and they cut capacity just as new responsibilities

[5] William Stanton, former Ohio congressman, in World Bank Oral History Project, cited in Kapur, Devesh, J. Lewis, and R. Webb, *The World Bank: Its First Half Century*, Brookings, 1997.

were being assumed (for the environment, the promotion of the private sector, and Eastern Europe).

A Staff Association report in March 1988, after the reorganization was completed, stated that staff saw three main problems, which were essentially the same problems as before: lack of direction, ineffective leadership, and unclear goals. There was, it said, a lack of communication, a lack of transparency, and a lack of trust in management; the board, staff, and management were pulling in different directions. 'The reorganization' it said, 'has cast doubt over the idea that there is a reason to plan and work together .... Reorganization has led to disorganization and insecurity'.

Conable's reforms were a response to the revolt over the budget and also a response to Congress in support of a large increase in authorized capital for the continued expansion of the institution. Regardless of the quality of the reform process, the capital increase duly arrived, expanding the IBRD's lending ceiling by 75%. Yet five years on, in 1992, the Wapenhans report could still conclude that there were serious problems of eroding quality and effectiveness. Its diagnosis was reminiscent of that of the 1983 consultant's report: a rush to approve loans and inadequate concern with the quality. Essentially, the Conable reforms had achieved little or nothing in terms of improved organizational efficiency despite the certainties of the reformers.

Following the 1987 events, the most important adjustments, which occurred under Conable's successor, Lewis Preston, included the appointment of managing directors in 1991 to run the organization, and the introduction of 'thematic' vice presidencies in 1992, partly responding to outside pressure by the United States to cater more directly to the private sector, skills, and the environment but without direct operational responsibility.

These changes had little to do with the traditional aims of reducing bureaucracy and increasing focus. Rather, they ran contrary to these objectives and increased the weight of the organization at the center and at the top, and confused the reporting lines. Under the pressure of the 1992 Wapenhans report, the U.S. Congress, and the 'fifty-years-is-enough' campaign, Preston laid out a need for further change at the

Bank's Annual Meeting in 1994. He was not able to implement his proposals because he was forced to retire shortly thereafter because of ill health. James Wolfensohn thus assumed the reorganizational responsibility in 1995.

1995: WOLFENSOHN TAKES CHARGE

Jim Wolfensohn was a man of wide-ranging talents, and had risen near to the top of a series of important financial institutions,[6] but he had no regular public sector experience, and he had no experience with the kind of foreign assistance activities that the Bank conducted. His fitness for the job stemmed to a large extent from the perception of him as a transformational figure from the financial world who would somehow make an impact on a large organization that somehow would not change. He is said to have read fifty books on the Bank before his arrival, of which only one was favorable, and he assumed office with that in mind and with the multiple outside pressures to move ahead with reforms.

Wolfensohn signaled the start of a new order when he announced to the staff on his arrival in June 1995 that, 'I will regard externally-voiced criticism of the Bank – of ourselves – as an indication of a desire to find alternative employment'. This was alarming and unprecedented, but it signaled a new energy that attracted support from many who wanted good leadership and meaningful change. At the same time he also wrote: '[F]rom what I can see we are blessed with a group of dedicated and highly-qualified people – diverse and caring, with a long and unique collective experience'. It turned out, however, that Wolfensohn in fact intended to seek changes in that group of dedicated and highly qualified people.

After returning from a program of exploratory visits to client countries he set up two top-level internal task forces to develop change visions and they reported back to him later in 1995. The Bank had a

---

[6] He had been an executive partner of Salomon Brothers in New York and head of its investment banking department, deputy chairman of Schroders Ltd. in London, president of J. Henry Schroders' subsidiary corporation in New York, and managing director of Darling & Co. of Australia.

choice, they said, between 'slow death and irrelevance' on the one hand and an enhanced role as the 'global premier development institution' on the other. The Bank, they said, faced external threats: dissatisfaction with its performance, competition in lending, and 'aid fatigue'. It faced broad internal problems of eroding skills, remoteness from the client, obsession with process, low morale, lack of clear goals, and resistance to genuine culture change.

Following the task force report, in late 1995 change initiatives duly got under way with a ferment of discussion and proposals throughout the organization, and the start of a change process with a pilot in the Africa regional area.

Under pressure to deliver, the new president wanted overt signs that things were happening. But change could not be immediately visible. In March 1996, impatient at the seemingly slow pace, he summoned 300 managers for a meeting. He implored them to break through the 'glass wall', to get enthusiasm, change, and commitment. 'Unless you give the leadership and unless you have the belief ... we cannot win', he said. And he concluded his address with a by-now characteristic gesture of despair: 'I don't know what else to do,' he said, 'I just beg you to think about it'. His *cri de coeur* puzzled his listeners because most were already well aware of, immersed in, and quite committed to serious action. Wolfensohn was seemingly detached from the details of what was actually happening.

There was a rapid formation throughout the organization of change management groups, and an equally rapid introduction of change rhetoric. To assist the process, the head of external relations, Mark Malloch Brown, was elevated to the rank of vice president and change bulletins were launched to explain what was going on, since most people were not focusing much on the details but waiting for what was to come. The general attitude was still positive if cautious.

In line with much outside management thinking of the time, the pilot project that went ahead in 1996 in the Africa regional department introduced an experimental matrix management system consisting of country units and a skill pool, initially just in the area of human development. The previously smaller, specialist divisions became a larger,

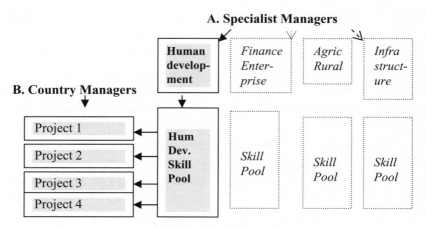

Figure 1. The Africa pilot matrix.

regional skill pool that was called a Technical Family. The idea is set out in Figure 1.

The skill pool was the total of the specialized human development resources available within the regional department. Management authority was to be channeled both through projects under the control of country managers and through the skill pools under the specialist managers. The pilot initially balanced management power on each axis of the matrix.[7] While the pilot only applied to the human development specialists in one region, a full matrix would apply to all the other regions and specializations as well.

THE REFORMS DERAIL

While the 1996 pilots showed some promise, they did not however have a chance to show either their strengths or their weaknesses before the pressure built up to roll them out institution-wide. Within months, in February 1997, their replication institution-wide was formalized in the Strategic Compact, Wolfensohn's proposal for greater organizational

---

[7] Other matrix options allowed for weaker or stronger control on the task/project axis (balanced and unbalanced matrices). In the full version of the Bank's system applied later, strong task control prevailed – through the country managers who had control over budgets, as explained in Chapter 4.

effectiveness in return for a short-term investment and a redundancy program to 'adjust its staffing smoothly, equitably and cost effectively'.

The Compact was put to a board of directors reluctant to sanction large expenditures against more plans. Nevertheless, it was successfully maneuvered through and the required increase in the administrative budget was agreed on. But then, from the moment of approval, the top management appeared to see their task as complete. Their immediate goal had been to ease the budget constraint, and that had been achieved. The inconvenient details and effective leadership of the detailed changes were then passed down to the regional chiefs and below.

Signs of distress emerged quickly. The reforms were not well planned from the start. One of the indications of this was a Cost Effectiveness Review, the latest in the series of consultants' reports commissioned by successive Bank presidents. This review was, however, largely conducted after the Compact was already launched[8] to confirm the results that had in effect already been promised to the board of directors. Its terms of reference restricted it to process issues such as savings in office space and computer systems, and it did not look at the organizational restructuring that had already started. One former consultant involved said that some of the top Bank managers did not understand its purpose and were hostile to the review. It projected cost savings of 14% by the fourth year, largely through the new integrated information system. However, it was nearly impossible for an outside consultant with limited access to make firm estimates in an atmosphere of organizational stress, and with most important changes not on the table for assessment.

The Review findings bore little relevance to reality. Among the benefits it predicted were 'just-in-time resolutions procedures ... quick hearings and decisions on the interpretation of policy'. It said that there would be simpler processes, better information systems, and clearer accountability. Above all, clients would benefit from 'more efficient and higher quality services'.[9]

The top management who had concurred in the initial reforms were not intimately involved in the execution of the reform plan. The

---

[8] The Cost Effectiveness Review was carried out by the consulting firm, KPMG.
[9] The Cost Effectiveness Review, ibid, pp. 3, 17.

president himself seemed to see his role as one of passionate exhortation and admonition while he pursued other interests that caught his kaleidoscopic attention. While the basic concepts of the changes were planned collectively and were approximately standard across the organization, each region developed its own version subject to three declared principles. These principles were a) increased focus on countries, b) less fragmentation, and c) de-layering of the staff. Otherwise, they were free to let a thousand flowers bloom. The board of directors, meanwhile, once it had been co-opted, was seemingly content to monitor the course of the treatment with polite and diplomatically worded queries to the top management's regular optimistic change progress reports.

Just as interest eroded at the top, the energy, the support, and the understanding of the Compact's meaning also weakened within the organization as a whole. The Compact was increasingly viewed as a deal with the board to get a budget increase, not a coherent reform strategy, while the process itself decomposed into a series of initiatives many of which had already been under way from before. There was ostensibly a democratic process of dialogue up and down the organization, but in reality major decisions had already been made within a small group on the reform task force. Very soon a staff survey gave the process a very bad report. Less than one in five thought that the management system that was being introduced would meet its goals.

Unable to discern what exact progress was being made, the top management seemed to layer on more and more initiatives to try to create some of the expected overt signs for their boss and for the puzzled shareholders, while the employees became increasingly unimpressed with slogans and non-actionable mission statements.[10] One senior

---

[10] A typically inoperable regional declaration of purpose said: '[W]e will build teams that include the client through greater decentralization to the field, greater reliance on and empowerment of our national staff, more intense consultation and frankness in dialogue with our client, and greater participation of the various stakeholders in our work . . . . Building and sustaining team spirit is an art which we need to learn to appreciate and practice'. It went on: '[L]earning events will be customized and closely aligned to business needs . . . . Programs will be developed on a just-in-time basis, and will be refined based on experimentation; i.e. pilot, evaluate, strengthen and roll out more broadly'.

manager, Manual Conthe, who was in charge of financial sector development and was not part of the reform inner group, circulated a memorandum that was leaked to the *Financial Times* newspaper. It said, '[W]hat the Bank staff regularly identifies and decries in developing countries, few people have the courage to recognize at home; as in the fable, it is not always easy to announce that "the emperor has no clothes."' Here was groupthink in operation.

Predictably, by 2001, at the end of the Strategic Compact period, only three out of nine areas of savings projected by the Cost Effectiveness Review were achieved, and the savings were largely in reduced office rent. A look-back review said: 'It is difficult to reconcile these overoptimistic projections (which were endorsed by the Board and management) with the fact that the Review itself was finalized several months into the first compact year, and that even upon completion, it did not satisfy the requirements of a ready-to-implement plan'.[11]

Professor John Kotter, a well-known professor of change management at Harvard Business School, proposed eight steps for successful organizational transformation. They were to *increase urgency, build the guiding team, get the vision right, communicate for buy-in, empower action, create short-term wins, don't let up*, and *make change stick*. Such concepts were influential in the Bank in the late 1990s partly because of the number of managers that attended a retraining course at Harvard Business School. But following the first two steps, on few of others steps did it seem that the Bank's reform process measured up to the ideals.

REFORM AFTER THE STRATEGIC COMPACT

The Compact reform program formally ended in 2001. The following years were taken up by implementation, amendment, and reversal of the initiatives of 1997–2001 as the Bank struggled to rationalize the changes that had engulfed it. Selected aspects of the reforms were followed up by President Paul Wolfowitz over 2005 to 2007. As we will show later, Wolfowitz arrived

---

[11] 'Strategic Compact Review', World Bank, 2001.

with intentions that did not require further task forces or consultants' reports. Notably, in the face of opposition inside and outside the Bank, he continued, on a smaller scale, the focus on internal changes. He introduced formal anti-corruption mechanisms and he strengthened a watchdog organ known as the Department of Institutional Integrity (DII) to investigate possible corruption within and outside the organization[12] and announced plans to deploy anti-corruption experts to local offices to fight corruption at its roots rather than wait for it to emerge.[13] He explained the extent of the problem to the *Financial Times*: 'I mean very precisely clear-cut cases of bribes, kickbacks, manipulation of the contracting process, fraudulent procurement'. The Department of Institutional Integrity said that there were 387 unresolved internal investigations ranging from corruption to sexual harassment. It accelerated the disqualification of private firms from working with the World Bank and banned 112 additional private firms from supplying goods and services to the Bank in two years, an unprecedented increase.[14]

Wolfowitz's zealous pursuit of the Bank's supposedly corrupt heart led him to raise the bar on corruption both inside and outside the Bank to new heights. But, in May 2007 he personally failed to clear the hurdle and had to resign.[15] The culmination of the anti-corruption initiative, after his resignation, was a report by a commission under Paul Volcker[16] that proposed, among other actions, the elevation of the

[12] The DII head was Suzanne Rich Folsom, a Bush loyalist. Though originally hired by Wolfensohn in an attempt to co-opt external opponents, she was appointed by Wolfowitz to head the department.

[13] Wolfowitz's sensitivity to the World Bank's possible corruption may have stemmed from his disquiet at the Iraq reconstruction effort that had been part of his own responsibility at the Pentagon. Transparency International's 2005 Global Corruption Report (p. 87) said that failing urgent steps, Iraq would become 'the biggest corruption scandal in history'. Indeed, said Transparency International, 'the US has been a poor role model in how to keep corrupt practices at bay'.

[14] Balls, Andrew and Edward Alden, 'Wolfowitz Anti-Graft Mission Triggers World Bank Strife', *Financial Times*, July 12, 2005.

[15] In April 2007, Wolfowitz was forced to resign because of the leadership crisis that followed the revelations regarding his misuse of the personnel system in favor of his personal friend, Shaha Riza.

[16] Independent Panel Review of the World Bank Group Department of Institutional Integrity, Washington, DC, September 13, 2007.

watchdog department to the level of a vice presidency, giving it the highest operational profile.

Wolfowitz's successor, Robert Zoellick, endorsed the Volcker Commission proposals, and offered the job of the head of the DII to Leonard McCarthy, former boss of the elite South African crime-fighting unit known as the 'Scorpions'. Thus the Bank's employees, as well as nefarious outside elements, could potentially now be treated to the mafia-style scratiny that they apparently merited. Otherwise, however, he wisely and at long last began to close the book on years of internal disruption and to re-focus attention on the Bank's main purpose: development assistance and the development of the Bank's global products.

4

The 1990s – Re-Engineering the Organization

INTRODUCTION

This and the following chapters deal in more detail with the reform initiatives of the 1990s. Here we deal with the range of initiatives that were core elements of the reforms, that is, related to *organizational restructuring*. First the matrix management system is considered because that was the central element, and then it is combined with the next key element, known as the internal market. Associated with these two initiatives was reform of the structure of management. Closely intertwined were the new knowledge networks and the information systems, and related to all these organizational initiatives was the aim of *moving to the front line*. A specific organizational change, the merger of parts of the Bank and the IFC, is considered, and then finally we look at what the employees thought about it. The order of events is as follows:

- the matrix
- the internal market
- management structure
- knowledge and networks
- the front line and backline
- Bank/IFC corporate merger
- the verdict of the employees

THE MANAGEMENT MATRIX

In accordance with the proposals of the Strategic Compact, set out in Chapter 2, at the core of the 1990s reforms was a reorganization of the operational areas of the Bank, the purpose of which was to address the issues of excess bureaucracy – that is, the excessive *cost of doing business* with the Bank, and the *slowness and lack of response* of the organization, while at the same time increasing its focus on the country clients of the Bank and increasing the chances of country buy-in. A key element of the changes was the matrix management system, which was expected to deal with dysfunctional compartmentalization and hierarchy, which were two cardinal sins in the 1990s world of corporate re-engineering.

Since the 1980s many traditional hierarchical command-and-control enterprises re-engineered themselves into flatter, leaner organizations. Many adopted the matrix structure where staff was managed by multiple managers – typically organized along the specialist (or functional) and the country (or 'product') groupings that were depicted in Figure 1. The purpose of matrix management was to improve the use of resources. Rather than up-and-down line management with fixed resources, a good matrix was supposed to achieve both vertical and horizontal control. Cross-functional integration, coordination, and standardization can increase productivity. Team members can share information more readily across task boundaries while more specialization is encouraged.[1]

At the same time it was recognized that, if inexpertly handled, a matrix could also lead to an unintended relocation of power and conflicts within management that could impede rather than improve the flow of business and information. Employees within matrix structures were often told they have been empowered to take greater responsibility, but in fact they might face conflicting pressure from multiple managers. The primary problem was that the matrix broke the conventional rule that everyone should have a clearly defined reporting line. To neutralize such disadvantages, at the very least, a highly cooperative environment was needed.

---

[1] For an early reference see Knight, Kenneth, ed., *Matrix Management: A Cross-Functional Approach to Organization*, PBI-Petrocelli Books, 1977.

A senior manager, quoted by the Bank's Staff Association in their June–July 2001 newsletter, stated, '[A]ll the global consulting firms were becoming more matrixed, realizing that knowledge was the key to their success. . . . All the leading firms were telling Jim that most firms were struggling with the tension between client and quality'. 'It was being written up in the textbooks, taught at Harvard Business School. Everybody was doing it . . .'. One of Wolfensohn's main advisers, John Mcarthur, had been a professor and dean at Harvard Business School.

In contrast, the Staff Association had been dubious. In June 2000, three years into the new system, the association newsletter was asking continued questions. 'The idea of reorganizing an institution to cut hierarchy and promote team-based work', it wrote, 'comes from several exciting fields – aerospace and software development and other high profile engineering industries, computer and software development. In these industries workers gather into a team around a project, often a high profile or glamorous task. Stakes are high, time is critical and creativity flows'. There are, they said, no egos; there is value-added; there is trust in the organization; and there is no hierarchy. 'Is this the model for the Bank?' the association asked. 'Does it have practical applicability; does it have the right conditions?'

The matrix had been piloted with some apparent success in 1996 in the Africa area, but the conditions of the organization-wide introduction were different because they coincided with two other critical initiatives, budget cuts and the introduction of an 'internal market'. Furthermore, the budget was now allocated unevenly, transforming the balanced matrix of the pilot into an unbalanced one for the full roll-out.

Extending from the pilot depicted in Figure 1, which applied only to the human development specialization, the full matrix pooled technical skills in all the functional specialist areas, while the projects came under the jurisdiction of country managers who ran very small operational units. The idea was to get a critical mass of sector skills and the 'best teams' from across the organization, while the country managers channeled and coordinated assistance activities. The country managers also controlled budgets, so small groups of non-specialists dictated terms to large groups of specialists. The country managers contracted people from the skill pools to do the work.

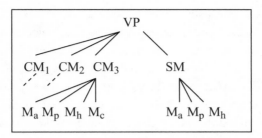

Figure 2. Old system pre-1997.

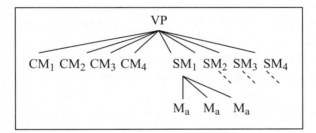

Figure 3. New system post-1997.

In addition to the new matrix system and in parallel with it, structures called 'networks' were created, run by their own vice presidents. These were to be knowledge centers serving the skill pools, and more will be said about them later. Figures 2 and 3 show the changes in the organization brought about by the matrix alone.

The essential change post-1997 was the consolidation of the specialist areas by moving personnel from the country managers (CMs) to regional skill pools under the specialist managers (SMs).[2] Whereas before 1997 the CMs had been in control of their own mini-groups of specialists, they were now left 'naked' while the SM area was multiplied and expanded. The naked CMs post-1997 were also more numerous, to allow them to focus on smaller groups of countries. The naked CMs, with minimal staff, now also controlled the whole budget, whereas before the budget had been allocated between country areas and specialist areas. Thus the matrix was deliberately 'unbalanced'.

[2] These are not the actual titles used in the Bank but are for illustration here.

The design was initially perceived to be acceptable, and management in general indicated that it knew what needed to be done to implement it. However, there proved to be a number of inherent flaws. The span of management control was much reduced in the case of the country managers and much increased in the case of the specialist managers.[3] The line of authority under the new system was that specialist managers reported upward to the vice president, but since the country managers controlled the funds, the specialists also answered laterally to the country managers.

The specialist groups had diffused and weakened management, large staff, complex reporting lines, large span-of-control responsibilities, and no funds, and the country units had defined management, few staff, a simple reporting line, narrow span of control, and all the funds. As for the individual specialists, they reported first to their own managers and second to the country managers, in line with a standard matrix. But the situation was confused because the specialist management was weak and the country management was strong. This led independent-minded specialist staff to try to assert independence from both. Unlike the textbook model in which employees were caught in a cross-fire from multiple management, these individuals dictated terms to management.

There was a particular flaw in the matrix concept in the conditions prevailing in the Bank. This was because the gain from skill pooling, if it was in practice achievable, would tend to be offset by a loss from the breakup of former mini-pools under country managers that had been dedicated to specific countries. There was a trade-off between skill-synergy and country-synergy. But this trade-off was itself not exact because, unlike a consulting firm or commercial knowledge organization, the Bank engaged many of its 'clients', who were also its members, in a dialogue relationship that put a premium on the continuity of assistance. Pooling of contracted skills might not reap gains when there was a need for this continuous, multidimensional relationship.

---

[3] Especially problematic when the managers were expected to be 'coaches'.

A matrix system in these circumstances might reduce effectiveness even if it were well executed.[4]

The one organizational change where there was by common consent a more positive effect was geographical decentralization. Decentralization had, as we have seen, been going on for years, but the difference was that it now received a renewed burst of energy. By 2003 three-quarters of the country managers were stationed outside Washington, where they could concentrate on development assistance, away from the political and bureaucratic pressures in the head office. But geographical relocation was not a product of the matrix as such. Furthermore, it increased costs because of the extras of running large numbers of fully equipped offices, and, as we shall see, this created the conditions later for the inexorable re-merging of countries into larger groups of three countries or more as under the discredited, old system. By 2005 some country managers (known formally as country directors) once more oversaw six or seven countries.

One of the first and most urgent revisions of the new system was to try and revive the middle management so as to re-establish control. But this was done inconsistently between regions, and in any case the new contracting system associated with the matrix removed much of the specialist managers' ability to allocate their resources properly. All management levels were restored after initial experimentation, and the same number of layers of authority existed as before. What was achieved by the disruption was in essence a re-allocation and re-labeling of resources. Another word for 'pooling' was 're-centralization'. In the head office a small number of employees were now more decentralized while the majority was now more centralized.

There had been skill pools under the old system, but they were smaller. The new system claimed to have created a 'critical mass' pool of technical people, but that was not clear since under the old system there had also been regional and central pools of expertise available. Skill compartmentalization had existed under the old system, but it was probably not as bad as imagined. The matrix might still have been

---

[4] One of the main complaints of the client countries was the lack of continuity on the Bank's teams. For example, this was one of the points raised by the government of Russia (see *Russia, Country Assistance Evaluation*, OED, May 2002).

manageable, and the expected synergy brought about by skill pooling might have been achieved with sensitive leadership. But this was also not in evidence. The matrix by most accounts effectively broke up the teams that the reorganization was trying to build.

THE INTERNAL MARKET MEETS THE MATRIX

The matrix system was only one of the main pillars of the new organizational edifice. Another was the internal market system. It was thought that the introduction of an internal market combined with the matrix would improve efficiency by simulating the advantages of market allocation within a non-market setting. A central idea was to move away from supply-determined activity and make the new country managers into filters of outside market demand for services. The idea was that this system would support a 'delicate new balance' of expertise and country focus.

In the new matrix system, where the country managers had the money and no people and the specialist managers had the people and no money, the work of the Bank was supposed to proceed on the basis of contracts between the countries and the specialists. So, while the country managers might well focus most attentively on their countries of responsibility, they had to go to the market to find technical specialists temporarily to share that focus before the specialists moved on to other things, as required by the matrix. So an asymmetry was created whereby one group was more focused and the other group (much larger) was less focused. The teams were now more difficult to keep together, while at the same time being more essential within a new emphasis on country buy-in. And, as mentioned, the budgetary limitations led to the re-merging of countries under each country manager, and the skill pool started to split into country groups, only less organized than before. The in-organization contract environment was not one in which either improved country focus or increased technical excellence would be expected to easily flourish, but rather one with a reduced sense of commitment to the objectives of the organization.

The possibility of improving efficiency in an organization by simulating a market internally bears further thought in any case. The Nobel Laureate economist, Ronald Coase, a pioneer of institutional economics, pointed out that organizations are created because they replace formal contracts between individuals with cooperative arrangements based on rules. That is, within an organization there are 'incomplete contracts' involving less formal relationships that work because there is a framework of rules. Now the rules could, with time, lose their effectiveness and need to be changed, but an internal market is a questionable way of making such a change because it introduces contracts into a system that is supposed to replace contracts. It is also difficult to create a genuine market because the providers and demanders of services are not independent of each other and cannot charge fees according to their merits. Furthermore, a market risks breaking the psychological contract that maintains employee morale and loyalty and which is particularly important in public organizations where employee motivation is as much policy- and service-oriented as monetary. The breaking of the psychological contract in turn encourages intensified competitive behavior among professionals who find themselves obliged to preempt such behavior in others.[5]

The place of competition within an organization is another issue. A distinction can be made between creative and dysfunctional competition.[6] Which type prevails depends on whether the system is open (infinite) or closed (zero sum). Open competition is subject to clear arbitration and under the control of competitors. Normally, professional competition is of this type. In the short run most competition tends to be more closed because of fixed budgets and staffing. In the longer run it is more open and more creative. But if there is a long-term budget squeeze coupled with uncertainty about resources, then even professional competition can become closed and dysfunctional. McNamara's tenure was characterized by open competition among professionals amidst budget expansion, while the 1990s saw closed competition amid a budget squeeze. Instead of using the best resources from the pools, it was often necessary to use the cheapest, most inexperienced resources, thereby rendering experienced

[5] An account of such effects is in Callahan, David, *The Cheating Culture: Why More Americans Are Doing Wrong to Get Ahead*, Harcourt, 2004. Callahan argues that aggressive behavior within organizations is fostered by incentive-driven structures.

[6] See Handy, Charles, *Understanding Organizations*, Penguin, 1983, p. 293.

individuals redundant. During the Bank's reorganization period, and beyond, the combination of budget cutting and reallocation together with the internal market system seemed to create a strong element of dysfunctional competition.

Finally, to implement the contractual system required defined budgets based on work norms, time recording, and work program agreements in place of the previous negotiated system. Time now had to be accounted for under specific task codes based on projects because specialist departments had to have some basis for charging themselves to country units. But the typical work flow of an organization like the Bank included a considerable amount of time spent on strategizing, planning, policy making, and general research and development, which was not billable. With the introduction of the new system the non-billables had to be entered into timesheets under categories such as 'self-instruction' for which no money was allocated, and those who had too much uncategorized time knew that their jobs were at risk. This could be justified as a neat way of cutting personnel, but in the circumstances of the reforms, including especially major budget stringency that was imposed at the latter stages of the Strategic Compact period, the few who held budget power over the many were effectively able to make personnel decisions, sometimes even to settle scores.

The rushed reforms not surprisingly created an environment characterized by perverse incentives.[7] The unintended adverse consequence of the internal market on employee attitudes was one example. The potential for score-settling created by the unbalanced control over the matrix and budget was another. A further example was the time-recording system, which became a battleground for two or three years. The Staff Association wrote in June 2001: 'Everyone who could began to charge everybody else to bolster their budget and also to prove the need for their existence'. The internal contract (work program agreement) system was a very resource-intensive exercise creating more than 1,500

---

[7] Incentives in organizations are increasingly used as explanations for organizational behavior. Perverse incentives, where incentives produce adverse results, have been examined in, e.g., Laffont, Jean-Jacques and David Martimort, *The Theory of Incentives: The Principal-Agent Model*, Princeton University Press, 2002.

agreements. It required a major expansion in administrative staff. The system put intense pressure on individuals to compete for work in the internal market, impacting morale and stress levels, and provided a disincentive to knowledge sharing. The desire for fully costed products, said the Association, led to a complex and expensive budgetary system for what was really a simple cost structure.

WEAK OR STRONG MANAGEMENT?

In addition to the problem of lost synergy, there were questionable changes to the managerial span of control that had been reduced to a minimal level in the country units and increased to an unwieldy level in the specialist departments. Organizational theory proposes a norm for span of control of about six, or perhaps eight, at the senior management level.[8] In the Africa specialist pool for finance and business development in 1999 almost 100 staff reported to two managers. As many as twenty directors reported directly to one vice president, who also had his own office and numerous lateral reporting and coordination functions. Knowledge network chiefs had the same rank as operational chiefs, and so large groups of vice presidents in both staff and line functions had to report directly to the same managing director.

At the middle management level, span of control was initially rein- terpreted as 'span of advice'. The weak management of specialist departments was consistent with an unbalanced matrix form, domi- nated by the project area rather than by the skill area, that is, by the country managers, in contrast to McNamara's 'creative tension', which gave equal weight to each. But the manager-as-advisor concept in the specialist areas was inappropriate per se because operational decisions were needed all the time, not just advice and mentoring, and because weak management was being applied precisely to those units that were the largest and needed the most coordination. In contrast to, say, a consulting business, where management-as-coach may be an appropri- ate idea, the Bank was not providing disinterested advice, or responding

---

[8] See, for example, Urwick, L. F., 'The Manager's Span of Control', *Harvard Business Review*, May 1956, pp. 39–47.

to externally provided assignments, or working to an externally given terms of reference or budgets. It was not a pure knowledge server but also a proactive programmer of development assistance that needed operational decision makers. There was a lack of understanding of the disconnect between broadening the span of control and weakening the management.

The manager-as-coach concept was being taught at a retraining program arranged for the Bank's managers at Harvard and other business schools. The management retraining program responded to Wolfensohn's reported surprise on finding that many Bank managers were former academics now applying theory in unfamiliar practical situations. But the former academics were themselves not necessarily impressed with the advice of the other academics. Said one skeptical retraining program participant in a Staff Association newsletter in 2001, '[E]verybody knows that HBS sells one big fad per decade. We even came in on the end of the current fad. In the beginning it was so touchy-feely that we weren't even responsible to those above us. The infantry-men were responsible. It seemed to us a copout'. The training program aimed at refocusing the Bank's traditionally reluctant management to management roles that were, perversely, in the process of being diluted in many cases.

The retraining program started in 1996 and lasted seven weeks spread over several months. It looked at strategy and competition, strategic management, leadership, and culture. By the end of 2000, more than 700 people, nearly 10% of the total staff, had gone to this course at a cost in excess of $12 million, excluding the cost to the organization of their absence. More than half of the participants in the courses were over the age of fifty, and as few as a quarter were below forty-five, an age group that might in a private company have been expected to contain the high flyers of the future. The courses were general to all participants, regardless of specialization. In effect they took the form of a 'perk' rather than a strategic executive development effort in the sense known in private industry. In fact, 20% of the participants were either let go or demoted later on.[9] Whether the courses achieved their goal of 'changing

---

[9]   Source: Strategic Compact Review.

culture' or recharging relevant skills is doubtful, but in any case, like so many elements of the reorganization, the concept was ill thought out, the timing was poor, and it created division when teamwork was otherwise being urged.

FACING MARKET REALITY

After more than three years of the matrix system, a letter from a group of staff in the Middle Eastern department that was leaked, once more, to the *Financial Times*[10] said that it had failed: 'We have', it said, 'experienced all the pitfalls of the matrix and are yet to see any benefits. It continues to be a cause of confusion and stress amongst staff and managers alike. The failure of the matrix system as originally envisaged has naturally led to the introduction and accumulation of corrective processes and controls. Bank processes, far from being simplified as was promised ... are more complex than ever. The responsibility for decision-making today is even more diffused than it was three years ago. The system has been a disaster ...'.

The executive director, Valeriano Garcia from Argentina, also spoke up at his farewell address about the new system: '[M]atrix management' he said, 'has substantially weakened the Bank's effectiveness. I think that the very important function of the Bank has been hindered by its new internal organization .... Matrix management has weakened accountability because the line between you and to whom you are accountable has become a labyrinth. The shortest way to accountability is one straight line. Now we have a maze'. The Bank, he said, is involved in too many things – '[W]e have 123 thematic groups .... We really need to be more focused'.

Teamwork, which was critical to the new matrix system, thus deteriorated during the reorganization. The Staff Association complained that the management had little understanding of the concepts and kept breaking up the actual teams.[11] In the new system, it said, everyone had to be generous with their chairs in the game of musical chairs. The enthusiasm

---

[10] *Financial Times*, January 31, 2001.
[11] Staff Association newsletter of June 2001.

for downsizing virtually doomed efforts to create a teamwork-oriented, low-hierarchy culture. Little effort was made to prepare the ground for the likely confusion caused by the loss of the traditional hierarchies.

The look-back review of the Strategic Compact in 2001 largely agreed. It stated: '[C]ontrary to beliefs that the individual internal market would contribute to achieving client responsiveness, indications soon began to appear that instead it inhibits teamwork, knowledge sharing, cross-organizational work, and creates a preoccupation with individual objectives rather than client objectives'. Teamwork and the internal market were working at cross-purposes, while loss of skills was preventing the possibility of making lower ranks more accountable. Managers struggled to find the time needed to mentor and develop staff appropriately. It concluded, contradictorily, that to make it work, the matrix needed a different mindset – a 'matrix in the mind'. The report confided that measures were now under way to address this need.[12]

Despite the realization that expectations had not been fulfilled, an official Bank newsletter, Bank's World Today, of 2001 still said that the matrix system could be credited with an increase in country focus, improved technical quality, and rapid response capacity. A board presentation in the same month intoned comfortingly: '[T]he theme for the next phase is convergence'. 'Convergence means harvesting the lessons of experimentation, identifying the principles that make for effective matrix functioning, providing feedback on their implementation and then holding key players accountable for judiciously applying these to their units'. '[W]e now have a common understanding', it said, 'of what these good practices are and how they will work . . .'. '[T]he good news is that the Bank has come a long way in learning how to manage its matrix'. The bad news was that this statement was largely untrue.

The emerging realities caused mounting concern, which led to a Budget Reform Group being appointed to recommend changes in the internal markets, budgets, country norms, the costing of corporate initiatives, and the charging system. Following the Bank's Strategic

---

[12] 'Strategic Compact Review', op cit.

Forum in January 2001, nearly four years after its introduction, it was announced that the internal contract process would be reformed to reduce the number of contracts and fix the budgets in advance for each year, allowing skill pools to plan their work, albeit still in the longer run dependent on the country managers.

THE NETWORKS: KNOWLEDGE AND ITS BUREAUCRATIZATION

The strengthening of knowledge and information was closely associated with the skill pooling measures taken through the matrix. As we have seen, the Bank's twin pillars of development assistance are through finance and know-how, and the know-how pillar was becoming increasingly important while financing was tending to be reduced in status. Wolfensohn formally announced a 'knowledge bank' at the 1996 annual meetings. The idea was reportedly triggered for Wolfensohn by a conversation with two senior managers (Jean Francois Rischard and Steve Denning) from his car as he sat in a New York traffic jam.[13]

Despite its opportunistic introduction, the knowledge bank initiative had far-reaching organizational ambitions, in alliance with the matrix and internal markets. It was to change the way in which the Bank operated, and transform its relationships with clients, partners, and stakeholders. It was supposed to require a shift from an individualistic mode of working and storing knowledge toward a team-based, sharing mode, opening up archives, filing cabinets, disparate computer systems, and personal know-how. The knowledge system was to be developed around help desks, information databases, statistics databases, a directory of expertise, Web sites, and team-based electronic platforms.

In 1993 three 'thematic' vice presidencies had been created, known as ESD (environmentally sustainable development), FPSD (finance and private sectors), and HRD (human resources). These creations were

---

[13] Steve Denning and Jean-Francois Rischard received Wolfensohn's call for ideas for his upcoming Annual Meeting speech when they were discussing how to get the Bank to take notice of the new concept of knowledge management (as told by Steve Denning, in Davenport, Thomas H., and Lawrence Prusak, *Working Knowledge: How Organizations Manage What They Know*, Harvard Business School Press, 1998).

prompted by outside pressure. The broad environmental lobby, increasingly insistent over the course of the 1980s and culminating in 1989 in legislation in Congress, was one main outside pressures, while the IFC capital increase of 1991 nearly failed over U.S. pressure to force the Bank to pursue a private sector development agenda. The three vice presidencies were advisory and control structures; they had no authority over lending operations and their role in relation to the Bank's core business of financing and knowledge production was obscure.

The 1990s reorganization found a role for the thematic vice presidents. They were to take charge of 'knowledge networks'. This idea was pushed particularly by one of the recipients of Wolfensohn's telephone call, Rischard. The thematic vice presidencies would become internal 'centers of excellence'. The principal MDs went along with the idea. Thus was created an infrastructure of advisory departments, quality control, and expanded support departments, paralleling the operations functions contained within the matrix and replacing the less ambitious and more decentralized previous formations. The networks were the central element of the new advisory infrastructure. They were supposed to integrate the Bank's knowledge into a widely usable resource through, for example, 'communities of practice'. They had a wide remit besides – to reduce fragmentation, increase information flow, set priorities, manage quality, run the information system, consolidate external partnerships, vet staff promotions, disseminate 'best practices', and, generally champion knowledge management.

By 2001, at the end of the reorganization, about 1.000 people were located in five networks. These were now known as economically and socially sustainable development (ESSD), private sector and infrastructure (PSI), human development (HD), financial sector (FIN), and poverty reduction and economic management (PREM). They supported 4,000 or so professional employees within the matrixed area, with some overlap. Each had a hierarchical structure, headed by its thematic vice president. Under the vice president was a council; under the council were sector boards, and under the sector boards were thematic teams, clusters, and/or groups. The network officials ranged from sector board heads down to members-at-large, representatives from other networks, and support staff. They had overlapping functions, so that many of the same faces (largely from middle management) met in the various inter-locking groupings, and areas of focus were often duplicated.[14]

This hierarchical structure was not readily consistent with best prac-tice as recommended by the knowledge management profession.[15] Rather, it was mainly the result of the attempt to integrate the poorly defined thematic vice presidencies into the Bank's organization. It also superseded relatively simple previous arrangements whereby the advi-sory units were partly decentralized and closer to operations. In the more informal system, knowledge had a better chance of being acquired as part of the learning experience of actual operations as well as through smaller expertise pools. This was a case where the scale advantages of centralization of resources were apparently expected to outweigh the innovation advantages of decentralization.

The reorganization pilot in the Africa regional department had estab-lished semi-informal working groups across disciplines, sectors, and countries that produced good results when coordinated by enthusiastic individual people. Formalizing such entities into networks did not nec-essarily increase their effectiveness. Instead, the creation of formal knowledge sharing structures risked bureaucratization. Knowledge might become supply-driven rather than demand-driven, a commodity waiting for a chance to be used. 'Knowledge' in fact might become something to be avoided. Formalization introduced minuting, report-ing, position-taking, time-filling, territory marking, and politics, activ-ities that raised transaction costs and barriers to knowledge transfer.

Four years after the foundation of the networks, a board report on the use of knowledge for growth in fact pointed to 'the need to better integrate capacity enhancement into mainstream lending and analytical work, drawing closer linkages between internal knowledge sharing, staff learning, and operational quality'.[16] The networks were tending to

---

[14] For example, the ESSD network had a council under which were three sector boards including a 'social sector board' in which there were 'thematic teams' such as teams on social policy and social capital; the HD network had a council that included three boards among which is a social protection sector board.

[15] This hierarchical structure was inconsistent with the textbook notion of democratic idea generation, as set out in, for example, McElroy, Mark W., *The New Knowledge Management – Complexity, Learning, and Sustainable Innovation*, KMCI, 2003.

[16] November 2001 edition of *Banks World*.

operate in parallel with, rather than partnering with, operations. In 2005,[17] nearly ten years down the reform road, an evaluation still complained about 'institutional silos' that prevent cross-sector dialogue, and inadequate links between knowledge and core business. At the extreme, operations were taking place without knowledge, and knowledge was being generated without operations. It was exactly the kind of problem that the reorganization was intended to solve.

The bureaucratization of knowledge, according to one of the leading thinkers, McElroy,[18] is a typical distortion of what is supposed to happen. McElroy divides the knowledge industry into supply-siders (KM phase 1, or KM1), who see knowledge management as the integration of information (collecting, classifying, and sharing of information), and demand-siders (KM phase 2, or KM2), who see it as knowledge enhancement. The former, he says, think that knowledge management is about the provision of existing knowledge using various technologies – getting information to the right people at the right place at the right time – while the latter is concerned with structuring the organization to maximize the generation of new knowledge, which is a social process rather than a structural one. There is a tendency for KM1 and to a lesser extent KM2 to be seen as a sort of closed system with little direct impact on business performance, rather like an internal think tank that has to be left alone to come up with new ideas.

Lack of integration combined with replacement of the previous more informal approach by a knowledge bureaucracy could well have been value-subtracting to the organization. There is strong circumstantial evidence that the Bank's knowledge departments have been unable to fulfill the potential of a KM phase 2, or possibly even KM phase 1, while the network structure has aggravated institutional complexity.

The flaws in the formal knowledge structure were aggravated by the character of the matrix to which it was supposed to be providing services. The Compact look-back review in 2001 recognized that there was a widespread perception that the internal market was a disincentive to knowledge sharing. Similarly, budget cuts and job insecurity created

---

[17] 'Improving the Banks Development Effectiveness – What Does Evaluation Show?', World Bank OED, Nov 2005, op cit.
[18] McElroy, Mark W., *The New Knowledge Management*, op cit.

incentives to hold on to knowledge as a form of power. Despite some progress, it stated, the system was 'unhealthily supply orientated and needed to be rooted far more directly in client and country office demand'.

NEW INFORMATION SYSTEMS

The new knowledge bank structures had to be equipped with the appropriate technology, and this was one area in which by general agreement the reorganization saw progress. The Bank established an intranet system as a significant information resource.[19] In 2000 the Bank was judged to be one of five global best-practice information technology users,[20] and received a Most Admired Knowledge Enterprise award based on the nominations of Fortune 500 executives. At the same time the Global Development Learning Network was established to exploit the major advances in communications for worldwide distance learning and participation in dialogue.

The Bank spent $54 million on information systems renewal over the Compact period, somewhat over budget. A high return in savings was expected from a new project documentation system, improved procurement, budgeting improvements, information systems/database, and accounts streamlining. An information systems renewal bulletin[21] on May 21, 1999, just before the system came on line, quoted the head of the information solutions group: '[W]e know when we turn it on in July it will work. The challenge is to reap all the benefits of the new system'. He said that it would change the long-held Bank group metaphor of 'managers should trust no one' to 'managers should trust everyone and hold them accountable for doing their own transactions'.

The head of the information systems group was somewhat overoptimistic. While the technology of Web sites was heavily funded and supported, its implementation was less so. A review of the intranet in

---

[19] Though the most popular resources on the intranet turned out to be newsfeeds and staff service information (three-quarters of hits received in 2000) rather than substantive development knowledge.

[20] The award followed a six-month benchmarking process that considered eighty different organizations.

[21] 'Update – Improving the Way We Work', World Bank memorandum, May 21, 1999.

the same year the knowledge enterprise award was received said that
the central information system remained fragmented and of doubtful
quality[22] and was encouraging 'rogue' sites to be set up that created
maintenance problems and reduced the operational value of the system.[23] The results were never adequately measurable, but while most of
the expected savings were claimed to have been achieved, they were
more costly and much delayed. Extensive overtime by systems specialists and harassed administrators was needed to understand the complexities of the new information systems, and major processing delays
occurred while systems were de-bugged. For example, savings had been
projected from on-line travel arrangements, but the system was so
difficult to use that extensive technical support was needed. Tearful
office assistants sometimes just abandoned deadlines.

The bugs in the new system also initially caused serious budgeting
mistakes. It failed to capture and update data on time, let alone 'just-in-
time', and sometimes it lost it. In 1999, just before its introduction,
spending was under budget by $90 million. In 2000, the new system
predicted under-runs again, as a result of which expenditure was stepped up. But this was a mistake, and all across the operations area over-
runs actually occurred. Then, in 2001, as a result of warnings of
managers being held to account, the pendulum swung back again and
there was an excess of caution. Layoffs of staff reached a peak, hiring was
frozen, and there was an under-run of $69 million or about 5%, equiv-
alent to the cost of more than 300 professional jobs. The interaction
between flawed data and management under pressure was doomed to
fail. Said one manager,[24] 'CFOs in Lucent and many other companies
have been sacked on the spot when they presented financial figures

[22] Shaines, K., 'World Bank Intranet Content Quality Review', World Bank, October
2000.
[23] This was the view of Larry Prusak, a leading knowledge management expert, hired
from the IBM Institute of Knowledge Management, in a 1999 review of the Bank's
system. In setting up such a system there is a choice between a centralized approach,
for transparency and consistency, and a customized approach to meet the local needs
of particular groups. Local solutions, or rogue sites, tend to create maintenance
problems and discourage use as employees become increasingly unwilling to contribute knowledge to a 'black hole'.
[24] Staff Association newsletter, August 2001.

which were hopelessly out of line with their earlier projections'. Some of the blame was put on the information system, some on the internal contracting system, and some on management. The budgetary see-saw was a cause of excess numbers of people being fired under the Bank's redundancy program.

One of the principal items in the new facility was an integrated management information system that was intended to replace 65 systems and 100 databases. An integrated SAP/Lotus Notes/PeopleSoft system was to allow consolidation, streamlining, and standardization of tools and reduced maintenance requirements. The main information system selected, from SAP of Germany, was judged the best choice on its 'state-of-the-art' technical specification, and the organizational implications were treated as secondary. But for three years after it was implemented it was necessary to maintain parallel systems to validate the numbers, and in some cases internally constructed interfaces and reports had to be used.

The management information system had been effective in process industries such as chemicals. But the Bank was not a processing industry and the system was not well tailored to its needs. Its introduction was also rushed to completion in eighteen months, by July 1999, compared to the thirty-six months usually needed, so as to preempt the need to make changes in existing systems for 'Y2K compliance'. This turned out to be a serious false economy. An independent review of the project showed that the implementation was successful from the technical point of view; but the accompanying organizational changes were not, and training fell well behind. Michael Hammer from Harvard was invited in April 1999 by the Bank to give a lecture on the social and organizational changes that would be required with the new system. He stridently warned his listeners to expect a 'U-curve' performance dip after the new system went live. His prediction was correct but optimistic; the short-term dip was more of a long-term recession.

User interfaces had to be changed to be consistent with the organization's terminology and processes. Main menu pages contained links to inventory control, something of little importance to the operations of the Bank, even if of critical importance on a BMW assembly line. 'How', said one new user, 'am I to remember what a dump truck icon does, or a sun over a mountain or a piece of a puzzle. In order to use it one would have to memorize it as though it were a dance routine'.

Savings in costs and increases in benefits through knowledge sharing required modified behavior. For example, the new project documentation system provided templates and checklists, and guides on maximum report length, aimed at simplifying documentation. Yet in 2001, said an internal assessment, appraisal reports still reached in excess of 100 pages, something that Ernie Stern, the Bank's celebrated former operations chief, had tried hard to prevent back in 1976. '[E]ffective immediately' he wrote in a circular, 'I will no longer accept … any Staff Appraisal Report the principal text of which exceeds 50 pages or the total length of which exceeds 100 pages'.[25]

The 2001 Compact look-back review seemed to blame the mistakes on unrealistic expectations and a defective project management process. Its proposed solution was that all future systems projects should be owned and led by 'business sponsors' supported by a small group of dedicated staff. 'Scope control' it declared profoundly, 'is a key management tool to ensure that projects meet their initial objectives'. But the management of the IT process was not the cause. To the rank-and-file staff all this was predictable, and indeed predicted. The ultimate cause of the problem was the demand for too many major, untested changes within an inadequate time frame, and with little regard to sequencing, under outside pressure, with the inevitable perverse results and unintended consequences.

Almost three years after its launch, the Staff Association ran a survey of opinions about the information system. The Hammer warning of a performance dip was more than confirmed. While opinions were by now beginning to stabilize and even in some areas to improve, the survey results showed that detractors still outnumbered supporters. One called it 'a beautiful way for two persons to do the job of one, recent modest improvements notwithstanding'. Another said, '[T]he original (travel) system was an absolute shambles, an absolute diabolical disgrace'.

Information technology was also a large part of the U.S. 'reinventing government' initiative that took place during the 1990s. As a Brookings

---

[25] Kapur, Devesh, J. Lewis, and R. Webb, *The World Bank: Its Last Half Century*, Brookings, 1997, p. 1183.

report on the initiative pointed out, if information technology offers a high return in improving governmental performance, it also poses high risk.[26] The U.S. General Accounting Office found that opportunities for using technology to improve cost effectiveness and service delivery in government were great. But they could also produce dramatic failures. A consultant found that one-third of all private sector information systems projects were canceled before completion because of problems in planning, designing, and implementing. Government has been plagued by problems 'ranging from poorly designed requirements, poor contractor oversight, and inadequate system design to managerial and technical skill deficiencies'. Indeed, half of the government's biggest information technology projects are at high risk for management problems. The Bank was thus hardly alone in facing problems with information systems, but it did have precedents elsewhere at the time to draw lessons from, and it could have adopted a more sensible strategy of phased introduction.

THE FRONT LINE AND THE BACK LINE

As we have seen, the Strategic Compact stated that the Bank's processes were inadequate. There was an excessive *cost of doing business*, and *slowness* and *bureaucracy*. Information was not shared across the organization and was instead confined to 'silos' and 'cylinders', and lengthy project processing coincided with inflexibility in design and inability to respond to evolving county needs. The Strategic Compact proposal showed front-line services as declining in proportion to the total administrative budget from 56% to 52% over 1994 to 1997.[27] To help remedy this situation it was proposed to reduce overhead and back-line resources and increase those devoted to front-line work, where they could respond directly to demand. The Compact projected that the front-line share would rebound and reach 60% of the net administrative budget by 2001. Is there evidence that overhead resources were in fact switched to the front line?

---

[26] *Reinventing Government – A Progress Report*, Brookings, 1998.
[27] *The Strategic Compact*, op cit., 1997, p. 7.

It is difficult to categorize processing costs clearly into operational (front line) and non-operational (back line), but the data that are available provide persuasive signs that the Bank's expenditures went to increasingly non-operational ends. Over 1999 to 2001, only about a three-quarter (and declining) share of the funds earmarked for operations (the regional budgets) actually included core operation costs. The rest was for the networks, internal advisory, support and quality control, for some other support areas, and for training and research.

The networks' main spending was on knowledge management (IT), quality control, operational support, and external outreach, and it was these areas where costs rose especially fast. Some of these areas backed up operations, but a significant part of their role was internally oriented. Reclassifying these as at least partly non-operational, the share of expenditure on direct operations fell over 1996 to 2003. Furthermore, inside the regional operating budgets themselves (the claimed front line) there were also elements of overhead cost,[28] which doubled their share of the total operating budget over 1999 to 2002.[29] Employees working on so-called fiduciary and safeguard oversight, who were part of the regional budget, more than doubled[30] and regional quality control organs expanded rapidly. Even in 2003, when the overall budget expanded significantly, direct 'front-line' expenditure as interpreted was flat and in real terms below the pre-reorganization levels.

Some of these developments can be determined by looking at the Bank's overall administrative budget over the relevant period (see Table 2).

The shares of the networks, the 'other' support categories, and the regional overheads rose rapidly[31] while the share of operations fell. Reinterpreting these numbers as well, there was a switch away from core business. On this interpretation of core operations expenditures, the bread and butter of the organization fell significantly, from about

[28] These were known as 'regional functions'. They include financial management, loan accounting, and procurement, which are not strictly operational but are more connected with the burgeoning oversight, fiduciary, and safeguard obligations.

[29] From 7% to 14% of the regions' costs.

[30] The number rose from 48 in 1998 to 119 in 2002 and 139 in 2003

[31] They rose from about 6% in 1996 to about 21% of the gross administrative budget (as defined in Table 2) in 2003.

Table 2. *The administrative budget, IBRD and IDA ($ millions)*

	1997	1998	1999	2000	2001	2002	2003
Regions (direct operations)	651	710	740	779	708	775	816
Of which 'regional functions'			*50*	*78*	*83*	*100*	*140*
Regions less 'regional functions'			690	701	625	675	676
Networks	61	86	107	124	119	147	159
Other (quality and support)	2	11	13	19	23	24	31
Training and research	88	92	97	87	93	97	110
Other net overheads[a]	354	357	366	364	387	365	396
Administrative budget[b]	1156	1256	1322	1373	1330	1407	1511
Administrative budget plus Board costs[c]	1226	1329	1397	1453	1414	1490	1604
Of which OED (IEG)	*15.5*	*16.0*	*16.8*	*18.5*	*19.2*	*19.8*	*20.3*
Board and Secretariat	*54.2*	*57.1*	*58.1*	*61.8*	*64.9*	*63.2*	*72.8*

[a] Consists of finance administration and management services and contingencies.
[b] There are various different measures of administrative costs. This figure is before counting reimbursable fees, and the last line excludes the development grant fund and the costs of pensions.
[c] These include the board, corporate secretariat, and IEG (OED).
Source: Annual reports and estimates.

58% in 1996 to about 45% in 2003, or to an even lower level if the costs of governance (the board and its secretariat) are taken into account. By 2004 there was a relaxation of the budget stringency, but the share of core business apparently did not rise.

Figure 4 reduces regional operations to purely the front line (both lending operations and knowledge products – analytical studies) and aggregates networks, quality control, and fiduciary/ safeguard expenditures, all of which are essentially 'back-line' tasks, over the critical period of 1999–2003. It shows a near doubling of 'network costs' while direct operations expenditure fell overall over the period.

There are also other areas that are of questionable relevance to operations. For example, expenditures on external relations grew rapidly during the Strategic Compact period, 1997–2001,[32] to a level larger than the Bank's average expenditure on research (separate from

---

[32] External relations expenditures rose from about $24 million in 1997 to about $29 million in 2001.

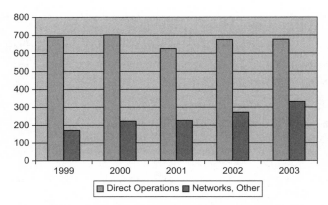

Figure 4. Front-line and back-line costs ($ million).

training), which was heading in the opposite direction. Of special interest is governance and evaluation, that is, the board, its secretariat, and the evaluation units reporting directly to it. These areas all increased their shares.

Governance costs were excluded from the Strategic Compact budget agreement and not subject to limit under it. Thus the share of expenditures for the directors and their supporting secretariats rose just as those for core business expenditures fell. By 2005, more than $100 million per annum was being spent on the board, its committees, its advisory staff, and the evaluation organs that reported directly to it. Expenditures for core business (loans and analytical reports) were about $750 million. The total number of personnel involved in the 'governance industry' was about 500, almost entirely paid for by the Bank. Thus a significant share of the institution's costs was to provide information to the board and its staff – the 'transparency costs'.

The growth in the Bank over the period was therefore in areas that were either 'off the table' for discussion (i.e., governance costs were not part of the Compact) or were in a gray area that was not directly related to operations. If we count the board costs as part of the administrative costs, then the direct operating costs of the frontline country and sector units – those in the trenches who actually designed, prepared, and managed the projects and carried out analytical studies – declined to significantly below half the total by 2003.

The conclusion that operational focus was reduced is confirmed by interpretation of the Bank's numbers for what it called 'business processes'. These also show that front-line activity (lending, loan management, economic reports, and technical assistance) declined as a proportion of the total operating expenses.[33] In 2001, as the institution struggled to meet its artificial final-year Strategic Compact target agreed to between the CEO and the board of executive directors, financial stringency was so tight that the budget was in the end underspent.

The major casualty of the final Compact year budget stringency was knowledge products. These were the analytical reports, on which expenditure in 2001 fell to only half of what it had been nearly ten years earlier, in 1993.[34] The analytical reports were the backbone of the Bank's economic information offering, a key part of what was proclaimed as the Bank's second or principal service pillar. Expenditures on lending and analytical reports together received far less than they had received in 1993 before the coming of the knowledge bank.[35]

While the Bank refocused its strategy on knowledge services, whether out of necessity or out of design, during the reorganization period core knowledge products, that is, the detailed reports on economic sectors and country economic reviews, running at around 350 reports per annum, in fact fell rapidly behind even normal requirements while the advisory skill pools grew. Thus knowledge capacity rose but knowledge production fell. The lack of basic reports was offset partly by short policy and strategy papers, but these were less knowledge-intensive. The Bank's so-called country assistance strategy and poverty reduction strategy papers were not expert knowledge products but planning documents. The HIPC debt relief papers fell to a trickle while they waited for poverty reduction strategy papers to be completed. A major effort was made to catch up when it was realized that only a small proportion of countries had the full suite of up-to-date basic economic reports on which country strategies were supposed to be based. Over 2003 to 2005, output doubled to about

---

[33] From about 50% in 1993 to about 40% in 2001.
[34] $51 million against $99 million.
[35] $150 million against $250 million. Between 1996 and 2002, the cost of lending and analytical studies fell from about 28% to 22% of administrative costs.

700 'ESW reports' to try to get rid of the backlog, with a concomitant rise in expenditure to $128 million in 2005 from $51 million in 2001.

Thus in terms of both of its main outputs – financing products and knowledge products – the reorganization period and after saw a retreat, not an advance, on the 'front line'. The emergence of Internet-based information sources and distance learning has changed the technology of knowledge production and its accessibility, but the basic analyses and reports still have to be done. This poor start for the 'knowledge bank' that had been announced in 1996 was caused by the budget cuts of the Strategic Compact, the very instrument that was supposed to strengthen knowledge production within the Bank's product range and enhance its front-line performance! In 2001, when the budget crunch was particularly acute (since the board was holding Wolfensohn strictly to his promise under the Strategic Compact) it was the front line that suffered most acutely.

Ultimately it is not credible that the Bank grew under the Strategic Compact in a way that was consistent with an improved delivery of pro-poor development projects, either financing or knowledge products, evidence of which was borne out repeatedly by the anecdotal opinions of the people who worked in it. The process penalized the front line and the core business and therefore reduced client focus. In a 2001 paper called 'Refueling Current Business Activity', the Bank claimed that the front-line staff ratio increased from 58% to 61% over the reorganization period, and thereby met the goal of the Strategic Compact. But, on a realistic definition of what the front line really is, this was absolutely not the case. At the same time, this situation was not one that could have been normally expected to result in the widely proclaimed major performance improvements, which we will discuss later.

PURSUING CORPORATE MERGER – THE IFC AND THE BANK

While it was not one of the issues explicitly laid out, the Strategic Compact proposal addressed the need to merge Bank institutions. Accordingly, another re-engineering initiative to reduce the *cost of doing business*, improve the *slowness* and *bureaucracy*, and make the organization more responsive to its clients was the linking of parts of the IFC and the Bank, apparently with a view to an eventual merger.

Early on in its history it was realized that the IBRD would not be able to easily finance the private sector despite the need to promote private enterprise, because of its requirement for government guarantees.[36] This is why the IFC was established, after five years of discussion, in 1956. Key features of the IFC differentiated it from the Bank – it did not require guarantees (though it is protected under the Bank's informal umbrella). It was deal-oriented, and it did not try to promote policy reforms. It was required to make a profit on a normal commercial basis, and thus it was also much more sensitive to business risk than the Bank. It does not carry out 'developmental' investment except out of special grants, and its private focus is by definition inconsistent with the Bank's role as a provider of public goods.[37]

The two institutions differ in objectives, culture, and working methods. The IFC is impatient with the Bank's consensus-driven and academic style, and skeptical of the Bank's ability to promote the private sector. William Ryrie, a previous head of the IFC, said 'the Bank is intrinsically incapable of using its influence to bring about a reduction in State activity ... funds that are subject to full commercial risk are likely to be more efficiently used'. On its side, the Bank stereotypes the IFC as narrow dealmakers.

The report of the Task Force on Multilateral Development Banks of 1996[38] discussed the possibilities for a merger. It pointed out that separation had costs in terms of lack of coordination. For example, the IFC might pursue a commercial opportunity in a country where the Bank is trying to change economic policy in a way that might damage the IFC's commercial interests. But on the other hand, there was an operational advantage in separating guaranteed and non-guaranteed lending, and separating risks and functions. On balance it came out against merging the two organizations.

---

[36] In 1963, George Woods had for a time considered the possibility of waiving guarantees for possible private sector loans from the Bank.

[37] Most recently, its increased net profits have been channeled through trust funds into technical assistance services. The diversification of IFC activities into free technical assistance raises issues for its own corporate strategy.

[38] 'Serving a Changing World, Report of the Task Force on Multilateral Development Banks', IMF/World Bank Development Committee, Washington, DC, April 1996, p. 14.

But the pressure for coordination finally prevailed in 1999, when a partial merger went ahead in what were called global product groups,[39] a joint private sector advisory service, a small and medium (SME) enterprise unit, and one joint operational region, East Asia. To try to avoid a sense that the Bank would dominate the merger, the new IFC chief, Peter Woicke, was put in charge of the merged units. Still, lengthy discussions ensued to convince a doubtful IFC of the rationale for such a joint venture considering that it was in a successful period when such a strategy change seemed counterproductive. The governance structure for the newly merged organization was complex. Woicke supervised a network vice president, Nemat Shafik, who in turn managed the network that provided oversight of the merged departments, as well as other non-merged units.[40]

Woicke, who was appointed from J. P. Morgan by Wolfensohn, set to work happily free of the burden of too much knowledge about the two organizations. Interviewed by *Euromoney* in April 1999 he was asked, '[W]hy should you succeed when in the past others have failed?' He replied accordingly: 'I don't know why, or if, other people have failed in the past, but I do think that there is now an increased recognition that the private sector is more important than it was five or ten years ago'. Woicke circulated an article on the Bank Web site in 1999. He wrote: '[T]he topic of greater Bank group cooperation has come up before. In the past there was no shortage of rah-rah rhetoric, but also no real incentives, no convincing answers to questions of "what's in it for us?" And the dynamics of a close partnership were never right in the (previous) era . . .. But things are different now. (Our client countries) are tired of duplication, lack of coordination and even open conflict between the Bank and IFC'.

Corporate governance theory and practice, as espoused by the Bank, was at the time calling for disaggregating the functions of public

---

[39] The groups were in telecommunications, mining, oil and gas, small enterprises, and a joint private sector advisory service, which incorporated several units from both organizations.

[40] The Vice President, Nemat Shafik, in a 2001 newsletter to the new conglomerate mysteriously quoted one of the five principles of management of Juergen Schrempp, head of the Daimler-Chrysler merger: '[A]void the danger of a deadly wish for harmony!'

institutions in order to clarify and realign their non-commercial and commercial functions. This merger drive instead tried to pull together disparate functions in pursuit of central coordination. There were also potential conflicts, such as the handling of confidential commercial information. A task force was set up in 2000, which in turn recommended the setup of a special 'conflicts office' to deal with this. But conflicts of interest might be easier to resolve when negotiated between two separate entities rather than, non-transparently, within one.

The merged departments found some mutual interests but in general had little in common. Each continued to do what they had always done, essentially separately. The global SME department started its life with a dispute over management that ended with the IFC largely adopting it. The new department 'boxed in' a function that had already existed throughout the Bank for years, a reversal of the usual approach to a pilot project. That is to say that a pilot usually leads to mainstreaming while in this case the direction seemed to be from the mainstream back to the pilot. Most of the other merger initiatives were put into reverse within two or three years of their unveiling, reflecting the fact that they were impractical and unnecessary corporate moves in the first place.

THE VERDICT OF THE EMPLOYEES

One way of measuring the success or otherwise of the reorganization is by the responses of the organization's employees. Research has suggested that public sector employees, in government and elsewhere, tend to be relatively long suffering when faced with the constraints of organizational structure and process, because they have interests and objectives that are beyond the organization. The U.S. Federal Employee Attitude Surveys, for example, have shown that employees are largely influenced by the chance to have an impact on public affairs and do something of worth to society and relatively little by remuneration.[41] At the same time, public service motivation also requires a greater degree of trust in management, and the 'psychological contract'

[41] Crewson, Philip. E, 'Public Service Motivation – Building Empirical Evidence of Incidence and Effect', *Journal of Public Administration Research and Theory* 7(4): 499–518.

between employees and management is more important than in the private sector.[42] This 'contract' is an implicit agreement between employer and employee that each party will treat the other fairly, based on presumably shared expectations.[43] Compliance is not based on the fear of legal reprisal but, rather, on the desire to maintain mutual trust. It thus constitutes partly an emotional bond, and strong feelings are provoked when the bond is compromised.[44]

The opinions of the employees who were the main target of the reorganization can be deduced from staff surveys carried out every two to three years. Problems started with the reforms of 1987. The consultant employed by the Bank to run the 1987 staff survey stated that he found the results seriously of out of line with what would be expected in a well-run organization: 'These results would normally be considered disturbing to any organization known to me' he wrote.[45] There were further surveys in 1990 and 1993 showing some recovery as Conable and then Preston restored morale, but in October 1997, two years into the reform process, a survey showed the worst results ever.

The voter turnout in 1997 was 50%, down from 70% in 1993. Only 21% thought that the Bank was a 'well coordinated and internally cooperative organization'. Only 18% thought that the top management was 'trustworthy'. The 'institution's climate' was satisfactory to less than one-quarter of the employees, and relations and trust between employees and senior management were particularly poor. Within all this negativity the scores were relatively high on the work itself and the ultimate goals of the Bank, which seemed to mean that these people, pilloried as self-serving, were in fact quite dedicated and largely doing their best within the system they had to work with.

Two years on, in 1999, the results improved a little but were still very poor by the standards of a supposedly top-rank organization. The voter

---

[42] Perry, J. L. and L. R.Wise, 'The Motivational Basis of Public Services', *Public Administration Review* 50(3), May–June 1990.

[43] Robinson, Sandra L., 'Trust and Breach of the Psychological Contract', *Administrative Science Quarterly* 41, 1996.

[44] De Meuse, Kenneth P. and Walter W. Tornow, 'Leadership and the Changing Psychological Contract Between Employer and Employee', *Issues and Observations* 13(2), 1993.

[45] Communication from Robert Wade.

turnout was still only 55%. Well under half of the Washington employees expressed themselves as being 'generally satisfied'. Most lacked trust and confidence in the institution and considered it to be poorly coordinated. Less than a quarter believed that the senior management operated as an effective team. About a quarter believed that the matrix management system was effective in improving quality. In some regions things were better; in others, things were worse. In one particularly badly managed department in the former Soviet Union area, only 7% thought that the Bank was a well-coordinated organization. The only area consistently getting higher scores was information technology. The president tended to be less criticized than the top management under him. There was a residual sense at this stage that his intentions were right and that it was the people implementing his program that were responsible for the mistakes.[46]

Despite results that were historically poor, and poor by the standards of high-performance organizations, a report to the board[47] said that the 1999 staff survey confirmed that leadership practices had improved in a number of areas. The president wrote: 'I am heartened by the improvements I see in this year's staff survey'; he thanked the staff for their 'extremely valuable insights' and 'critical' and 'invaluable' contributions and said that the responses showed better access to information and demonstrated more confidence in the direction the organization was heading. 'We have got a lot right already but more needs to be done'. The situation remained poor for the next two years, during which time the management did not feel inclined to risk a further survey. Stephen Fidler, in the *Financial Times*, wrote,[48] '[O]ne reason for the low morale is a botched previous attempt at reorganization'. The time and money were used in part to increase hiring and move into new business areas. Three years later, with the budget returning in real terms to its 1997 level, he said, 'the bank is going through a hurried and poorly planned effort to rein in costs'.

---

[46] A number of incidents, including Wolfensohn's appointment of Nicholas Stern as chief economist in breach of the Bank's strict hiring rules, suggested that he was disengaged from the details. The issue was that his brother Richard was a staff member.

[47] In the Bank's Corporate Strategic Directions Paper for 2001–2003.

[48] Fidler, Stephen, *Financial Times*, January 30, 2001.

In December 2000, returning buoyed up from a high-profile foreign trip, the president learned of the continuing dissension. Despite what was by then nearly five years of efforts at reorganization, the workforce did not seem to share his upbeat vision of the way the organization was headed under his leadership. He called a 'town hall meeting'. Warned in advance that there was trouble brewing, he had returned, he said, 'with the internal criticisms ringing in my head'. However, unfazed, he turned to talk at length about his achievements overseas. 'I am made to feel very humble by the "voices of the poor"', he said. The problem for some of his listeners was that he did not seem so interested in the voices of his employees. He explained to them the need 'for us to act like adults'. He talked of a 'sense of responsibility'; he spoke of their 'need to blame someone else', and 'enormous cynicism'. Only one member of the audience stood up to challenge, though that was barely discernible – he asked for an honest review and stocktaking, and also asked why, if external partnerships were so important, internal partnership was not also.

Following the town hall meeting, the president spoke at a corporate strategy meeting ('corporate day') about 'negativism, cynicism, lack of teamwork and lack of loyalty'. He bemoaned the disjuncture between the progress with outside partnerships and the lack of trust internally. 'The highs of visits are contrasted with the downers at home', he said. He asked for a 'new climate of inclusion, transparency, and internal partnership based on trust at all levels'. He challenged the staff to 'speak out'.

Wolfensohn's challenge provoked the letter from a group of staff in the Middle Eastern department leaked to the *Financial Times*.[49] It said that his leadership and management style prevented open debate, sowed resentment, and resulted in poorly coordinated work. 'We do not think that the President receives honest feedback from his senior managers,' it said. 'He does not welcome criticism or tolerate dissent, be it from the Board, or the managers or the Staff Association. Managers at all levels live under fear'. 'Despite pronouncements from time to time that staff is our most valuable resource, Mr. Wolfensohn continues to have a low opinion of Bank staff and often expresses it to outside audiences'.

---

[49] *Financial Times*, January 31, 2001.

The letter continued: 'Some Managing Directors have no clear or useful roles and responsibility. Only one has any real Bank experience. MDs are isolated from staff and have few occasions for substantive or meaningful interaction with staff'. Finally, it said, '[W]e fully agree with the President that the Bank is in deep trouble. Bank staff today are more demoralized than ever . . .. There is need for better management and leadership at all levels, starting with the President himself'.

The Bank's enlarged external affairs office put out an assurance that the letter-writers were a disgruntled group whose jobs were under threat. And undeterred, two months later, in a presentation to the board, Wolfensohn said: '[W]e have emerged from the Strategic Compact period delivering a higher quality and broader range of services – both lending and non-lending – to our clients. The quality of our portfolio is at its highest level in two decades – which by itself translates into billions of dollars in more effective development spending for the people we serve. In fundamental ways, this is a different Bank doing more things, and doing them better, than four years ago'.

What President Wolfensohn seemed to be seeing were privileged employees trying to maintain privileges, and what employees thought that they saw was a leader uninterested in leading. The ensuing misconceptions and frustration eventually fuelled an attack by Stephen Fidler in the journal *Foreign Policy* in September 2001. This was probably Wolfensohn's lowest point and one of the low points in the institution's history thus far. Wolfensohn picked himself up, assisted by allies like Britain's Clare Short, then the minister for international development and a lifelong fighter for employee rights. She had risen to the chief executive's defense with a letter to the *Financial Times*. Defying the 'modern day kulaks', she wrote: 'these critics ignore the considerable progress that has been made and are seeking to promote a narrow and reactionary agenda that could return the Bank to the mistakes of the past . . .. Reactionary forces are at work, wanting to undermine the paradigm shift in development practice. They cannot be allowed to succeed'.[50] Managing Director Zhang also wrote to the *Financial Times* in his boss's defense.

[50] *Financial Times*, September 5, 2001.

But the correspondence in the *Financial Times* was overwhelmed by events. A few days later the New York and Washington terrorist attacks occurred. Attention was diverted to bigger things and in a sense never returned to the issues of mishandled reform. Suddenly the role of the Bank in the world seemed more relevant, even to the Bush White House. The shock of the terrorist attacks and Wolfensohn's public statements of concern helped to suppress the now trivial-seeming internal issues. In April 2002, the survey showed, six years after the start of the reorganization, finally the start of an improvement. The voter turnout was 76%, closer to the norm for high-performance organizations.[51] Two-thirds said that their general morale was good. The consultant (Allen Kraut) said: 'These are truly outstanding results, especially in light of declines in scores on those items in benchmark organizations'. On September 3, 2002, in a 'looking ahead' letter, Wolfensohn wrote: '[T]he events of (September 11) made me realize, more than ever, that we have the very best people in the world working right here . . .. I am proud of you all and look forward to working with you in the period ahead'. And following a strategic planning forum in 2003 he wrote even more fulsomely: '[T]his year's forum reminded me of just how far we have come in recent years. The organizational culture is different now. It also reminded me of what an incredible group of people we have here – talented, committed and passionate about our mission. As we enter 2003 with all its challenges and uncertainties, I feel very privileged to be leading this fine institution – and I am very proud of you all'. The 2003 survey confirmed that things had turned around.

The rise in morale was partly the desire for a united front following the terrorist attacks, assisted by Wolfensohn's politically sensitive reaction to those events. It was also because nearly half the employees had no memory of the former situation, and otherwise there was relief that the disruptions were over and repairs were in progress. Wolfensohn's now regular and fulsome tributes to his employees also reflected relief on

---

[51] There was, however, cause for some doubt about the 2002 results. Some questions were not directly comparable to those of 1999 or could be interpreted differently. Missing from the survey were questions on 'trust'. There was continued pride in the institution, but that was the norm, since even in 1997 it had been relatively high. The least positive group was the longer term professionals. Some of the worst results were in the corporate secretariat that worked most closely with the board of directors.

his part. His political antennae seemed to tell him that it was time to move on from phase one, when the U.S. government and others expected him to wield the axe on the pinstriped bureaucrats and re-engineer the corporation, to phase two, when they expected the axe-wielding to have finished, and the re-engineering to have been completed. Without a doubt it was time now to declare victory and move on.

RE-ENGINEERING ELSEWHERE

The style of the race to change had its roots in the so-called re-engineering of corporate America. From the public sector viewpoint it also had some parallel in the National Performance Review (NPR) or 'reinventing government' initiative in the United States during the early 1990s. A passing knowledge of the NPR, which was coming to its conclusion at the time the Bank launched its change initiative, might well have informed the Bank's efforts. The NPR also drew its ideas from the U.S. business theorists like Drucker and Hammer.[52] The reformers envisioned a government without obsolete structures, archaic processes, and inadequate leadership. They proposed replacing top-down, rule-based government with bottom-up, customer-driven entrepreneurial government. They promised a stronger focus on information and customer service. But, said Drucker, '[I]n many if not most cases downsizing has turned out to be something that surgeons for centuries have warned against: amputation before diagnosis'. The government, he argued, needed to confront the basic questions: What is the mission? Is it the right one? Is it worth doing? Others dismissed the change effort as more style than substance.[53] Public sector reforms, they said, have tended to lag behind the most innovative private sector practices. 'Careful studies of private firms were warning that downsizing improved profits at only half of the companies where it was tried, and that only

[52] A guiding text was also by David Osborne and Ted Gaebler, *Reinventing Government: How the Entrepreneurial Spirit Is Transforming the Public Sector*, Addison-Wesley, 1992; another important reference was Donald F. Kettl, *Reinventing Government? Appraising the National Performance Review*, CPM Report 94–2, Brookings, 1994.

[53] Wooldridge, John and Adrian Micklethwait, *The Witch Doctors: Making Sense of the Management Gurus*, Times Books, 1996. The authors describe the program as a jargon-ridden series of management-reform fads.

one-third of companies reported improved worker productivity . . . .
The federal government's reform efforts have replicated the mistakes
that crippled many industries in the 1980s'.

Some of the NPR experience sounds rather familiar to the Bank's
experience. The artificial nature of the cuts under the strategic compact,
and the insistence of a Board in sticking to them, resulted by the final
year in a situation where the staff, already severely overstretched, had
been cut to a level at which emergency action was needed to get the
numbers back up again.

THE END OF RE-ENGINEERING

The Staff Association newsletter of June–July 2001 stated: '[T]he senior
management is now changing or even dismantling many of the new
ideas imposed on staff in only the last few years, grade telescoping,
dance-card (contracting), performance awards, SAP, flat management,
and sustainable decentralization'. Along with the major reversals went
minor ones. Even the preferred airlines policy was put into reverse.[54]

On a Corporate Day in June 2002, the Bank's vice president for
operational policies and client services, Jim Adams, spoke, ten years
after Willi Wapenhans had said the same things, of 'the complex, costly
and time-consuming procedures which have sprouted up around
investment lending – making life difficult for our clients and staff'.
'Most of the processes', he said, 'are self-imposed by the institution.
We have met the enemy and he is us'. In October 2002, well after the
reorganization had formally ended, the president wrote a letter to staff
saying, '[W]e need to simplify our policies and processes . . . we simply
must push harder and cut through the needless bureaucracy that places
such a heavy burden on our staff and task managers'. The complaint

---

[54] In an attempt to lower travel costs, a preferred airlines policy was introduced. However, it did not target the airline agents but rather the airlines themselves in what was
already a highly competitive market. Interference in a highly competitive market is
likely to make it less rather than more competitive as hard-pressed suppliers seize the
opportunity to secure safe, long-term contracts. Long negotiations took place. The
oligopoly of four airlines selected excluded British Airways on a technicality, although
it had previously been the most frequently used airline. In Latin America travel was
going to be difficult, as only one airline was allowed.

was the same as it had been in 1987 but by all accounts the 'bureaucracy' was now much worse, and, characteristically, the president still appeared to expect the employees to sort out the mess. In November 2002, Managing Director Zhang wrote that it was necessary to act urgently to roll back the bureaucratic processes. 'A set of new management procedures has already been announced . . . . There are no silver bullets and these issues will not be resolved overnight'. A simplification drive was thus launched, with simplification awards for good ideas. The wheel had come full circle.

In its 2005 review, the Bank's quality assurance group (QAG) reported on the good progress the institution was making in project processing. 'The Bank has continued to simplify its internal processes in order to improve its responsiveness to Borrowers' needs'. The Modernization and Simplification Agenda had resulted in two significant changes', said the QAG: 'First, a new report format (Implementation Status and Results Report) to emphasize results and flag issues, and, second, faster approval for incremental funds to existing projects. These measures, the QAG stated, were beginning to have an impact though they would need more resources for training. But such initiatives hardly constituted substantive progress on a path along which the Bank has been struggling for so long. In fact, the same report stated that longer delays were occurring elsewhere, in producing advisory reports. It said, '[D]espite Bank management's commitment to accelerate delivery in response to clients' requests, average elapsed time from task inception to delivery to client has continued upward in FY05 . . . performance in FY05 indicates further backsliding'.

In November 2005, an evaluator's report highlighted once more the costs of doing business. Ten years down the road from the first reorganizational moves and several years even after the later simplification initiative, the report made this statement: '[T]he costs of doing business with the Bank are high and its procedures are very bureaucratic. More intelligent application of safeguards and fiduciary requirements is needed' (p. 24). An administrative staffer who had worked within the Bank for twenty-six years described the internal processes as 'absolutely terrible', with a loss of institutional memory and a breakdown in mentoring and control over project execution.

The lack of progress made in streamlining the system illustrated the inability of the complex and costly reforms to address even one of the first objectives of the Strategic Compact, reducing delay. As the Strategic Compact look-back review put it: '[T]he simultaneous introduction of de-layering, relocation of work, empowerment, team-based work, matrix, systems renewal, suggests that the organization's capability to implement was not sufficiently factored into the design'.

The negative impact of the matrix and skill pooling is now almost an accepted historical fact. A 2007 report on World Bank assistance to agriculture in Sub-Saharan Africa, for example, makes this unequivocal statement: '[T]he sectoral organization of the Bank has impeded interaction among staff across sectors. As a result, good quality analytical work produced in other relevant sectors, such as trade and transport, is also not adequately considered in informing agricultural lending'.

How did the renewal process rate against Kotter's eight-step cure (*increase urgency; build the guiding team; get the vision right; communicate for buy-in; empower action; create short-term wins; don't let up;* and *make change stick*)? Not well. The evidence of what actually happened suggests that the level of achievement dropped steadily as the process moved from the first step. There was urgency. There was a guiding team but not a good one. Vision existed but it was flawed. Communication generally was unsatisfactory, sometimes acutely so. Empowerment never was much more than a slogan. Short-term wins were difficult to identify and were offset by losses. The seventh step was fulfilled but should not have been. And finally, some of the changes had to be put rapidly into reverse and the sustainability of the rest is debatable. Why was this deplorable process allowed to continue? These questions we explore later.

5

Changing Culture and Changing People

Closely parallel to the organizational re-engineering efforts was the attempt to restructure human resources. The restructuring exercise had two goals. First, it was intended to renew the organization's skills, and, second, it was intended to assist in changing the organization's culture.

The Strategic Compact spoke of a lack of *systematic knowledge building* and decline in knowledge generation, a *lack of expertise*, and an under-investment in training. The board of directors provided a restructuring fund that was supposed to allow redundancies to be phased in order to '*allow the Bank to move away from large, one-time redundancy exercises, which had caused serious disruption in the past*', and to '*adjust its staffing smoothly, equitably and cost effectively*'. With regard to culture, it was supposed to change the attitudes and approach of the workforce, make them more participatory and less insular and elitist. How far were these twin aims of re-skilling and cultural change achieved?

'CULTURAL CHANGE'

One of the keys to increasing the effectiveness of the Bank in the 1990s, like many other organizations both private and public, was supposedly to create a more effective culture. Members of the U.S. Congress and other outside observers thought this, and were loud in their belief in the need to change what they considered was the arrogant, insular, and elitist character of the Bank's staff, the 'culture of pin-striped bureaucrats', which, apart from offending the sensitivities of Congress, was regarded as dysfunctional for the Bank's work in reducing world poverty.

The concept of organizational culture gained attention during the corporate re-engineerings of the 1990s. Culture turns out to be quite a complex phenomenon. One leading theorist conceived of it at three levels – first at the subconscious level, where it involved the organization's learned assumptions, attitudes, and beliefs; at the next level it was the overt strategies and mission statements; and at the third level were the formal structures and procedures or 'cultural artifacts'.[1] The first level included the hidden drivers of how things actually work, observable only to those on the inside for long enough. To be sustainable cultural change would have to be effective at this first level, changing attitudes and beliefs. If the organization's employees, the pin-striped bureaucrats, were the ultimate bearers of the organization's culture at 'level one', then one way to change the culture could be to get rid of them and find new people.

The earlier years of the Bank were where the 'elitist' label originated. Kapur et al.[2] describe it as an 'exclusive, merit-ridden, prudent, quite civil, and cerebral club'. Albert Waterston, a long-time senior staff member, commented: '[W]e had an extraordinary arrogance in those days . . .. We were coming from Washington, which we thought of as the center of civilization, and we had money . . . of course, I didn't know what I was talking about half the time, but it was a wonderful feeling'.[3] But under President Eugene Black the organization was still very small and its insularity could be sustained because it was remote from view. Shades of such attitudes still survive. Evelyn Herfkens, a board director, commenting on the Bank's attitude to its overseas clientele, said: '[A]ny transnational corporation, like Royal Dutch Shell, would make you go through a training program before sending you to a foreign country, but that's not how the Bank works'.[4] The Bank's staff in fact still goes on

---

[1] This is the approach of the well-known management authors, Edgar Schein and Warren Bennis, in *The Corporate Culture Survival Guide*, Jossey-Bass, 1999, Chapter 1.

[2] Kapur, Devesh, J. Lewis, and R. Webb, *The World Bank: Its First Half Century*, Brookings, 1997, pp. 1174ff.

[3] Caufield, Catherine, *Masters of Illusion – The World Bank and the Poverty of Nations*, Henry Holt., 1996, p. 170.

[4] Ibid., pp. 225, 229.

'missions', not visits or business trips, suggesting a diplomatic or evangelical exercise. Bank missions are certainly cultural artefacts with their own peculiar sociology.[5] Brian Urquhart, a top UN official, wrote in 1994: '[I]t remains ... extremely difficult to envisage the scope of reforms in the World Bank that would make it a compatible and appropriate specialized agency of the UN system. Beyond austerity air travel, not only the Bank's present lavish meeting style, but staff remuneration would have to be brought into line with the UN common system. The heavy handedness of Bank loan approaches ... is equally incompatible with the principles of respect, cooperation and partnership on which all UN development activities are based'. [6]

But the expanded and diversified Bank under McNamara was filling up with different kinds of people, agricultural engineers and education planners as well as financiers and economists, and one would have expected them to bring changes if, indeed, it was the individuals that determined the organization's culture. But the perception of insularity and elitism continued, which suggested that the institution was determining the individuals' attitudes, rather than the other way around. It was not the elitist agronomists who determined the behavior of the institution; the organization was the collective framer of the attitudes required of the agronomists. If, for example, relatively inexperienced agriculturalists or engineers fresh out of Western or other organizations or academic institutions were expected to negotiate complex and often controversial programs in poor countries at the top government level, then the institution itself was demanding and instilling a certain elitist arrogance. Similar pressures to conform to institutional demands apply

[5] Typically in the past, and currently, especially for adjustment-type projects, the receiving government was expected to 'drop everything' and form a special team to deal with major missions, and the mission itself usually developed a solidarity around shared experiences of living in strange places. The government was burdened at one end and the mission arrangers were burdened at the other end with feverish activity just before, during, and after larger missions. Sometimes the two sides developed a sympathy for each other from the shared burden. But sometimes the missions marked an unwelcome imposition after which the reluctant government teams reverted to their normal business of government, until the next time.

[6] Urquhart, Brian and Erskine Childers, 'Renewing the UN system', *Development Dialogue* 1, 1994. In fact, in 1993, outside pressure finally ended first-class air travel for Bank staff, while in 1994, fifty-seven luxury hotels around the world were declared off-limits to Bank travelers.

to other international financial institutions (IFIs). Scandizzo, for example, wrote[7] of the aggressive culture of the IFIs compared to the UN. He
wrote: '{a} tough stance and soft operations corresponds to a basic
ambiguity in their mission of suppliers of public goods'.

The evolution of attitudes therefore changed slowly according to the
demands made by the institution. Under McNamara from 1969 to
1981, while professional staff increased nearly fourfold,[8] there was an
increasing sense of professionalism and a rigorous analytical style based
on that of the Ford Motor Company and the Defense Department. He
hired numerous top-class professionals[9] and developed a formal mission for the Bank as a center of excellence but champion of the poor. As
Kapur et al. put it: '[U]nder McNamara, the Bank was proud of its
mission and (however critical) proud of its leader in the 1970s. It had
the world class number one that staff thought it deserved'. There was a
relatively high professional morale and optimism that submerged or
compensated for elitism and insularity.

Under Clausen as president and Ann Krueger as chief economist in
1981 a more confrontational style emerged, centered on the new intellectual certainties of free market orthodoxy, spilling over on to the
outside world through the entrenched attitudes of the emerging
Washington Consensus. Krueger's research department earned a particular reputation for dogma in relation to the Bank's client countries.[10]
Elitism and insularity were associated with these certainties. Inside,
economists came to be rated according to their loyalty to such ideas.
Clausen did not curb the oppositional attitude because he needed to
maintain relations with a right-wing Republican U.S. administration
that supported the thinking of Krueger.

In 1987 Conable sought to change the institution, believing that it
was a privileged, elitist 'organization out of control', but nine years later
little had changed and Wolfensohn arrived at the Bank with similar

---

[7] Scandizzo, Pasquale. L., 'The Purpose, Management and Governance of IFIs: A Case
Study of Ambiguity', *EIB Papers*, European Investment Bank, 3(2): 90–100, 1998.
[8] The number of employees rose from 750 to 2,550.
[9] These included such people as Rotberg, Clark, Chenery, ul Haq, and Stern,
[10] A critique of this attitude is in Ben Fine, 'Neither the Washington nor the Post-
Washington Consensus: An Introduction', paper for the UK Economic and Social
Research Council (ESRC), 2000.

preconceptions about inflexible and conservative bureaucrats. His early addresses were about failure to share information and learn lessons. 'You're all very intelligent!' he announced with a hint at mockery when he addressed a staff retreat at a Virginia country hotel shortly after his arrival. He was thinking in terms of administering shock therapy to jolt the organization out of its apparent complacency.

If there was intellectual elitism in the Bank, it was very much an American variety. Out of approximately 2,000 PhD holders in 1999 (more than a third of its professional employees) and 3,000 holders of one or more masters degrees, the majority were trained at U.S. universities, with most of the rest from Western Europe.[11] Only India and Russia among non-OECD countries provide even marginal numbers of those with postgraduate accreditations. The U.S. cultural influence seems to have been important in some ways to how the Bank conducted business. For example, the preference for conditions over understandings seems to derive from a relatively rule-bound national culture along with a latent suspicion about the intentions of foreigners. Up until 1986, U.S. employees had even been subject to loyalty controls.[12]

Top academic qualifications, preferably PhDs, are sought by many international assistance agencies as well as the Bank, probably to a greater proportion than those generally sought by the private professional sector. This is partly because of the academic orientation of much development work, but also because it is often more difficult to assess abilities across societies than within one society, where greater homogeneity allows signals of merit to be more easily picked up. As a result, the currency of individual worth in the international development field has come to be based heavily on formal academic record with special emphasis in the Bank on the identity of the U.S. university attended. Yet, while some areas such as macroeconomic and financial reforms may need top-level academic inputs, the design and delivery of welfare-increasing projects in poor rural

[11] Nearly 80% received degrees from countries in which English is the first language, and nearly 90% received their degrees from six Western countries (United States, UK, Canada, France, Germany, and Holland).

[12] Starting from the McCarthy era of the early 1950s up until 1986, newly hired U.S. nationals had to obtain loyalty clearances from the U.S. government.

and urban communities does not demand top postgraduate honors from Ivy League colleges; rather, it needs smart and energetic program designers and implementers.

The intellectualization of the development process has spread applied social science terminology to the farthest corners of the earth. By illustration, in one Kenyan village in 2003, a notice was pinned to the mud wall of a local artisan group's office. Its title was 'Empowering Communities and Stakeholders to Participate in and Increase Value-Added Within Product and Service Delivery Chains'. Thus African blacksmiths learn the terminology of applied social science that would be unknown among U.S. or European blacksmiths, an achievement of no value whatsoever to their business performance.

Both by the character of the work that it demands and the backgrounds of the people it hires the Bank, like other similar organizations, frames the behavior and 'level one' attitudes of its employees. During the reorganization the overt focus was, however, at 'level two'. In 1997 a visitor to the Bank would be confronted with a sign on entering the building that read: 'Our Mission Is to Fight Poverty with Passion and professionalism for Lasting Results'. The institution issued many statements about its mission, and the external affairs department expanded rapidly to support this and to combat outside criticism. In the *Washington Post* of March 20, 2000, an anonymous Bank staff member said: '[W]hat you have to understand is that the PR people at the Bank are insanely paranoid – they believe any admission of mistakes . . . will be used as fuel by right wingers in Congress who hate the whole notion of foreign aid. Bank officials are just terrified of Jesse Helms'. Expenditures on public relations thus overtook those for economic research, while idealistic mission statements became a currency within the Bank.

How far could mission statements change the attitudes of the Bank's employees? If there was no change in the basic demands of the institution on its employees, then this could only be to a limited extent. The assumption remained, for example, that inexperienced people could work on complex issues at top levels.

Could the new hires have personality characteristics more appropriate for the Bank's culture? This would have been unlikely. Myers–Briggs personality typing prior to the reorganization showed that the 'INTJ' personality profile was unusually frequent.[13] J's indicate rational, logical thinkers driving for results, as opposed to P's, who are negotiators and consensus builders.[14] The annual staff assessment included criteria such as 'drive for results'. In a complicated decision-making environment, 'drive' tended to be all-important. Robert Clymire, a testing expert, suggested that the J attitude might also account for the perception of arrogance.[15] It was J's who went to the Harvard retraining program, which therefore tended to reinforce the J approach even if some of the courses ostensibly emphasized the P's.

The presence of J personalities – indeed, the necessity for J's in the Bank's operating environment – was another factor framed by institutional demands. The Bank not only framed the attitudes of its employees through the kind of work it demanded but to some extent hired the personalities that would be consistent with those attitudes, provided that they had the right academic record. Mission statements alone were not going to alter the fundamentals.

A DEMANDING WORK ENVIRONMENT

The supposedly driven attitudes of the Bank's officials toward the outside world contrasted with the forbearance required within the organization, deriving from the increasingly complex and indeterminate processes and procedures. In terms of our earlier definition, these processes are the 'artefacts' of the Bank's culture ('level three'). Rather than change this aspect of the Bank's culture for the better, however, the reorganization period saw a greatly worsened situation. Thus, while the mission statements were urging a new simplified, client-centered

---

[13] Isabel Briggs Myers developed the index (based on the ideas of C. G. Jung) in the 1940s. MBTI results indicate the respondent's likely preferences on four dimensions: Extroversion (E) OR Introversion (I), Sensing (S) OR Intuition (N); Thinking (T) OR Feeling (F); Judging (J) OR Perceiving (P). There are sixteen possible ways to combine the preferences, resulting in sixteen MBTI types: ISTJ, ISTP, ESTP, ESTJ, ISFJ, ISFP, ESFP, ESFJ, INFJ, INFP, ENFP, ENFJ, INTJ, INTP, ENTP, and ENTJ. The type descriptions summarize the underlying patterns and behaviors common to most people of that type.

[14] The Bank and Myers–Briggs, 'Why We Are the Way We Are', Staff Association newsletter, December 1996.

[15] Ibid.

approach, the processes were pulling in the opposite direction, toward increased complexity and inflexibility. The confused signals also negated any impact that mission statements could have had on basic attitudes.

Specifically, there were several new or reemphasized organizational artifacts that evolved during the reform period. For example, during the 1990s the Bank adopted numerous operational directives or policies, often the result of outside pressure. Complexities increased because of the accumulation of mandates just as instructions from the top at the same time demanded simplification. A note that had circulated around the Bank in July 1992 was entitled 'OD'ing on ODs' (operational directives). In it an employee complained that 'the organization is enmeshing itself in rules and regulations'.[16] Things got even worse thereafter.

Safeguard policies and procedures were introduced to cover the environment; natural resources; forestry; pest management; cultural property; indigenous peoples; involuntary resettlement; the safety of dams, international waterways, and disputed areas; and AIDS. Where the safeguard policies were concerned, the issue is not that such factors, each of which is in itself of importance, would otherwise be ignored. Rather, they were now the subject of procedures rather than informed judgment. The unnecessary burden was partly relieved when the concept of 'materiality' was introduced in 2002. Only those safeguards that were actually relevant to a project now needed to be addressed, but the burden remained.

Along with the safeguards there were fiduciary policies and procedures introduced, initially because of the mismanagement of some procurements and the need to tighten up project financial controls. It has been estimated that fiduciary compliance increased costs of loan preparation by 6%, or by about $81 million a year, in 2001. To the borrowers the extra costs were estimated at $118 to $215 million. The administrative costs 'have little to do with lending, and a lot to do with the bells and whistles that keep many other constituencies satisfied', wrote Kapur.[17] The

---

[16] Attempts followed for some years to transform ODs into advisory OPs, but this also created outside suspicion that safeguard policies (e.g., on the environment) were being diluted.

[17] Kapur, Devesh, 'Do as I Say, not as I Do; a Critique of G7 Proposals on Reforming the MDBs', Department of Government, Harvard University, February 2002, p. 17.

number of employees working on fiduciary and safeguard areas tripled between 1998 and 2003.

Along with the fiduciary policies there were intensifying review and quality control processes that often required extensive documentation to be prepared and which encouraged gaming to avoid oversight. These will be discussed in more depth later. Time was also increasingly required for mediation, reviewing, mentoring, and evaluating.

Outside fund-raising became a further procedural burden. As the internal budget was cut in the 1990s, outside trust fund money became a major source of funds for project development, described by one official as a 'phantom economy'. Many of the 900 currently active funds (out of 6,000 on the books) have their own procedures, eligibility rules, clearances, and deadlines. Said an interviewee in the April 2000 Staff Association newsletter: '[F]ully twenty percent of time is spent seeking new sources of financing for preparing projects that were (already) agreed with the client'. A large amount of time was also spent trying to manage the complexities of the numerous funds. A special trust fund department expanded steadily to deal with the complex situation, drawing in valuable professionals from other areas. Problems arose, such as misappropriations, people were fired, and time was spent in conference with the donor organizations that had entrusted the Bank with fund management.

In 2003, well after the end of the reorganization period, the simplification awards were introduced. A twelve-month standard processing time for certain loans was urged. By the end of 2003, a year after launch, the initiative was said by its chief[18] to be one-third of the way down the road, with a long way to go.

There were also the procurement regulations and procedures, often the main interest of board directors who wished to see a share of contracts going to their own countries. The procurement rules were left to be interpreted by specialists, since project officers could not take the time to understand them, while governments sometimes had even less insight. Following Wolfensohn's departure from office, his successor Paul Wolfowitz' anti-corruption agenda saw the procurement rules

---

[18] The simplification initiative chief was Jim Adams, a vice president.

aggressively reinforced, with some unintended consequences.[19] Private
vendor firms were zealously scrutinized, complex enforcement rules
were drawn up, and the new Department of Institutional Integrity
boasted that it chased down and publicly blacklisted a record number
of firms over 2005–2006.[20] In 2007, the Volcker Commission recommended that the integrity group be elevated to a vice presidency,
potentially creating additional distraction and diversion from the core
work of designing and managing development. The operations staff
found its ability to contract outsiders increasingly restricted and complicated even as the Bank was forced by budget restrictions to use more
and more outside consulting resources.

A staff member in 2002 wrote this on a Bank hotline: 'We say a lot
about this (client responsiveness) but if our management could hear the
real message it is that we let our drive for perfection ruin our chances for
really making a difference'. In 2003, well after the reorganization had
been completed, a new hire wrote: 'I cannot believe how much process
we have to go through all the time. Quarterly reports, monthly reports,
trust fund reports, management meeting reviews, program leaders meeting, human development meetings, team meetings, meetings with regional
operations, meetings with the network, meetings with the evaluation unit,
meetings with the partnership unit, reviewing documents from the country pillar, and an unbelievable amount of e-mail correspondence relating
to information sharing. Then we have multiple information systems that
do not seem to be able to talk to each other so we are constantly having to

---

[19] For example, small firms (lacking in-house lawyers), especially from developing
countries, can face difficulties with Bank contracts because of asymmetric information and unusual norms and definitions (e.g., on conflict of interest) designed to 'set a
higher standard' while the Bank itself operates comfortably beyond the jurisdiction of
the courts. Thus it is not obliged to make market-appropriate rules, but it is free to
publish 'blacklists' of firms deemed to have breached the rules. For a discussion of the
insecure status of private contractors dealing with international institutions, see
Suzuki, Eisuke and Suresh Nanwani, 'Responsibility of International Organizations:
The Accountability Mechanisms of Multilateral Development Banks', *Michigan Journal of International Law* 27, Fall 2005, e.g., pp. 182–183.

[20] While it proclaims the cause of private sector development in theory, as a public
sector entity the Bank's attitude toward the private firms with which it actually
transacts business as suppliers of services seems to remain in practice one of distrust.

check to make sure everything is up-to-date. I have worked in academia, in the private sector, and in Bank operations and I have never seen anything like this . . . . Do we actually have time to do real work?'

But it was not only the employees that had to spend a lot of resources dealing with the complexities. The effect was felt by the clients as well. A departing executive director for Ireland, Terrie O'leary, who was a supporter of Wolfensohn, said in October 2002: '[I]t has been painful to watch the administrative burden placed on countries when dealing with all of us who want to help them in their quest to develop their econo- mies . . . .. We simply do not understand the magnitude of the difficulties we bring to the table with costly reporting standards, numerous and large mission visits, and duplication of effort across the board that can diminish the good we are trying to accomplish'.

The Bank was not the only organization facing these problems. Scan- dizzo[21] also wrote about the IFI work environment. He described it as a 'case study in ambiguity and stress' where professional excellence often went along with alienation. But the Bank seems to be in a class of its own. Robert Wade, a one-time staff member and now a professor at LSE[22] said that disconnects facing everyday decisions resulted from the split between the 'action' and the 'political' character of the organiza- tion. The employees, he wrote 'are likely to experience the organization as a confusing noncompliant, out-of-control, or puppet-on-a-string kind of place'. They and the external entities expect an orderly align- ment of ideology, goals, procedures, decisions, actions, and feedback. Yet the logic of the political organization makes it impossible to main- tain this orderly alignment'.

Ambiguity and stress also arose from the perverse incentives intro- duced. The reforms created a rich tapestry of such perversity. Wolf- ensohn wanted first responders – firefighters – but his workers were required to operate as a policy-making elite. The Bank asked for sim- plification but rewarded sophistication. People were urged to work in teams, but the effects of the matrix and internal market were to

[21] Scandizzo, Pasquale. L., 'The Purpose, Management and Governance of IFIs', op cit., p. 97.
[22] Wade, Robert, 'The US Role in the Malaise at the World Bank; Get Up Gulliver', *Proceedings of the APSA Annual Meeting*, August 2001.

emasculate the teams. The creation of an information bureaucracy impeded the flow of information. The time-recording system did not increase efficient use of time but rather hoarding of time. Projects were to be simplified but became relentlessly more complicated.

People may embody the culture, but the culture in the end does not shape the organization. Rather, the organization will in the end shape the culture and how individuals must behave. Thus, the extraordinary demands of the system of mandates, fiduciary requirements, safeguard policies, fund-raising procedures, procurement rules, and integrity checks, along with the compressed schedules and multiple constituencies, combined with the requirement for new recruits to perform at top level in unfamiliar foreign environments, tended to dominate the posture of an individual within the organization and shape an institutional personality. The removal of the mythical pin-striped bureaucracy was irrelevant to the cure for the Bank's operational problems. What were needed instead were changes in the way the institution worked and the demands it made.

THE RE-SKILLING

If cultural change was not likely to be sustainable no matter how many employees were fired and replaced, then getting rid of staff was in essence largely irrelevant to cultural change. Thus the reason for cutting staff was in the end restricted to the purposes of re-skilling the organization. Did the organization become re-skilled?

Up until 1998 the numbers of employees increased in line with the expansion of the Bank's business and its various diversity targets.[23]

---

[23] The Bank, unlike other UN organizations, does not have nationality quotas. But a statistical review is submitted to the directors each year, which reports on 'over-' or 'under-' representation of employees in relation to national shareholding. Americans account for about a quarter of all professional employees. This is about four times the next highest – Britain and India. Rich countries have for some time comprised slightly more than half of the total professional staff. English-speaking countries, including the United States, Britain, India, and Pakistan, have tended to be over-represented in relation to shareholding. There are also gender targets that led to an increase of women professionals from 22% in 1990 to 36% in 2002 in Washington, particularly from the United States. The American orientation is increased by short-term consultants.

Under the reorganization, for the first time the numbers of people employed on a long-term basis at the Bank fell, from a peak of more than 9,000 in 1998.[24] It is worth repeating that this was a small number in relation to the workforce of many comparable private investment finance institutions, but it was a large number for the political opponents of the organization. The cuts were tentative at first, and the numbers actually climbed back up in 2000 as new entrants exceeded exits. But then, through determined axe wielding, the total employee headcount was brought down by 10% to below 8,400 by 2002. The fall occurred entirely in Washington, which was the most exposed to public scrutiny, where the total number fell 16%. Out in the country offices, the numbers rose. Indeed, one area where the reorganization achieved restructuring goals was decentralization.[25] The cuts also reduced tenure, which for a manager had averaged more than twenty years. Staff turnover rose from a usually low 4 to 5% per annum to a peak of 12% in the critical year of the Strategic Compact in 2001, before falling back to its long-run level.[26] Post-2001, the overall employment numbers started to move back up.

The Wapenhans report[27] had found in 1992 that three-quarters of the employees felt that they were overwhelmed with responsibilities for which they had little or no experience or training, and were expected to take on administrative, managerial liaison, and negotiations responsibilities outside their areas of technical proficiency. The report cited gaps in internal skills like contract administration, accounting, and 'management'. A report that followed stressed the lack of auditing capacity.[28] Sixty percent of the project audits were late and 7% never arrived. Unfortunately the Bank had rid itself of a third of its financial specialists

---

[24] The peak headcount was 9,262 in 1998, or more than 11,000 including temporarily hired consultants.

[25] The proportion of all staff working in country offices outside Washington rose from 18% to 25%, and the increase of country professionals was higher than that.

[26] The slow natural turnover of employment is partly because of the large proportion of non-U.S. citizens. Their status prohibits them from staying in the United States if they leave the Bank's employment and so they have to disrupt their families and homes to take another job.

[27] The Wapenhans Report, 'Effective Implementation: Key to Development Impact; Report of the World Bank's Portfolio Management Task Force', pp. 19, 20.

[28] 'Report of the Financial Reporting and Auditing Task Force', World Bank, 1993.

around the time of the 1987 reorganization. The report called for more new skills, in private sector development, the environment, and the financial sector, more 'social scientists' and people who knew about public sector reform. The list was, however, quite general and difficult to operationalize while the requirements were continually changing with changes in development assistance policy.

The Wapenhans skill renewals materialized in some form in the late 1990s. Over 1997 to 2002, in the general renewal quest, or in the cause simply of dramatic change, nearly half the staff left, through normal 'wastage', exit packages, and redundancy, and more than one-third of those present in 2002 were newly hired. Nevertheless, three years into the process, in December 2000, the Staff Association quoted a manager who said: '[I]n some fields our staffing is now shockingly thin, but no one seems to have noticed or care. This issue deserves mention at least as a corporate strategy concern, and as an antidote to all the chatter which seems to equate knowledge with tele-coms and technology'.

In 2000, when the numbers went back up instead of falling, a central hiring freeze was imposed to force them down. In some departments emergency action was taken to find redundant staff, assisted by the perverse incentives of generous severance packages. The rate of exit rose especially among UK and German nationals,[29] continuing a trend that started with the first major reorganization of 1987. Meanwhile, a group of nearly 3,000 existing staff known as 'non-regulars' were put through a fast-track and vaguely targeted weeding out process that cut out one-third of them.

One approach to redundancy had been based, implicitly at any rate, on the concept of a vitality curve. This was another appealing manage-ment idea used by GE, Enron, and others, colloquially known as the 'rank-and-yank' system. At one stage in the process Bank managers were asked to identify the lowest 15% performers on the curve, the news of which had an electrifyingly adverse effect on employee–management relations. However, the situation in 2001 did not allow

---

[29] According to the Bank's statistics, over 1995–1999, donor country employees exited more than proportionately with their share in total numbers (62.5%), and UK and German staff more than other donor countries.

time even for this approach to be used since it was necessary to find candidates at short notice.

A large proportion of leavers were over fifty years old. The firing of older staff is understandable from the usual argument about bringing in 'new blood' and new ideas, even though these were also the ones that had by and large attended the management retraining program. But the drive for new blood at all levels was not necessarily appropriate because there was a particular need for institutional memory and the continuity of client relationships, unlike the innovation-oriented technology company with which the Bank was keen on comparing itself.

The year 2001 was when the budget was supposed to fall back in real terms to the level of 1997 in order to meet Wolfensohn's undertakings to the board. The fallback was so effective that in 2002 the axings left gaps and understaffing of several hundred, which then required an immediate rehiring program to get the numbers up again, based on what was now called a strategic staffing program. Strategic staffing was a concept that appeared to be designed to provide credibility to the need to plug gaps in skills. The program proposal claimed that the redundancy program had been a success. At the same time it said that the institution needed what it termed integrator skills, that is, people who could lead teams, integrate work, and deliver work programs, and who were difficult to find outside. What this meant was a lack of experienced project managers, that is, the type of people of whom many had just been fired or let go.

The proposal also announced a multi-sector learning program to 'break new ground in integrating learning into the operational work of teams'. After five years of re-skilling a skill need was discovered that was the same as the one that had just been discarded. As Wolfensohn explained it at a strategic planning meeting, more expertise was needed 'to enable us to respond to the specific and practical needs of the clients . . . .. In particular we need to fill critical skill gaps in operations'. To kick-start that process, he said, there would be an immediate 'batch recruitment' effort in key sectors. He told the board: '[W]e identified this strategic staffing issue in our quarterly business reviews and we are moving aggressively to address it'. The new concepts that entered the institutional lexicon to deal with the situation – cluster or batch hiring, anticipatory recruitment, and strategic staffing – were part of the re-engineering revolution.[30]

In March 2002, three-year staffing plans linked to the budget were announced to help avoid 'stop-and-go staffing'. Human resources were to be better aligned with the emerging business so as to deal with 'issues of employment stability with flexibility, and maintaining cutting edge skills, given the new directions of lending'. The announcements stated that more effective and responsible recruitment was essential to meet strategic staffing expectations, to find new staff 'with scarce skills drawn from non-traditional sources'.

The Bank's strategic staffing was not successful in predicting changes in demand for skills. Indeed, it seemed to have problems coping with the well known demands of the type of work that the Bank was already embracing. The new participatory development programs in particular needed 'integrative' skills, the P skills as much as the J skills. A 2001 assessment of poverty reduction strategy papers by the IDS in Britain said: '[T]he traditional domination of technocrats and their expert knowledge is being challenged and enhanced by a range of different kinds of poverty knowledge, including experiential knowledge'.[31]

Just as the cultural deficiencies of the Bank had been blamed on the individuals who worked within it, the implication of the re-skilling effort was that the people, not the institution, were the problem. More skills were needed. Yet a key finding of all the Bank's client surveys, starting in Africa in 1995, of government officials, donors, private businesses, and civil society organizations has been a high level of satisfaction with skills and a high level of dissatisfaction with the institution – its lack of flexibility and slow response. In one set of African surveys in the late 1990s, satisfaction with individuals averaged about

---

[30] Cluster hiring normally refers to hiring for interdisciplinary teams – for example, to carry out a research project. Strategic staffing is a concept invented during the 1990s that means hiring according to a long-term corporate strategy, rather than short-term filling of vacancies. (But in practice the 'filling short-term vacancy' approach never existed in the Bank.)

[31] For example, see McGee, Rosemary, Josh Levene, and Alexandra Hughes, 'Assessing Participation in Poverty Reduction Strategy Papers; a Desk Based Synthesis of Experience in Sub-Saharan Africa', Draft, Institute of Development Studies, October 2001.

90% while satisfaction with the institution was less than 30%. The message from these surveys was not inadequate staff skills or unacceptable individual attitudes, but inadequate organization. The Staff Association said:[32] '[T]he goal was to get the right person to the right place at the right time. But the Bank's implementation rates a D minus'.

At the same time it was a common complaint that after some time in the Bank de-skilling set in. Peabody[33] describes a similar phenomenon in the WHO resulting from rigid organizational structure and displacement of developmental goals by internal process objectives, that is, internal process demands and confusion of work objectives deskills people. Thus re-skilling appeared to be needed not so much because the existing people did not have the inherent skills or potential skills, but because a supposedly skill-hungry organization actually dissipated the skills that its employees came in with and then looked outside for more.

INCENTIVE ENGINEERING

Motivational redesign complemented re-skilling. Performance bonuses were introduced in 1999. However, the idea was dropped two years later because it was seen as another divisive piece of human engineering. The human resources department in 2001 intoned about the need to explore differentiation in applying merit increases and the speed of growth through the salary scale, to get a more strategic utilization of existing tools by managers with attention to long-term effects. As for the de-layering of management, broad-banding, or grade collapse, as it was known, on balance did not work either. It reduced the incentive to perform by those who worked hard for the longest time because it weakened the signals of recognition of performance or career success, thus offsetting the incentives supposedly provided by performance bonuses. Incentive design is important, but clumsy incentive design is counterproductive.

Many Fortune 500 companies had reformed their hierarchical structures in the early 1980s to increase effectiveness and teamwork. But a

[32] Staff Association newsletter of June 2001.
[33] Peabody, John W., 'An Organizational Analysis of the WHO; Monitoring the Gap Between Promise and Performance', *Social Science and Medicine* 40(6), 1995.

few years later many of these companies and others besides had reversed the process. The general view that it had failed emerged at just about the time the Bank introduced it. In 2003, the organization started re-layering through a process called 'in-grade progression'. Paul Dorf, head of a human resources consulting firm, pointed out that one of the problems had been that broadbanding needed financial resources to provide rewards where grading could not, but that the Bank implemented it at the same time as budget cuts.[34] In many respects incentive engineering created the wrong incentives. It succeeded in doing the reverse of what it was intended to do, largely as a result of ill-thought-out and hastily implemented reforms mainly to satisfy an external audience.

THE ROLLER COASTER RIDE

From mid-1997 to mid-2002, more than 4,500 people left and more than 3,800 new people joined the Bank. Having recruited so many people in five years, the further room for maneuvering, even if the right strategies were in fact known, was limited. The institution was in a position where it would either have to inflate its staff once more, fire more people, or wait for natural wastage to allow it to pursue strategic goals. The restructuring had three major problems. First, it was done under artificial budget pressure, especially in 2001, when across-the-board axings violated the very undertakings of the Strategic Compact to *'adjust its staffing smoothly, equitably and cost effectively'*. Second, the definition of what skills really were regularly required was very confused. Third, the effects of the 'new paradigm' of development assistance, institutional and capacity building, which the Bank had espoused prior to the start of the skills restructuring, was not broadly adopted until after the main redundancy program had finished, so that the restructuring could not take it into account.

In August 2002 the senior manager responsible for strategic staffing wrote in a circular about skill gaps and the shortage of 'deep technical skills'. He said that centralized control, that is, recruiting managed by

---

[34] Staff Association newsletter, 'Broadbanding: An Idea Whose Time Has Passed?', May 2003.

central advisory boards rather than through individual managers' judgments, would now be the solution. The institution 'would be more easily able to 'identify the difficult-to-find skills from non-traditional sources'. The main areas of skill gaps were now thought to be fiduciary officials (e.g., auditors), country economists, trade economists, staff with skills to work on poverty, and skills related to the millennium development goals. The all-important team leaders, or integrators, who could not be easily recruited from outside, would have to be created though 'multi-sector team learning'.

While the staff restructuring had been done too early in relation to the 'new paradigm' of participatory and dialogue skills, it was also out of time in other ways. For example, for years the Bank had reduced its infrastructure skills, especially in the energy sector, where capacity fell by more than half. But now the board asked for a revamping of infrastructure lending to meet a looming investment gap in developing countries. As a result, what was called a groundbreaking infrastructure action plan was announced to 'meet the challenge of rebuilding the Bank's support to its clients'. Thus, almost as soon as it was announced, strategic staffing had been rendered redundant by actual events and replaced by a new 'groundbreaking plan'.

The main corporate strategy document for 2004–2006 called for 'a replenishment of the core technical staff that was eroded over the past several years and to supplement the need for technical expertise with broad based multi-sector integration skills'. But the strategy document also reassured its readers that the batch recruitment program, which started in early 2002, was supporting efficient recruitment'.[35]

There was, meanwhile, an even worse decay of agricultural sector skills that was hardly consistent with a poverty-focused institution. In its report of 2007 on Assistance to Agriculture in SubSaharan Africa, the Bank's evaluation group stated that there were only seventeen agricultural specialists left in the Bank's agricultural and rural department, less than half of the already low number of 1997. If this gap had been exposed, then that would have further complicated matters for 'strategic staffing'. However, it was not clearly exposed until the Bank was

---

[35] Strategic Update Paper 2004–2006; op cit., p. 13.

ready for it. The 2008 World Development Report focused on agriculture for the first time since 1982, by chance at the same time that a serious food crisis threatened to reverse the precarious advances in world standards of living. Affirming the long gap in assistance, the head of the UN Food and Agricultural Organization, Jacques Diouf, at a press conference on April 27, 2008, blamed two decades of poor policy decisions.

Apart from the abandonment of technical skills, the skill mix of the Bank's new recruits stayed largely in the old, traditional, safe categories – economics, finance, and 'operations', as well as the environment, information technology, and external affairs, and, finally, the Bank found itself in the unexpected position of having to rehire its infrastructure and now agricultural expertise. The skill restructuring could not meet the promise or the expectation of the Strategic Compact.

THE CUTS; EPILOGUE

The institutional memory of the Bank is a serious concern because, unlike a commercial firm, where learning is imbedded in products and technology, much of its effective memory lies within the process of dealing with clients, that is, country governments, knowledge that is difficult to codify in a knowledge management system. In 2002, just about half of the Bank's staff had five years' experience, whereas at the end of 1997, at the start of the renewal process, it had been three-quarters. Only a third of the staff in 2002 had what might be called long-term experience, of ten years or more. Just as the processes were becoming more complicated, and fiduciary responsibilities were widening, the experience of the people in operating them was being significantly reduced. The same had happened in 1987 when staff was cut as new responsibilities were being assumed. By the end of the period of cuts it was realized that the high levels of turnover were putting a premium on explaining the basics. 'New employees have to be submerged in the Bank persona' stated one strategy paper. The Bank's learning agenda was to be refocused to address these needs.

Facing the final crunch year of the Compact that he had maneuvered past the board, the president wrote to the staff in March 2000: '[W]e cannot go back to the board for additional funding because it will not be available. And therefore we have to react rather like a family does when they find they are short of money. We've got to come together. We've got to say we have a job to do, that we have a billion two hundred million dollars in the Bank ... with which to run our institution, and we have to get through this year within the framework of a billion two hundred million .... If a program requires three trips we have to try to do it in two. If six people typically go maybe its three or four. If there are ten different projects we may have to do six or seven. We have no choice so we've got to do it, but let's do it together with good will and with a sharing of the burden amongst us'. The allusion to family values illustrated the psychic distance between the president and the impact of his Compact on the ground. Many of his family members were under unnecessary redundancy notice.

Early on in the story the Staff Association wrote a polite article entitled 'Please Stop Criticizing the Worker Bees'.[36] 'We'd like to see Mr. Wolfensohn and (the external relations department)', it said, 'talk about staff as allies in this fight rather than enemies'. 'We hope Mr. Wolfensohn will remember that the ultimate frustration is not the staff; it's the goal we have set for ourselves ...'. By 2001, the association was less polite. 'The enthusiasm for downsizing doomed efforts to create a teamwork-oriented environment and low hierarchy culture'. Management, it said, should have had enough insight into human nature to foresee that – it was only common sense.[37]

The real problem was wider than goals. It was institutional failure, characterized by confused objectives, unplanned budget cuts, dysfunctional funding mechanisms, poorly planned reorganization, burdensome procedures, and de-skilling. The institution blamed its employees for its problems, while the real responsibility lay with its inadequate direction.

An observer of the U.S. corporate re-engineering experience wrote: 'Now, a few years later, companies are beginning to understand the price of their decisions. They had sacrificed many of their best people. We are now witnessing reemployment of those who are considered to

---

[36] December 1996 Staff newsletter.
[37] World Bank Staff Association newsletter, July 2000.

have significant skills. Or in other cases the same people are being retained as consultants or playing a part in outsourcing . . .. The degree of radical change called for and often implemented was in reality disastrous to the long-term interest of the organizations involved'.[38] These kinds of realizations were part of the widening critique of business process re-engineering at the time the Bank was just starting to re-engineer.

[38] MacDonald, John, *Calling a Halt to Mindless Change; a Plea for Commonsense Management*, American Management Association, 1998.

6

Reforming the Bank's Assistance Product

There were many flaws in the processes of reform of the 1990s. But even if the processes were per se flawed, this does not necessarily mean that the product was also flawed. The new organizational structures and processes were the immediate outcomes of the reforms, but the actual products delivered, in terms of both type and quality, would reflect the ultimate impact of the reforms, and it is in the final analysis the impact that is important.

The Strategic Compact called for change in the quality and types of products, within the overall objective of poverty reduction. The aim was both a process one, to make the Bank's products more responsive to the needs of clients, and one of content. Stemming from Wolfensohn's 1996 'knowledge bank' announcement, the principal content change was to accelerate the diversification from lending projects to knowledge and information projects and services. Following the Strategic Compact, another key process change was the emphasis on projects that used a participatory development approach. How far in fact did the reforms put in place under the Strategic Compact improve or worsen the product menu?

THE BANK'S PRODUCTS – A RECAP

As discussed in Chapter 1, the Bank's rationale for assistance can be conceived as having evolved essentially through three stages: a) capital deficiency; b) capital deficiency and related skill/know-how deficiency;

and c) capacity, know-how, and 'information' deficiency. In accordance with this evolution the Bank has shifted from its initial role as a financier of infrastructure and industry. It has diversified into the social sectors, macroeconomic reform, market regulation, public management, legal and judicial reform and institutions, and anti-corruption programs.

To deliver these products the Bank uses a range of financing and non-financing vehicles. On the financing side these include loans for sector investment, adjustment, development policy and poverty reduction loans and credits, budget support, and several others including grants for capacity building. The main vehicle has continued to be sector investment loans used largely for infrastructure lending. Adjustment lending, now also known in the form of development policy loans and poverty reduction credits (that is loans-for-reform), has comprised over time an average of about 30% of the total.

Knowledge assistance has incorporated technical assistance projects, advisory services (including what has been called economic and sector work, or ESW), training, research, and advocacy. Knowledge products have also evolved from a focus on technical project issues to country economic policies, and in more recent years to advocacy on world economic problems. The Bank produces a range of basic macroeconomic and sector reports; policy papers; sector, country, debt relief, and poverty reduction strategy papers; and a range of publications such as the World Development Indicators and the World Development Report.

One of the most important products in the Bank's menu over time has been structural adjustment lending, recently renamed as development policy lending and extended into poverty reduction support. While conditions apply to all of the Bank's loans and credits, one of the particular features of adjustment loans up until the reorganization period was extensive reform conditionality.

As discussed in Chapter 2, loans-for-reform were an idea that arrived with the oil crisis of 1979–1980. Loan conditionality was one of the key issues cited by Wolfensohn in the Strategic Compact proposals as requiring urgent remedial attention.

LOAN CONDITIONALITY AND STRUCTURAL ADJUSTMENT

To what extent were loans-for-reform amended or discontinued in the 1990s? Reform conditionality through adjustment loans, especially in the 1980s, had been extensive, and increasingly controversial, particularly as regards the lack of buy-in from recipient governments. In this respect the Wapenhans Report had held a borrowers' workshop in 1991 in which representatives of a number of governments gave their confidential views. One stated: '[T]he staff rigidly insist on as many conditions as possible – some of which reflect insensitivity about the political realities in the borrowing country – to convince the Board that the project will be successful. Yet those very conditions make it impossible for the project to attain its objectives'.

African adjustment lending received most of the critical attention, but the problem applied generally. In 1991, at the break-up of the Soviet Union, for example, many former republics faced severe macroeconomic imbalances and the Bank and Fund moved in with adjustment-type programs. There was an idea that a group of key economic adjustments were the basis on which structural change would occur. The adjustments would galvanize dormant markets in the former Soviet Republics and thereby encourage a responsible capitalist class to arise and lobby for their market rights. Some western economists thought that shock-therapy tactics would create a free market in Russia. 'Russia became a free market economy on January 1, 1992' they said, and they raised their expectations accordingly.[1]

Far from being phased out, adjustment-type programs remained very much on the agenda. Russia and the Ukraine for example received billions of dollars in adjustment loans throughout the 1990s[2] despite increasing scepticism of the reform conditions. A Bank evaluation for the Ukraine in 2000 reported: '[P]ublic cynicism about the transition reform agenda

[1] As explained in William Easterly, *The White Man's Burden: Why the West's Efforts to Aid the Rest Have Done So Much Ill and So Little Good*, Penguin, 2006, p. 61.

[2] During 1992, Russian inflation rose to 1,350% and recorded output and employment fell substantially for six straight years up to the financial crisis of 1998. By 2002, a total of $12.6 billion had been granted for fifty-five projects, of which only half of those completed were rated satisfactory. In the Ukraine, inflation rose to 3,400%. The Ukraine received over 1993–2002 a total of twenty-five IBRD loans worth $3.4 billion.

is high. Abstract notions of economic liberalization and the benefits that ensue ring hollow to anyone exposed to the decline in living standards over the past five years'.[3] In 2000 the Russian government criticized its $1.5 billion third structural adjustment loan. It said that the experience had 'laid bare serious problems in preparing such structural adjustment loans, problems that could be important to the Bank as a whole; these include, in particular, inefficiency caused by excessive loan conditionalities and excessively broad coverage of many sectors simultaneously'.[4] $1.1 billion of the loan was later canceled.

Along with other former Republics, the Republic of Belarus received its first adjustment-type loan in 1993, one that is illustrative. The government had little economic policymaking experience. The loan was nevertheless accompanied by a 'policy matrix' asking for progress on unifying the exchange rate at a free market level; reducing food, energy, transport, and rent subsidies; liberalizing interest rates and credit; breaking up wholesale distribution monopolies; reducing profit and price controls; removing various barriers to business entry; freeing up the laws on housing transactions and leasing of real estate; submitting a draft law on the privatization of urban land; privatization through auctions for 120 businesses and preparation of others for leasing; creating regulations to implement voucher privatization; eliminating the state order system for non-government producers; making an action plan to ease the entry of new trading firms; eliminating export licensing, quotas, and foreign exchange retentions; submitting a new customs tariff code; drafting a new labor code; reorganizing social security accounts; creating a unit to prepare pension system reform; and, finally, making a list of potential state enterprise board members.

---

[3] *Ukraine – Country Assistance Evaluation*, World Bank OED, November 8, 2000. According to the evaluators' assessment in 2000, the Bank overestimated the level of consensus and the speed of reform in the Ukraine. In eight years only two reform actions – small enterprise privatization and liberalization of prices – were regarded as 'satisfactory'.

[4] '*Russian Federation – Country Assistance Evaluation*, World Bank OED, April 2002. In Russia, which had been the location of Soviet-era governance and policy-making capability, up to the financial crisis of 1998 three Bank-Fund–supported structural adjustment programs were deemed to have largely failed to achieve their objectives.

Progress on these issues formed the recommended program for *the remainder of 1993*.

In this particular case the proposed measures were not actually conditions of the loan. However, many of them were benchmarks against which the Bank later rated the government's performance under a 1997 'memorandum of understanding', an instrument that actually reflected no understanding but which became the guide for Bank lending policy. In other countries such programs comprised the actual conditions of loans.

A key element of Bank and IMF adjustment programs during the reform period was privatization, but privatization was more complex than understood. In the absence of adequate institutions, accepted corporate laws, and judicial enforcement, it was inadequate to promote sales of companies and assets, especially at large scale. Instead of reviving the economy with the expected positive entrepreneurial energy, privatization in Russia after 1995 got mired in complex regulations, punitive tax administration, and corrupt practices.[5] After some initially hopeful signs that mass privatization by vouchers would be successful in countries like the Czech Republic and Russia, it soon became apparent that they too were failing in their central objective, which was wide distribution of ownership to small shareholders.[6]

In the former Soviet States, disentangling economic problems needed far more sustained and intensive collaborative input than was allowed under typical adjustment programs, yet adjustment loans remained the primary policy instrument. There was no equivalence between Zambia's attempts to adjust to copper price changes and Russia's attempt to reconstruct an economy distorted by the complex adverse effects of

---

[5]   Jeffrey Sachs was a leading advocate of rapid privatization; see 'Privatization in Russia; Some Lessons from Eastern Europe', *American Economic Review* 82(2): 43–48, May 1992. Critical positions on the privatization programs were taken by, among others, Stiglitz, Joseph, *Globalization and Its Discontents*, W. W. Norton, June 2002. See also Black, Bernard, Reinier Kraakman, and Anna Tarassova, 'Russian Privatization and Corporate Governance: What Went Wrong?', Stanford Law School, September 1999; John M. Olin Program in Law and Economics, Working Paper No. 178; and William Davidson Institute at University of Michigan Business School, Working Paper No. 269.; Svejnar, Jan., 'Assistance to the Transition Economies: Were There Alternatives?', World Bank OED, 2002, and Nellis, John, 'Time to Rethink Privatization in Transition Economies?', IFC discussion paper no 38, 1999, p. 9.

[6]   Pistor, K. and A. Spicer, 'Investment Funds in Mass Privatization', World Bank, Viewpoint No 10, April 1997.

seventy five years of central planning.[7] Policy performance targets for the short to medium term were often far in excess of what the donor governments themselves could possibly have delivered through their own national legislatures or executive bodies, with the result that the Bank's conditionality was not taken seriously and compliance was poor.

The structural adjustment approach toward the former Soviet Republics was driven by the political perceptions of the main voting member countries of the Bank, and ill-judged reform pressure at a critical time from the 'West' was part of the external environment that encouraged the re-emergence of authoritarian nationalism. In other regions, loan conditionality did not have such a potential for damaging international relations, but it was increasingly recognized to be an unproductive approach to assisting countries to escape from economic difficulties. Paul Collier, a former senior Bank economist, wrote that the most effective model of development assistance is that of a 'partnership between two agents', not an unequal relationship based on conditionality.[8]

DIALOGUING ON ADJUSTMENT

The conditionality issue thus called into question the Bank's neutrality, credibility, and its technical capacity. While structural adjustment lending continued unabated, by the latter part of the 1990s increasingly this message began to be accepted by the Bank and IMF, with the reservation that economic imbalances still required complex packages of remedial measures.

Wolfensohn in fact took a personal role in the conditionality discussion shortly after joining the Bank as part of his program of reaching out to the Bank's civil society opponents. In 1996 he started a dialogue with the members of the Structural Adjustment Participatory Review Initiative (SAPRI), which claimed to coordinate hundreds of civil society groups.[9] A second dialogue was started with a group of non-government

---

[7] See Svejnar, J., 'Assistance to the Transition Economies' op cit.

[8] Collier, Paul, 'Conditionality, Dependence and Coordination; Three Current Debates on Aid Policy', in Christopher L. Gilbert and David Vines, *The World Bank: Structure and Policies*, Cambridge University Press, 2000, p. 299.

[9] These were in Mexico, the Philippines, Bangladesh, Ecuador, El Salvador, Hungary, Ghana, Mali, Uganda, and Zimbabwe.

organizations (NGOs) in February 2001.[10] SAPRI issued a report in 2002, but by this time the argument was largely over.[11] Prior to meeting with the group before the U.S. launch of the report Wolfensohn said: 'I wish some of them would change their tune and tell us that we haven't done enough on the next level of the things that we should be doing, rather than going back to things that were addressed five years ago and to which I think we have been particularly responsive'.

The activist participants complained that although the Bank had acknowledged the importance of local consultation in the formulation of economic policies, it did not seem prepared to learn from the meeting. The Bank team had been obstructionist, they said, and almost always found extensive faults in the draft reports, including fifty pages of objections to a report on Bangladesh covering four or five topics. To their annoyance, at the conclusion of the forum, the Bank immediately closed down the SAPRI process without any commitment to follow up or any recognition of the SAPRI analysis in any of its internal documents'.[12] The limits of the Bank's willingness to dialogue with the activists had been reached.

Even if the SAPRI felt it had been given the brush-off, the original adjustment idea was now diluted. Aid-for-reform was now seen as long-term, and not just a response to a temporary shock; reform programs had to be designed around social protection; there had to be an emphasis on growth and poverty reduction; and, above all, the programs had to be developed in such a way that the people of the country understood what they were for and accepted their main principles. Thus, while this type of lending continued at a high rate, its character was changed, and

---

[10] The Banks issues paper was 'From Adjustment Lending to Development Policy Support Lending; Key Issues in the Update of World Bank Policy', OPCS, June 2002. The notes of one dialogue participant (from the Bretton Woods Project) claimed that there was annoyance on the part of Bank officials when confronted by NGO members, a lack of an advance agenda, and that the Bank was formally in the chair rather than in a participant role. Nevertheless, it conceded that there was a dialogue.

[11] Structural Adjustment Participatory Review Initiative (SAPRI), 'The Policy Roots of Economic Crisis and Poverty', Washington, DC, April 2002. The report criticized trade and financial liberalization, privatization of utilities, user fees in social services, and unregulated labor markets. Its solution was to increase the power of the state and control global trade and investment.

[12] SAPRI report, op cit., p. 24.

this was a qualified plus point for the overall reform of the Bank's assistance products.

REPLACING CONDITIONALITY

The antidote to reform dictation from Washington was local participation. Attempts to establish stronger participation had preceded the 1990s reforms. In 1991, the Bank established a participatory development learning group, and in 1994, a fund for innovative approaches in human and social development to promote participation. In 1994, the Bank introduced a 'participation action plan'. Twenty projects were designated participation 'flagships' and external partnerships such as an NGO working group were established. A senior managers' committee was appointed to oversee the introduction of participation. In 1995, a review of economic work in Africa had found that, 'by far the most striking and general attribute of success had been the increasing involvement of the government, local consumers, and stakeholders in its preparation and discussion'. In 1996, a 'participation sourcebook' was published. But the initial enthusiasm weakened and the committee was disbanded by 1997. As the evaluators put it, 'the Bank declared victory and moved on'.

Wolfensohn's experience as a relationship banker told him that, without strong client commitment, efforts to implement new projects would fail. He was also frustrated by the seeming compartmentalization of foreign aid into donor fiefdoms that in turn tended to prevent meaningful local participation. In early 1999, returning after a stay at his home in Jackson Hole, Wyoming, he presented to the Bank staff the first draft of his Comprehensive Development Framework (CDF). The aim of the CDF was to harmonize development efforts. In essence it proposed a joint approach to development projects in which each of the stakeholder institutions, including international financial institutions, donor agencies, government, civil society, and non-government organizations (NGOs), would provide services or focus on areas according to its comparative advantage. His aim was to provide a platform for a comprehensive, 'holistic' view of economic development.

Initially the intelligentsia of the Bank scoffed at what seemed a simplistic and not very original proposal, foisted on them at a time when they believed that sorting out the internal disorder in the Bank should have been the first priority.[13] The project managers suspected that this was just another kind of planning gimmick, when what were needed were actual results. As desirable as participation and dialogue really were, they doubted that participation was either understood or achievable in the Bank's timetable-driven programs. The CDF idea also contained an anomaly. It appeared to imply that a *necessary* requirement for development was for countries to form partnerships with 'aid' when the large bulk of development spending in most developing countries comes from their own resources. The CDF was really a CDAF, with the 'A' standing for 'assistance'. But despite the doubts about originality, purpose, and style, the organization fell into line remarkably quickly and no less than sixteen country 'CDF pilots' were initiated within months of the announcement. By 2000 the Bank had mainstreamed the CDF.

The participatory process constituted an important innovation in the way Bank products were delivered. But it was not without problems. A board review of forty-six countries in 2001 found that the link between the CDF consultations and national policy-making was weak (national parliaments were largely ignored). There was a tension between the need to meet targets and the need for countries to commit themselves. Fewer than half of the countries had 'medium term strategies well anchored to their visions'. Said one board member: '[W]e need to have a more realistic assessment of the extent to which we can obtain consensus or should seek to obtain consensus on what are the core political issues of budgets, of priorities ...' It was difficult to avoid the process becoming bureaucratized. A year later, a doubting letter to the editor of the *Financial Times* said[14] that the comprehensive development framework was becoming a factory for churning out reports/strategies and generating useless meetings.

---

[13] Wolfensohn had changed the original name, which was the 'New Development Framework', to accommodate some of the doubters.

[14] Ruderfer, Emil, 'Receivers of Development Aid Should Run Own Show', *Financial Times*, October 4, 2002.

BUILDING LOCAL INSTITUTIONS

Increasing local participation requires local capacity to participate, which in turn requires stronger institutions in and outside government, including administrative capacity and legal, regulatory, and enforcement systems. The switch to institution building was another logical product development away from adjustment lending, consistent with the Bank's shift to knowledge projects and services.

However, institution building is also a difficult area. Moises Naim wrote: '[I]nstitutional reform is a field with much action and little theory . . . . What passes for knowledge about institutional reforms is often nothing more than a series of partial findings with little capacity to provide universal prescriptions to guide efforts aimed at improving institutional performance in reforming countries'.[15] Similarly, Rodrik et al. wrote that recognizing that institution-building is central to development does not necessarily imply much in terms of operational guidance.[16] The Bank's World Development Report (WDR) for 2002 states that in institutional reform best practice is a flawed concept.[17] Another study, part of a Bank conference on institutional reform,[18] emphasized the difficulty of defining institutional quality. The authors wrote: '[O]ur understanding of reform strategies remains in its infancy, especially in the light of the growing understanding that different institutions might be appropriate in different circumstances'.

[15] Naim, Moises, 'Fads and Fashion in Economic Reforms; Washington Consensus or Washington Confusion?' op cit., pp. 525–528.

[16] See, for example, Rodrik, Dani Arvind Subramanian, and Francesco Trebbi, 2004, 'Institutions Rule: The Primacy of Institutions Over Geography and Integration in Economic Development', *Journal of Economic Growth*, vol. 9(2), pp. 131–165. Later, however, Rodrik lowered his expectations for institutional reform. See Rodrik, Dani, 2006, ' "Goodbye Washington Consensus, Hello Washington Confusion? A Review of the World Bank's Economic Growth in the 1990s: Learning from a Decade of Reform', *Journal of Economic Literature* 44(4): 973–987. 'Desirable institutions', say the authors, 'have a large element of context specificity, arising from differences in historical trajectories, geography, political economy or other initial conditions'.

[17] World Development Report, 'Building Institutions for Markets', World Bank, 2002.

[18] Djankov, S., R. La Porta, F. Lopez-de-Silanes, and Andre Schleifer, 'Appropriate Institutions', paper presented at the World Bank Conference on Appropriate Institutions for Growth, September 13, 2002.

Nevertheless, in corporate strategy discussions the Bank's management reassured the board that, '[T]he way we build institutional capacity in countries has also improved development results. We are not only delivering learning opportunities, we are also working together with our clients to exchange and adapt knowledge'.[19]

One illustration of the difficulties of institutional capacity building is in the reform of civil services. Some projects have relied on the government to reduce its own staff as a condition of a loan, and the conflict of interest has led to poor implementation. In other cases donors have set up special project management units that have drawn away the best people from the departments they are trying to strengthen.[20] In 2005, an evaluation of fifty-five African countries pointed to this as a serious problem for building genuine capacity, because the short-term advantage of efficient project implementation was offset by the long-term adverse effects on the capability and morale of units of government.[21] In Malawi the evaluators found that the Bank had financed training, counterpart advisors, and equipment to build capacity in public agencies in nearly every project for ten years with little significant long-term impact. The Bank's efforts just temporarily relieved the symptoms rather than addressing the real causes of the problem.[22]

Another element of institution building, creating regulatory institutions, has also been problematic. In the former Soviet Republics outsiders worked on regulations to improve corporate governance. Early attempts to help rewrite laws came up against a lack of consensus on what made good law, an example being appropriate accounting standards where it was not clear whether the United States or the European principles were more appropriate.[23] Generally, the European civil code approach differed from the U.S. and British common law approach in

[19] 2004–2006 World Bank Strategy Update Paper: Questions and Answers.
[20] 'Best-practice' incentive bonus systems in a civil service often cannot compete with the remuneration of a relatively lowly position in an aid donor's office. In some former Soviet Republics young graduates in local donor agency offices in the 1990s were earning more than government ministers.
[21] 'Capacity Building in Africa: An OED Evaluation of Bank Support', World Bank OED, 2005.
[22] 'Malawi – Country Assistance Evaluation', World Bank, 2000.
[23] The U.S. system is more rule-based while the Europeans put more weight on intent.

corporate legislation. It was unclear how far it was urgent to formalize bankruptcy law when all the enterprises that needed to be closed were government owned. One of the results of the lack of a perceived need for new regulations was that they were prepared by outsiders without meaningful input from the local legal profession or legislative bodies, something that would not be acceptable or have any chance of success in the United States or Europe.

It is difficult to observe and measure the quality of institutions. The Bank uses measures of governance, public financial management, the investment climate, the quality of checks and balances, public procurement, statistical systems, and administrative reforms. But the classifications are not rigorous.[24] An April 2006 report to the development committee of the board[25] claimed that Ghana, Mali, Senegal, and Tanzania all achieved substantial improvements in a critical area of institutional development, financial governance, between 2001 and 2004, and that with political commitment many countries should be able to achieve reasonably strong public finance management within a five- to ten-year period. However, the 2005 internal evaluation of fifty-five African projects had stated that particular difficulty occurred in putting into place complex systems such as public financial management systems. It stated that 'there is little empirical evidence to clarify what part of the problem international capacity building support can best help to solve; in what order capacity needs should be addressed; what can be expected of different kinds of interventions and why' (p. 18).

In 1996 Wolfensohn brought the issue of corruption on to the institution building agenda with his speech to the World Bank/IMF annual meeting. He described the 'cancer of corruption' as a tax on the poor in developing countries. The aid community had up to then steered clear of the issue, on the grounds that corruption was inherent in all poor societies and rich donors had little understanding of its nature, and that it had a neutral, or even beneficial, effect on investment and growth.

[24] These include the so-called Kaufmann–Kraay (KK) indicators compiled by the World Bank Institute on the basis of a large number of (mostly external) assessments, Transparency International (TI) indicators, and Country Policy and Institutional Assessments (CPIA) compiled by the World Bank.
[25] 'Global Monitoring Report 2006: Strengthening Mutual Accountability – Aid, Trade and Governance', Development Committee Paper, World Bank, April 20, 2006.

Bank research helped to show that corruption was not a neutral phenomenon, but rather an issue of economic inefficiency and waste as well as unfairness, especially toward the poor and disenfranchised. Between 1996 and 2005, the Bank claims that it supported within its projects more than 600 anti-corruption programs in 100 countries, in areas such as financial and constitutional governance, judicial reform, civil service reform, decentralization, and latterly media freedom.

As in the case of institution building in general, however, it is by no means clear that corruption fighting is susceptible to Bank intervention. Subsequently, the donor community itself applied a dose of realism when Wolfowitz tried to introduce a new area of loan conditionality based on reducing corruption. The governors opposed the program on the grounds that setting the corruption bar too high could penalize the poor on account of the failings of their leaders.[26] Wolfowitz's zealotry was potentially counterproductive for the Bank's institution-building effort to the extent that it positioned institutional development as another focus of external conditionality.[27]

CAN ASSISTANCE TO INSTITUTION BUILDING BE SUCCESSFUL?

The record does not provide grounds for optimism about the effectiveness of institution-building products. Table 3 is an attempt at

---

[26] Giles, Chris, 'Governance Poses a Test for World Bank', *Financial Times*, September 26, 2006; FT.com. At the 2006 annual meetings in Singapore, Hilary Benn, Britain's Development Minister, threatened to withhold 50 million pounds of Britain's contribution unless the issue was resolved. Mario Draghi, governor of the Italian Reserve Bank, warned that anti-corruption programs should complement, and not substitute for, the commitment to development. The complaints were not only about the excessively onerous corruption conditions but also about country selectivity. For example, corruption in Indian infrastructure projects was targeted, but Pakistan remained unchallenged, leading to suspicion that the U.S. foreign policy agenda was influencing Wolfowitz's anti-corruption campaign. The plan that finally emerged after an unprecedented all-night sitting required board oversight 'to ensure that the Bank's decisions were broadly based (that is not arbitrary suspension of lending),' and an instruction to the Bank to improve the effectiveness of its governance indicator.

[27] An early reaction to the anti-corruption proposals from the Chinese authorities was to inform the Bank that it was considering stopping borrowing because the Bank was exceeding its mandate. Since by 2007 China was by far the largest single borrower, such an action would have been a severe test of the program.

Table 3. *The possibilities of institution building*

Assistance activity	Assistance content	Who does it?	Degree of difficulty	Time required
1. Create market regulatory agencies	Set up fair trade offices, utility regulators, securities commissions, etc.	Usually government	Relatively easy	Short term
2. Build regulatory agency capacity	Install equipment, develop procedures, train agency staff	Usually government	Moderately easy	Short to medium term
3. Create rules for agencies, to govern regulator and regulated	Draft contract rules, fiduciary rules, corporate rules	Government, parliament	Relatively easy, but prone to frequent revision	Short to medium term
4. Create enforcement mechanisms	For self-regulation, security services, police, judiciary, prisons	Usually government, can be private	Moderately difficult	Medium term
5. Implement effective market regulation	Develop and build effective regulatory agency programs	Government	Difficult	Long term
6. Develop and implement effective enforcement	Train and develop efficient enforcement and judicial services	Usually government, can be private	Difficult	Long term
7. Persuade the market and society to respect the rules	Combination of incentives, penalties, and a process of social evolution	Society and government	Very difficult	Very long term
8. Develop general respect for law, develop democratic institutions, and reduce corruption	Gain widespread acceptance of the rule of law, property rights, and contracts	Society and parliament	Very difficult	Very long term

making some 'degree-of-difficulty' institutional assistance categories, applied in this case to the measures to improve the business climate.

The areas in which aid can and has got involved are by and large the easier and quicker ones like the writing of regulations and the establishment of a regulatory agency, which can be implemented relatively fast with recordable results. But effective capacity building, regulatory enforcement, and the culture of acceptance are both critical and harder, and local buy-in is crucial, without which much upfront work can be a waste of time. There is an extremely wide gap between on the one hand describing and theorizing about corruption and on the other effectively dealing with it, and concern that outside pressure might hinder as much as assist the process.

There is definitely reason for caution in the reorientation of Bank products toward institution building. Without a good understanding of the processes at work and the way in which they unfold, institutional development may fail. There can be value-subtracting institutions and value-subtracting processes of building them. There can also be counterproductive attempts to enforce participation. Good policy must learn what good institutions are, and these are culture-specific. Rodrik writes that the policy-maker may be better advised to target the binding constraints on growth than attempt ambitious institutional reforms. 'Telling poor countries in Africa or Latin America that they have to set their sights on the best-practice institutions of the United States or Sweden is like telling them that that the only way to develop is to become developed'.[28]

STRUCTURAL ADJUSTMENT LIVES – POVERTY REDUCTION LOANS

The adjustment lending of the 1980s was replaced from 1999 by a new generation of adjustment-cum-social-investment programs. These were the multi-donor–driven Poverty Reduction Support Credits (PRSCs), which were tied to Poverty Reduction Strategy Papers (PRSPs), themselves in turn tied to the second phase of the Heavily Indebted Poor

[28] Rodrik, Dani, 'Goodbye Washington Consensus; Hello Washington Confusion?', op cit., 2006.

Countries Initiative (HPIC) launched in 1999. The PRSPs were not a Bank initiative as such, and Wolfensohn appeared to see them as supplanting his own CDF brainchild, but they became a core part of the Bank's new product menu.[29]

The PRSCs immediately faced challenges from academics, aid specialists, and laymen. Martin Wolf in the *Financial Times* wrote:[30] 'The World Bank is apparently calling for the restructuring of the political and social order of its developing country members – there is no reason to suppose that countries can be readily reordered to meet the demands of today's progressive sensibility . . .. The term suggests the presence of a benefactor prepared to dole out power to the deserving – but no such benefactor exists'. A research team from the IDS at the University of Sussex[31] concluded that the short PRSP timeframe meant that the process would end up like the one-sided communications of the past rather than the lengthy and unpredictable ones needed for genuine participation. The Bretton Woods Project, an anti-Bank activist group, reviewing the first PRSP in Uganda in 2001, contended that the Bank and Fund had repackaged past controversial adjustment policies in an attempt to co-opt the activist community and civil society into supporting the same traditional policies. These views were echoed by other activist groups.[32]

There was a fear that the coalitions convened by donor agencies to meet the donor's timetable would exclude meaningful participation

---

[29] Sebastian Mallaby writes that Wolfensohn was strangely uninterested in the PRSPs despite his avowed concern for participation and dialogue because he suspected that they might compete with the CDF. He was also apparently irritated when he heard {later} that there had previously been a type of CDF in use, known as a PFP (Policy Framework Paper), which bore some of the characteristics of a CDF. See Sebastian Mallaby, *The World's Banker: A Story of Failed States, Financial Crises, and the Wealth and Poverty of Nations*, Penguin, 2004, p. 236.

[30] *Financial Times*, September 13, 2000.

[31] This was the IDS Participation Group. See McGee, Rosemary, Josh Levene, and Alexandra Hughes, 'Assessing Participation in Poverty Reduction Strategy Papers; a Desk Based Synthesis of Experience in Sub-Saharan Africa', Draft. Institute of Development Studies, October 2001. See also McGee, R., 'Accountability Through Participation: Developing Workable Partnership Models in the Health Sector', *IDS Bulletin* 31, January 2000.

[32] 'The World Bank and the PRSP; Flawed Thinking and Failing Experiences', Shalmali Guttal, Alejandro Bendaña, and Helen Wanguza, Jubilee South, Focus on the Global South, AWEPON, and Centro de Estudios Internacionales, November 16, 2001.

from lawmakers. Larry Summers, a former chief economist and a guest at a Bank retreat in May 2001, said: 'I am deeply troubled by the distance that the Bank has gone in democratic countries towards engagement with groups other than Government in designing projects . . . there is a real possibility it seems to me of significantly weakening democratically elected governments'.

The Bank responded by starting to consult parliamentarians. It proposed even extending its reach to institutional strengthening in the parliaments themselves. Training seminars in the PRSP process for parliamentarians were mounted in 2001 in six African countries. A review for the 2002 Development Committee[33] claimed that, while the participation of parliaments had thus far been limited, there was some 'good practice' where individual parliamentarians had been involved or where progress was being reported to parliament. But while the PRSP needs broad participation including that of the legislature, the Bank's involvement with the legislature, if it in fact succeeds, will lead it into interference in the political process. But if it does not succeed, then the credibility of the PRSP will be in doubt.

Despite these issues the 2002 Development Committee nevertheless professed itself pleased with the way in which countries seized ownership of the PRSP process. 'The preparation of "interim PRSPs" (I-PRSPs) has served a useful purpose' said the Development Committee, 'by encouraging countries to take stock of existing data and policies, to launch a broader process of rethinking current strategies, and to produce a time-bound road map for the preparation of the first PRSP'. The implication seemed to be that policy development was something that countries would not otherwise do, and what is more, that the work involved in doing an I-PRSP would have a major benefit because 'time-bound road maps' could be created.

By 2005 an OED evaluation report warned, predictably, that client countries see the PRSP as a source of cash and not an expression of commitment to development. A status report to the Bank's Development Committee for the 2005 annual meetings concluded that the

---

[33] 'Review of the Poverty Reduction Strategy Paper (PRSP) Approach. Main Findings', Development Committee, World Bank, March 27, 2002.

PRSPs were lacking in operational details and showed a continuing tension between aid and government objectives. They could not eliminate the 'parallel parliament' problem, and they put further pressure on government planning capacity. By 2005 only one-third of PRSPs, which were clearly political documents, were being presented to parliaments, while to a large extent the 'poor' were not represented in the discussions.

Nevertheless, while the place of the PRSCs within the Bank's product menu remains in question, the weight of conditionality has certainly declined. A report to the Development Committee in 2005 said that the average number of conditions had declined to twelve, compared to the average of fifty-six counted in the second report on adjustment lending in 1988. The Bank's evaluators claimed that the PRSCs were doing better than the old SALs, with over 80% rated as satisfactory compared to 60% of SALs in the 1980s. At the 2006 annual meetings, Wolfowitz set a seal on the debate. 'On the subject of conditionality ... the whole approach has to be much more one of helping countries find what works and then embracing programs that they take ownership of'.[34]

The concept of loans-for-reforms lives on in an amended guise. The proportion of 'adjustment' operations has remained at an average of around 30% of total Bank lending since 2000, with a peak of 50% of commitments in 2002 and 44% of disbursements in 2003. The long-term average is well above the target of the original structural adjustment initiative of the 1980s, when the Bank's ability to support broad reforms was questioned by Burke Knapp. The decline in conditionality and the participatory nature of the programs cannot dispel the fundamental problem of how to judge the appropriateness of the reforms that are being supported with loans, and the way to ensure genuine and committed local buy-in.

WERE THE BANK'S NEW PRODUCTS PRO-POOR?

The new knowledge- and institution-building products were subsumed within the overarching Bank objective of fighting poverty. How far was the Bank's lending and knowledge product performance actually able to meet the poverty fighting objective?

---

[34] Letter from Wolfowitz in the *Financial Times* of September 29, 2006.

Poverty reduction was first promoted as a principal Bank objective by Robert McNamara in a speech to the board of governors in September 1973 at Nairobi, Kenya. McNamara's version of the fight against poverty was through 'poverty projects'.[35] Total poverty-oriented lending rose from an estimated 5% of the total in 1968–1970 to 30% by 1979–1980.[36] Agriculture, especially smallholder farms, irrigation, extension, crop development, livestock, fisheries, and agro-processing, was a major proportion of this. By 1980, more than $5 billion of annual lending was for agriculture and rural development. The assumption was that small agricultural producers would raise productivity in response to packages of improved inputs. Unfortunately, however, the projects were labor-intensive and complex and relied on enabling institutional conditions and buy-in from local elites, which was often not present. Some project ideas, in particular the Regional Integrated Development Projects, planned on the logic that sustainable rural development needed a multi-sector approach, had high failure rates despite the high expectations of the donor community.

The mixed success of poverty projects was a factor in encouraging the move away from direct interventions and toward adjustment lending. In 1990, the World Development Report was on the subject of poverty alleviation, and rural projects got a new lease of life around issues such as the environment and land reform. President Preston re-established the profile of poverty reduction by elevating it to the Bank's 'overarching objective'. But there was a lack of certainty about the vehicles for delivering poverty reduction, whether macro or micro. In 1995, a client survey of the Africa Region found that poverty alleviation was the least credible of the Bank's initiatives. With the arrival of Wolfensohn poverty reduction was once more given the central role.

Wolfensohn's version of the poverty focus was not, however, project-based. On the contrary, agriculture and rural development operations declined. The period 2001–2002, years in which poverty reduction was given more publicity than ever, at Doha, Monterrey, Johannesburg, and other international conferences, and at the annual meetings, when the

---

[35] McNamara was the main sponsor of the Consultative Group on Agricultural Research (CGIAR), founded in 1971, which supported agricultural projects.

[36] 'Focus on Poverty: A Report by a Task Force of the World Bank', World Bank, 1982.

Bank reiterated its poverty fighting objectives, was perversely also the period in which lending for agriculture and rural development fell to a record low share of the Bank's lending activity.

Under McNamara, 'Agriculture and Rural Development' reached 22% of overall Bank lending and 30% of IDA lending. Over 1986 to 1992, lending to this sector fell back to about 17% (IDA 20%), replaced by other lending that had a degree of poverty focus, for water supply, sewerage, urban development, population, nutrition, and education. Over 1992 to 1997, there was a further fall as average lending to agriculture dropped to 13.6% of the total. From 1997, with the start of the Strategic Compact and the renewed fight against poverty, rural development lending actually declined even faster, along with education; urban development; education; and investment in energy, fuel, and water, the sectors that had constituted McNamara's poverty focus.

A data reclassification made comparisons with the earlier years difficult,[37] but the acute decline in lending to agriculture (plus forestry and fishing) was clear. The 2001 level, reclassified, was a mere 4%, at the height of the reorganization period, before recovering to 6% from 2002. Combining the possibly pro-poor groups of water, health, and social services with agriculture, the reclassified numbers also confirm the rapid decline to 2002. Health and social services rose, but not enough to make much difference to the overall decline, and in any case the latter area targeted largely the urban sector. The numbers for the new categories post-2001 confirm the low emphasis on pro-poor expenditure, with 'rural development' overall falling to 8.2% in 2002 before rising on a fluctuating path to around 10% over 2003–2005.

The two largest and most rapidly growing areas during the reorganization period and up to 2002 were finance and public sector reform. In 2002 their combined share rose to a peak of nearly 40% of lending. The increase had been partly explained by the Asian economic crises of the late 1999s, but the major surge in projects aimed at financial sector reform came well after the end of the crisis. The rapid rise of public

---

[37] The new series introduced in 2002 was generally incomparable with the numbers from 1992 to 2001 except in four sectors. The new series for public sector management over 2001–2005 may still be an underestimate compared with the old series since the old series shows the 2000 expenditure share at 16%, and 2001 at 14.9%.

sector reform was a response to the Bank's institutional focus, on budget systems, accounting, civil service reform, customs reform, decentralization, judicial reform, and others. These types of projects were either neutral in their effects or tilting away from an explicit pro-poor orientation.

Figure 5 shows agricultural lending in relation to the latter two sectors. The vertical axis shows the percent of lending shares. The comparative trends over more than ten years up to the end of the Compact period are clear.[38]

Lending changed course again after 2001. This time it was precipitated by renewed concern for falling total lending business and a renewed realization that third-world infrastructure investment was severely inadequate. An infrastructure action plan was approved by the board which took off from the fact that energy expenditure had fallen to well under half its 1992–1997 average. The plan called for infrastructure lending to return to its historic levels of lending by 2008. But only well after the end of the reorganization period did agricultural lending start to recover ground, though it still remains at historic lows.[39]

About three-quarters of the world's poor still live in rural areas, dependent on agriculture. The need for a renewed focus on agriculture has been continually made, but without the capturing of donor attention. The Bank's annual report for 2002 said that 'agricultural growth

---

[38] Selected Bank lending by subsector (% shares)

	1986–1991	1992–1997	1998–1999	2000	2001	2002	2003	2004	2005–2007
Agriculture	22.0	13.6	9.4	8.8	8.4				
Agriculture reclassified				5.5	4.0	6.4	6.6	6.9	7.5
Finance	6.0	7.6	14.7	11.0	12.9	13.9	7.8	9.0	7.9
Public sector governance		2.8	4.4	16.0	14.9	21.8	13.3	16.5	14.0

Source: Annual Reports. (Note: Public sector governance based on different classification than finance.)

[39] In 2005–2007, agriculture forestry and fishing averaged 7.6% of total Bank lending while finance and public sector governance took 22%.

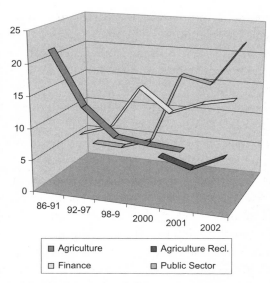

Figure 5. Trends in agricultural, finance, and public sector lending.

was identified as a fundamental pathway out of poverty' (p. 68), while at the Johannesburg summit Nitin Desai, of the UN, presented the keynote paper, which stated that '(agriculture) is the cornerstone for food security and poverty reduction'.[40] The USAID administrator, Natsios, asked at a Capitol Hill forum in 2003: '[H]ow can we possibly deal with the problem of poverty in the developing world without dealing with agricultural productivity?' Most recently, a 2007 report by the IEG on agricultural assistance in Sub-Saharan Africa states: '[A] major drag on Africa's development is the underperformance of the agriculture sector. This is a critical sector in the Region, because it accounts for a large share of gross domestic product (GDP) and employment'. 'The central finding of the study is that the agriculture sector has been neglected by both governments and the donor community, including the World Bank. Both arising from and contributing to this, the technical skills needed to support agricultural development adequately have also declined. . .'.

---

[40] 'A Framework for Action on Agriculture', World Bank, WSSD, September 2002.

Only now, after many years, is agriculture back into focus, with the 2008 World Development Report, which states that the sector must be placed at the center of the development agenda if the goals of halving extreme poverty and hunger by 2015 are to be realized.[41]

The meaning of pro-poor is not precise. Most development projects could be justified as pro-poor, from public sector management reform to small business development, on the grounds that all projects have some pro-poor effect. But taking explicit pro-poor lending by the economic sector, the trends show that the Bank's corporate strategy was *not pro-poor* throughout the reorganization period. In fact, at the peak of the anti-poverty fight, in 2002, it was Turkey, a middle-income NATO member and prospective EU applicant, who alone received nearly 20% of the Bank's lending (no less than 30% of IBRD lending) in a series of major adjustment operations partly to support the Turkish banking system. This was more than double the entire Bank expenditure on what it defined as rural development!

An overall indication of the level of continued support to middle-income economies, not necessarily those with major populations in poverty, can be deduced from the share of IDA financing in total Bank financing, since IDA loans go to countries with per capita incomes below a poverty threshold.[42] As shown in Table 4, over the period of the reorganization from 1997 to 2000, the IDA lending ratio fell substantially, largely due to increased IBRD lending to Asian crisis countries, and in 2001 and 2002, it increased largely due to the ending of the crisis followed by a sustained reduction in IBRD lending. However, even with the inclusion of the higher IDA ratio in 2001 and 2002, the annual average IDA lending share at 30.5% over 1997–2002 was still not appreciably greater than the pre-reorganization level of 1990–1996.

---

[41] Agricultural development took on special urgency in 2008 as cereal prices rose to record levels. 'Because you don't want everything to be a short-term response, we are really trying to upgrade our efforts in terms of increasing agricultural production,' World Bank President Robert Zoellick told Reuters. 'World Bank lending for agriculture has averaged some $500 million a year, but there are plans to push it up to as much as $850 million in coming years' (Reuters/Factiva) cited in *World Bank Press Review*, March 11, 2008.

[42] The assumed threshold is $2.36 per day at 2004 prices. This is somewhat higher than the absolute poverty line usually used and would encompass some 2 billion people.

Table 4. *Trends in IDA lending share ($ billion)*

	1990–1995	1996	1997	1998	1999	2000	2001	2002
IDA	6.2	6.9	4.6	7.5	6.8	4.4	6.8	8.1
Total Bank	22.1	21.5	19.1	28.6	29.0	15.3	17.3	19.6
% IDA	28.1	32.1	24.1	26.2	23.4	28.8	39.3	41.3

Neither did the total IDA lending over the reorganization period show a sustained increase in absolute terms (prior to 2004).

The Bank's lending did not focus in practice on the poor, but the fight against poverty did materialize in another type of product. Beginning in 1996, the debt reduction initiative for the Highly Indebted Poor Countries (HIPC) did focus on the poor. The Bank/IMF version of the HIPC moved forward slowly under complex eligibility rules and had to be re-launched as a multi-donor initiative in 1999 when it was linked to Poverty Reduction Strategies. The new initiative required producing Poverty Reduction Strategy Papers, and this caused a further slowdown in 2003, but by the end of 2005, twenty-eight countries had been approved for $33 billion in debt reduction. The HPIC was succeeded by the Multilateral Debt Relief Initiative agreed to at Gleneagles in July 2005, just after Wolfensohn left office, as a result of which IDA debt was forgiven of more than $37 billion for seventeen countries that had reached the 'completion point' of the enhanced HPIC program.

However, rather than going to the rural sector, Bank lending itself from 2003 returned to where it had been a long time ago, to Asian infrastructure. Infrastructure loans to India were among the first the Bank ever gave to a developing country, in the late 1950s. Since 2003 approvals have increased, particularly for transport and the neglected sectors of energy and mining, water supply, and sanitation, and they are expected to reach about $10.0 billion a year by 2008.

What are the implications of this lending strategy? First of all, there was a disconnect between the rhetoric and reality of how Bank funds were actually deployed. Second, because the actual path of lending was inconsistent with the overt strategy declarations, skills restructuring was left in a state of confusion. Third, the path actually taken was itself so inconsistent with the proclaimed rural poverty focus that it may in fact suggest a 'natural' role for the Bank that is very different from what is being currently promulgated by its owners. Debt forgiveness, while pro-poor, was a short-term palliative action, not a developmental program. The comparative advantage of the Bank is arguably still in large-scale lending, for infrastructure, reform, or budget support, and not in the intricacies of small participatory initiatives, which might be done more effectively by other small and locally based organizations.

HOW NOT TO SELECT PROJECTS

Despite the pro-poor rhetoric, lending patterns were in practice responsive to short-term demand and outside pressures rather than to a clear concept of the Bank's long-term strategic role. During the reorganization period the Bank in fact expanded its products on many fronts simultaneously. While there has always been a tendency to diversify, as Kapur et al. describe it,[43] it was previously better held in check. '[The Bank's] style was to cast itself as a major player on behalf of a new purpose only if and when the institution had developed a comparative advantage in the new field'. Jessica Einhorn, a top manager for many years, wrote in *Foreign Affairs*[44]: '[M]ission creep has led the Bank to embrace an unachievable vision of conquering global poverty instead of an operational mission to do so. Its mission has become so complex that it strains credulity to portray the Bank as a manageable organization'.

In 2001, at the board's session on the Strategic Directions Paper, the management talked of 'clear criteria' at the global level – poverty impact, efficiency, and the Bank's comparative advantage. The board in reply urged the Bank to be 'even more selective'. Later the Bank provided a qualifier[45]:'[T]here is substantial untapped potential for better selectivity to deliver performance improvements at all levels of Bank assistance'.

[43] Kapur, Lewis et al., op cit., p. 1216.
[44] Einhorn, Jessica, 'The World Bank's Mission Creep', *Foreign Affairs Journal*, September 2001.
[45] DevNews Media Center, September 2002 commentary on 'OED Annual Report on Development Effectiveness 2001'.

Sensitive to outside criticism, the Bank now adopted a formal goal of product 'selectivity'. In 2002 a 'selectivity guide' was issued to set this out. The guide, however, demonstrated the very problem it was purporting to solve, and in so doing provided a clue to the gulf between the rhetoric and reality in the poverty fight. 'Selectivity' it said, 'is currently exercised at three levels: within countries, across countries, and at the global level ... within countries: selectivity is reflected in the degree of strategy focus in the country assistance strategy. This would be in the PRSPs (Poverty Reduction Strategy Papers) using the CDF (Comprehensive Development Framework) as a guide to the respective contributions by partners. Within the CAS (Country Assistance Strategy) selectivity would be based on impact, likelihood of successful action, and additionally of the Bank's contribution. Across countries, selectivity would be based on poverty and policy performance. More resources would be devoted to countries that are both poor and have better policy performance. But at the same time the Bank is continuing to improve its support for countries with weaker policy and institutional environments. Finally, at the global level, selection will be based on global public goods priorities'. This framework did not provide a serious basis for selection but was loose enough to permit almost all projects that were not specifically banned, like tobacco, and waivers were even possible for the latter.

PUBLIC GOODS, AND BADS

As suggested in Chapter 1, the ultimate purpose of a global development agency should be to provide global public goods (GPGs). General poverty reduction could act as a global public good if it benefited the international community more than it benefited individual countries overall, through better health and lower criminality, including terrorism. Thus pro-poor projects that generate poverty reduction across borders could be consistent with the Bank's ultimate rationale. To the extent that the Bank's operations were pro-poor, it fulfilled such a role. Indeed, Wolfensohn suggested that international terrorism was ultimately about poverty. Historically, however, the Bank's projects have been national in focus, subject to sovereign guarantees, and increasingly at a sub-national level. The Bank's 'selectivity guide' still treated global public goods as just one category among many at the national and sub-national levels, and its strategic centrality has only been clarified relatively recently.[46] Important gaps exist in the GPG provision, such as global health research.[47] Furthermore, the Bank's pro-poor project record was flawed during the reorganization period. Did it during this time move toward a GPG focus in other areas?

Kapur writes: '[T]here is little substantive analysis that would help International Organization members to rank public goods in order of their relative contribution to global welfare. This analytical hiatus . . . allows' them to press for private interests in the guise of GPGs . . .'.[48] The Bank's public goods role was not in fact properly defined within the rapid diversification of product areas during the 1990s, and this created anomalies of the type that Kapur describes.

An example was the so-called Development Gateway project. Originating in 1998 as a small information Web site in Kyrgyzstan, the project was escalated to international status to project the Bank as a player in the 'New Economy'. However, the private sector was itself actively developing country information websites at the time. To counter the charge that it was competing with private interests, the Gateway was spun off as a non-profit foundation, but then it faced a legal challenge by two Uruguayan organizations with Internet interests that

---

[46] For example, see 'Improving the World Bank's Development Effectiveness', World Bank OED, November 2005.

[47] See Kremer, M., 'The Missing Mandate: Global Public Goods', in *Rescuing the World Bank, a CGD Working Group and Selected Essay,'* Center for Global Development, 2006. Some commentators have proposed curiously that the Bank and other donors in fact set up a special GPG trust fund in order to do what should be their core job.

[48] Kapur, Devesh 'Do as I Say, not as I Do; a Critique of G7 Proposals on Reforming the MDBs', Department of Government, Harvard University, February 2002, p. 17. Kapur continues: 'In seeking to reinvent the Bank's public image its management and staff have labeled all kinds of activities or "networks" as GPGs, meriting involvement on the basis of the moral claims that public goods invoke, and their ready slogan-appeal to Northern tax-payers. While many initiatives certainly do meet the criteria of public goods, the management also includes what one might call "Potemkin GPGs". A good example was the Banks initiative related to the World Faiths development dialogue'.

claimed that the authorities had been misled as to its independent status.[49] The activist Bretton Woods Project described it as 'a major land-grab on the internet'. The UK and U.S. directors essentially agreed and declined to support it, but the Gateway received funding from several other countries.[50] Wolfensohn's advisor, retired dean of Harvard Business School, John Macarthur, was made the Gateway's first head and it was given top-level status with oversight by Mamphela Ramphele, managing director for human resources. To widen its political constituency in 2002, the executive secretary of the Economic Commission for Africa was invited to head its 'editorial committee'. By this time the absurdly top-heavy and politically connected structure of the Gateway, apart from not being a public good, was also far removed from the New Economy business model.

Nevertheless, at the Bank's 2002 'strategic forum', the assembled top managers were able to report progress, including better poverty focus and better alignment with objectives. Global public goods were now incorporated into a complex set of priorities within what the Bank described at its *selectivity web*, and according to the top managers it was successfully being addressed. But it appeared that the selectivity framework was, again, so non-selective that it was possible to include almost any project under its rubric.

Thus there is evidence that the reorganization did not create a strategic ordering of the Bank's products, either financing or knowledge-based, around the public goods rationale. Instead, as Einhorn asserted, its mission became so complex that it strained credulity to portray the Bank as a manageable organization.

---

[49] The claim was filed by Roberto Bissio, coordinator of Social Watch and Latin American secretary of the Third World Network, and Dr. Carlos Abin, executive director of the Instituto del Tercer Mundo. They stated during consultations that the Gateway appears to represent unwarranted competition with existing country- and topic-focused portals that are genuinely independent.

[50] The Gateway management was obliged to defend itself, arguing that it was independent, that it had special features like 'global reach with local roots', and it was the next logical step for the private and public donor communities to coordinate on ICT. The spin-off company received $13 million of Bank funds in its first two years, and $60 million of member government funds were mobilized for Internet development support from Western Europe, plus India, Pakistan, Korea, and Mali.

THE DEVELOPMENT ADVOCACY AND
RESEARCH PRODUCT

International issue advocacy is potentially a global public good, but, apart from McNamara's efforts, up until 1995 the Bank had generally not used its 'bully pulpit' to seriously influence policy on global issues. This changed during the 1990s. The advocacy role played to Wolfensohn's strengths, and this was a change that can be credited to the reorganization period. When he assumed the presidency, neither debt relief nor corruption were yet on the World Bank's agenda, nor were they considered a priority by the international donor community, although they were being demanded by the many activist groups involved in the 'mobilization for global justice'. In 1996 he took on the issues of both corruption and debt relief. Later on, at the Monterrey conference and at other times he opened up issues of participation, trade fairness, and the removal of rich country production subsidies. Advocacy extended to the energy needs of poor countries, HIV/AIDS, education for girls, and climate change.

Adequate organizational resources are needed to back up advocacy, that is, policy analytical capability. By way of illustration, advocacy in multilateral trade reform would have needed a sustained research backup over several years before and after the stalled Doha talks. Similarly, lengthy research support would be needed to support the case for reducing rich country agriculture and industrial subsidies. Research capacity has been strong in the Bank since McNamara introduced it,[51] although it has also had its ups and downs, and views have differed on its role, quality, and objectivity.[52] Nevertheless, the annual World

---

[51] The research program started at the time of Hollis Chenery as chief economist. The research department has specialized over time, notably in issues such as growth, international trade and protection, economic adjustment, corruption, and aid effectiveness.

[52] There was an idea that the Bank was trying to build a research empire rather than spread research to borrower countries (according to Mahbub Ul Haq, in the Bank's oral history series). There was also some sense that the research capacity was 'captive' and not sufficiently independent. Ravi Kanbur, a senior former Bank manager, for example, resigned from the Bank over its insistence that the *World Development Report on Poverty* (1992), of which he was editor, should be amended to be more consistent with the Bank line. See Ravi Kanbur, 'IFIs and IPGs: Operational Implications for the World Bank', G24 paper, Beirut, March 2002.

Development Report is very widely disseminated and the Bank's Annual Conference of Development Economists, started in 1988, is a leading event in the development research calendar. The development research department, which houses 120 researchers, is in principle the Bank's analytical resource for policy advocacy.

However, the reorganization did not nurture research. Expenditure on research proper fell significantly, to a level lower than that of external relations, which was meanwhile on the rise. A 2006 report on World Bank research (the 'Deaton Report') states: '[W]ithout a research-based ability to learn from its projects and policies, the Bank could not maintain its role as the world's leading development agency. The 2.5 percent of its administrative budget that the Bank spends on research is surely too low given the multiplicity of tasks that research is expected to fulfill, including the generation of new knowledge about development, the collection and dissemination of data, the generation of knowledge to support and guide Bank strategy, operational support, and capacity building in client countries'.[53]

During the reorganization, the organizational muscle needed to produce convincing analytical support for advocated positions was weakening while the capacity to inform the public about success rapidly increased. Some commentators on the Deaton Report thought that its brief should have included proposals on strengthening the Bank's research capacity even further, into partnerships with outside organizations. Instead, the advocacy role of the Bank had emerged as a somewhat random process associated as much with publicity motivations as with purposeful organizational change.[54]

KNOWLEDGE PRODUCTS AND LENDING PRODUCTS; REALITY CHECKS

Wolfensohn proclaimed the 'knowledge bank' at the 1996 annual meetings, but the move from lending to knowledge was not simply a matter

---

[53] Banerjee, Abhijit, Angus Deaton (Chair), Nora Lustig, and Ken Rogoff, 'An Evaluation of World Bank Research, 1998–2005', World Bank, September 2006.

[54] See, e.g., Roe, Alan, 'Research on Development – What role for the World Bank?', OPM briefing notes, May 2007.

of proclamation. It had serious corporate implications, not least because relatively labor-intensive, small knowledge projects are often loss-making when overhead costs are taken into account. Knowledge services are not only small in scale but frequently do not generate any income, and they have to be subsidized through the Bank's loan or investment income, or alternatively financed outside the regular operations.

Little effort had been made prior to the knowledge bank announcement to develop financially sustainable knowledge services. Follow-up explorations of a system of charging fees took place in 1997, but there was little attempt systematically to research the market. Much of the Bank's existing knowledge products, such as its sector reports, are supply-driven, rather than based on the specific demand of a client country, and so sustainable market prices are not known. Charges are only made for special reports, and then only if they were not normally provided by the private sector, if there are no conflicts of interest, and if they are priced at full cost. Thus much work cannot be charged out. Only a few countries, such as Saudi Arabia, the Gulf States, and Chile, have regularly purchased the Bank's advisory services. Advisory income is a tiny percentage of the Bank's administrative costs.

Most poor countries cannot pay fees to cover rich country consultancy costs, except in specific commercially oriented ventures. A way of helping countries pay fees through vouchers was considered, but not adopted. Advisory services have never been designed with a commercial objective, and there is no clear idea of whether a large public sector consultancy service could work. Some have in any case opposed the commercialization of Bank knowledge services for fear of damaging the honest broker role.

Thus a pure knowledge bank would not be a financially sustainable entity, but would need to operate like a large think tank financed by an (eroding) endowment. It would have to seek out more subsidized funding, such as trust funds, and be more vulnerable to outside pressures. In reality, the transition to a knowledge bank would be hazardous, would require a renewed financial commitment from donor countries, and would most likely end up with considerable downsizing. The institution could evolve into the equivalent of a UN agency reliant on outside (UNDP) funds.

Lending provides a useful transmission vehicle for knowledge products by focusing the attention of ministries of finance on the need to use it cost-effectively. There is evidence that knowledge embodied in a financing relationship might be used more effectively than knowledge provided without cost. Wolfensohn told the Meltzer Commission: '[E]xperience shows that knowledge and advisory services are far more powerful in leveraging policy and institutional change when underpinned by a lending relationship'.[55] Even more, monetary flows may in some cases themselves fuel demand for institutional changes that institution-building projects fail to do.[56]

Thus lending is for a number of reasons likely to remain very important. The resurgence in infrastructure lending since 2003 is an indication of just how important the financing role remains. A 1996 Task Force report on the multilateral development banks[57] observed that even in the mid-1990s, when foreign investment was climbing rapidly, only 12% of major infrastructure investment was being financed by the private sector. The report said: '[W]ell into the future, the requirements of publicly financed infrastructure will remain large, and the MDBs will need to support such ventures as are developmentally important and not yet attractive to private finance'. Despite its significant expansion, private infrastructure investment has been cyclical, and in downturn periods private sector projects have been cancelled, leaving the public sector as the central player.[58] Further, a relatively new and expanding loan product, the Budget Support Loan, funds the borrowing country's treasury

---

[55] Wolfensohn's letter to the Meltzer Commission, February 28, 2000, supporting continuation of lending to investment-grade countries.

[56] During the 1980s, up to 25% of Bank lending used credit lines through local banking systems. These types of projects have been largely abandoned despite continued interest from many governments. When carefully designed, they may, however, act as effective institution builders while TA loans specifically for institution building often do not.

[57] 'Serving a Changing World', Report of the Task Force on Multilateral Development Banks, IMF/World Bank Development Committee, op cit., 1996, p. 10.

[58] About fifty private sector infrastructure projects worth about $24 billion were cancelled over 1990 to 2001 (this excludes facilities sold by the original investor to other private sector companies). The cancellations were concentrated in the road sector, especially in Mexico, because toll roads had difficulties making a profit.

and reduces or even eliminates the Bank's active involvement in knowledge transfer or institutional capacity building.

NEW FINANCIAL PRODUCTS

The Strategic Compact listed financial product diversification as an area of priority, and here the reorganization did see some progress. Historically the Bank's menu of loan products was extremely conservative. From 1980 to 1993, it only had one product, what it called the multi-currency pool loan. The principle involved was to spread the risks of the borrower who was not tied to service the debt in a particular currency. An innovation in 1989 allowed currencies in the pool to be targeted so that the true costs of borrowing were clearer. But only finally in 1995, after about four years of deliberation and a two-year pilot project apparently designed to determine whether clients were capable of understanding another product, did the Bank allow its clients to borrow in a single currency. The sensitivity to borrower understanding was despite the fact that the concept of the multiple currency pool was itself complicated and non-transparent.[59] From 1995 a number of new products were steadily made available, and the financial products broadened into a menu that consisted essentially of fixed spread loans (FSL) and variable spread loans (VSL) in any currency of the borrowers choosing accepted by the Bank. The current product range is shown in Table 5.

Outstandings comprise mainly FSLs and VSLs, but with a range of other types from the past. The excessive caution in diversifying loan products became clear when, as soon as new products were introduced, mass conversions took place. For example, the share of the old multi-currency pool loans dropped from 83% to 23% over 1997 to 2001, at which point they were discontinued. New loans represented by current undisbursed balances are almost 100% composed of FSLs and VSLs, as the earlier products have now been dropped entirely.

---

[59] In practice, the currency pool loans, intended to provide a simple way for clients to protect themselves by spreading their currency risk, were complicated. They were also non-transparent in that repayments had to conform to the Bank treasurer's sequencing requirements for specific currencies, which could negate the risk spreading benefits for the debtor.

Table 5. *The Bank's financial products in 2007*

Product	Outstanding ($ billion)
Fixed spread loans	32.1
Variable spread loans	42.1
Multicurrency pool (variable)	9.3
Single currency pool (variable	6.6
Single currency loans (fixed)	4.8
Special development policy loans	2.3
Other	0.6

Source: Annual Report 2007.

The difference between lending and borrowing technology seemed to reflect two 'cultures' that existed in the Bank, the funding culture that competed and cooperated with Wall Street and the private financial markets, and had innovated in frontier products such as derivatives, and the lending culture, marked by a slow-changing conservatism and paternalistic concern for borrower capacities. The changes of the reorganization period were consistent with a new, more inclusive and open approach to the Bank's clients. The menu of financial products in some views[60] could have been expanded further, but this is one area where the needed reforms were clear and where the reorganization period could chalk up a qualified victory.

REORGANIZING THE BANK'S PRODUCT: CONCLUSIONS

As we have seen, despite a few gains, the reorganization did not result unequivocally in productive reforms of the Bank's product menu. The new selectivity framework was practically meaningless. The product initiatives were not part of a clear strategy but more opportunistic and on too broad a front. By the end of the reform period, and beyond, despite the decades-long debate over adjustment lending, loans-for-reform remained a major feature of Bank lending, even though the

[60] Proposals have been made to introduce instruments for risk management, including commodity price hedging and risk-sharing loans, and to lend funds borrowed in local capital markets. See Birdsall, N., ed., *Rescuing the World Bank, a CGD Working Group and Selected Essays,* Center for Global Development, 2006, pp. 27–29. Under President Zoellick there were signs that this might happen.

average number of conditions dropped. The average percentage of total adjustment-type lending remained above the original 1980s target. With these types of loans the incentive for outside dictation remains strong. And, despite the CDF and attempts to encourage participation, the Bank still probably cannot work sustainably with open-ended, participatory processes not subject to a timetable.

The pro-poor strategy proclaimed during the reorganization was flawed, with the IDA's lending not increasing and knowledge products directed to sectors that were at best neutral in terms of income distribution impact, marginalizing the most critical poverty sector – agriculture. Debt reduction was pro-poor and significant, but constituted a one-off palliative action rather than a sustainable development initiative. The period 2002–2003, following the end of the reorganization period, saw record levels of adjustment lending, directed at the financial sector in Turkey, a middle-income EU accession country.

Institution and capacity building went ahead broadly as part of the new knowledge bank, accompanied by anti-corruption programs. But the results were mediocre and the basic concept of how far an outside agency, driven by time and results, could build meaningful local institutions remains doubtful. The knowledge bank is subject to restrictive limits as long as the Bank wishes to be financially sustainable. Unprofitable, small-scale knowledge transfer projects will in this case have to be subsidized by large-scale financing, and to do this the product profile will have to continue its reversion to that of the 1960s when infrastructure lending was the dominant element.

International issue advocacy became a more significant part of the Bank's product menu, but it was opportunistic and not supported by a proportionate increase in organizational resources such as research capacity. The one area of product development listed in the Strategic Compact that did make reasonably unqualified progress was the new financial products.

There has been a reversion to large-scale lending – both infrastructure and budget support, and an implication that this is still where the institution's comparative advantage, as well as its financial independence, ultimately lie. To the extent that large-scale infrastructure projects are also a (global) public good, this strategy is also consistent with the

Bank's long-term role. The new products of the reorganization period, on the other hand, need to establish their place, and their large logistical resource requirements and inadequate income generation potential could ensure that they remain secondary, dependent on subsidies from the large projects.

7

Changing the Quality of Development Assistance

As explained previously, the Bank's assistance focus has evolved in several stages, starting from the IBRD's initial role essentially as an investment banker financing infrastructure and then, with the IDA, moving into macroeconomic reform and increasingly into projects to develop skills, capacity, and institutional development, and in the process focus on advisory services and 'knowledge products' that are not necessarily combined with financing. This was an evolution that could also be described as a shift from hard to soft development products. The Strategic Compact aimed to both strengthen the Bank as a 'soft' knowledge provider and to improve the *responsiveness* and *relevance* of the Bank in both its hard and its soft offerings.

In addition to diversifying into new products that were more relevant to the needs of client countries, one of the principle undertakings of the Strategic Compact was to improve the *quality* and *effectiveness* of the Bank's products. The changes in these products during the reorganization period were ambitious, and, as we have seen, the shift has exposed numerous corporate strategic issues. Thus it is by no means clear yet that the Bank has established what new products are worthwhile or its comparative advantage in delivering them. Nevertheless, the Bank had to show improved quality and performance to justify the cost of its reorganization.

Regular and numerous claims were made of quality improvements. All the internal reviews made these claims with little qualification, and there were specific public statements that echoed these findings. For example, Joanne Salop, one of the Bank's vice presidents, wrote in

Euromoney in 2000[1] that the quality of newly approved operations had been improving steadily over the previous years, 'reflecting', as she put it, 'the internal renewal programme the Bank has carried out under President Wolfensohn'. Shengman Zhang, managing director, wrote in the *Financial Times* of September 7, 2001, that under Wolfensohn's leadership the World Bank had seen project quality rise to record levels; improved overall client satisfaction and strong support from shareholders for the Bank's strategic directions. The 2001 look-back review of the Strategic Compact, otherwise a relatively realistic document, also stated that the Bank's effectiveness as a development institution in reducing poverty had improved significantly. On the other hand, in March 2002, Adam Lerrick, a Meltzer Commission adviser and member of the American Enterprise Institute, wrote in one of his regular letters to the *Financial Times*: '[A]fter half a century and $500 billion of World Bank stewardship of aid, we have no measure of the World Bank's success except the one it chooses to promulgate, and no means of validating the wisdom of what is a collective investment decision'.

How far and when did the quality and effectiveness of the Bank's products in fact improve?

WAPENHANS ON PERFORMANCE

The quality improvement aims listed in the Strategic Compact had their origins in the poor results shown in the 1992 Wapenhans Report.[2] The report stated that 'the Bank must be no less restrained in diagnosing and seeking to remedy its own shortcomings than it is in seeking to help member countries recognize and address theirs'. It looked at more than 400 unsatisfactory projects, especially in the agriculture and water supply sectors, particularly in Africa.[3] The major culprits included the

---

[1]   Salop, Joanne, 'Has the World Bank Lost Its Way – au Contraire', *Euromoney*, March 2000, responding to an attack by Adam Lerrick (*Euromoney*, December 1999).

[2]   The Wapenhans Report, 'Effective Implementation; Key to Development Impact', World Bank, 1992. Initially, for external purposes, the Bank played down the findings of the report, claiming that 25% unsatisfactory project outcomes was acceptable, even expected, in a high-risk environment. But in the meantime it set about strengthening its evaluation capacity.

[3]   Unsatisfactory meant that they were judged not to be capable of earning a rate of return of 10%, or the equivalent.

Regional Integrated Development Projects (RIDPs) in Africa.[4] They appeared to have a coherent developmental rationale and were supported by the Bank and many other donor agencies. But they showed 60% unsatisfactory outcomes over 1978–1985 and are estimated to have accounted for half of the overall decline in the Bank's agricultural portfolio performance. Thus an initiative that initially seemed to be so promising was in the event unsuccessful.

In addition to design problems, the Wapenhans Report[5] found that project implementation was taking excessive time, stretching up to seven years, signifying often that government borrowers were not sufficiently committed to them. Long gestation was coupled with inflexible design. The report also said that borrowers wanted a shift away from 'blueprints' toward a more flexible approach whereby solutions could be sought to problems as they came up. Projects also had lengthy preparation periods before implementation, but when the time came finally to negotiate there was a rush to closure. As the previously cited Wapenhans interviewee from a borrowing country put it: '[T]here is so much pressure put on the responsible ministry by the Bank that, you know, you just have to get it done . . . the Bank tends to adopt a take it or leave it stance. The borrower agrees to conditions it has no way of honoring, and they end up with a contract that cannot be implemented'.[6] Governments often place more importance on sustaining the political relationship than on the potentially weak performance of one particular project.

The report also said: '[T]he problems we are encountering in today's projects are the same problems encountered in projects many years ago. We keep making the same mistakes because we did not learn from earlier experience . . .. Most project officers think that their project is unique and will succeed where others have failed'.

---

[4] The Operations Evaluation Department (OED) put their failure down to commodity price declines, the lack of government commitment, weak management, weak operations and maintenance, excessive complexity, lack of flexibility in design, inept public sector oversight, and, finally, the problems of the 1973 oil price shock.

[5] Wapenhans Report, 'Effective implementation; Key to Development Impact', op cit., annex B, p. 5.

[6] Ibid, annex C, p. 3 (box 1).

The Bank's 1995 Annual Report stated that a review of the first year's experience in implementing post-Wapenhans initiatives found significant progress but that, as per the standard disclaimer, further work needed to be done. Progress, it reported, had occurred in upfront actions, reduced complexity, and strengthened borrower ownership. From 1994 the measured quality of completed projects, that is, those that had been started at the end of the 1980s, did in fact start to recover. The reorganization of the 1990s, aimed at improving effectiveness, thus occurred as this reported upward movement in performance was already underway.

PERFORMANCE: ITS DECLINE AND RISE

The process of recovery and the longer run trends in lending project outcome evaluation scores are shown in Figure 6.[7] A long decline occurred between 1980 and 1988, when the rate fell to a low point of only 56% satisfactory outcomes. There was a revival and a second dip to 63% in 1994. There then followed a continuous eight-year rise from 1994 and 2002, a slight dip in 2003–2004, and a renewed surge in 2005. Thus, by the end of Wolfensohn's term, the completed project success rate rose to a record of 82%, and in 2006 to 83%.[8] The projects completed in 2001–2005 were measured as better than those of 1996–2000 in all regions except South America. In Africa, the percentage of satisfactory outcomes rose from 64% to 77%, while in East Asia it rose from 79% to 89%.[9]

---

[7]   Bank projects evaluated as satisfactory at completion (OED)

1980	1982	1984	1986	1988	1990	1992	1994	1996	1998	2000	2002	2003	2004	2005
81%	76%	71%	69%	56%	67%	66%	63%	69%	73%	76%	78%	75%	77%	82%

[8]   These are broken down by projects. The Bank also publishes results weighted by project value (disbursement amount) in which success with large projects counts as more important than success with small projects.

[9]   Transport projects improved the most up to 2004, while the 2005 results showed the biggest improvers were in energy, mining, and environmental programs, albeit from a poor start. Water supply projects also improved markedly from very poor results up to 2000. Those that recently got worse included particularly health and social protection projects.

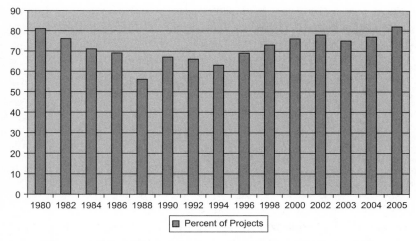

Figure 6. Percentage of satisfactory project outcomes (1980–2005).

The results in Figure 6 apply to projects as assessed by the Bank's Independent Evaluation Group (IEG), previously known as the Operations Evaluation Department (OED). In addition to the IEG, the Bank has a Quality Assurance Group (QAG), which was set up in 1996 to monitor quality during design and preparation.

The QAG was equally confident about the improving performance. 'The evidence is overwhelming' announced the quality chief in 2001, at the end of the period of the Strategic Compact,[10] 'that our portfolio today is much better positioned to deliver results on the ground'. Between 1996 and 2001, so-called 'quality-at-entry' overall rose every year, moving from 78% to 94% satisfactory, and 'quality-of-supervision' rose every year, from 63% to 89% satisfactory. By 2001, quality-at-entry was considered to be satisfactory for 100% of the projects in Latin America, the Middle East, and South Asia. The quality of project supervision had reached 100% satisfactory in the Middle East. Africa remained the laggard but also improved rapidly, from 58% in 1997 to 89% in 2000.

The measured quality of the Bank's knowledge products also rose strongly each year. Its analytical and advisory offerings rose from 72%

[10] In the publication *Bank's World Today*, March 13, 2001.

satisfactory in 1997 to 94% in 2002. Design and management quality was considered to have met its targets by the Bank's internal quality assessors. In 2005, the QAG reported that the quality of technical assistance projects was even more impressive, with more than 95% of the tasks identified as moderately satisfactory or better, and more than a quarter judged 'highly satisfactory'. A strength of these technical assistance activities, said the report, was their strategic relevance in support of the client's development agenda and the quality of dialogue and dissemination associated with them.

Such was the rate of improvement of entries that exit and entry quality began to show inconsistencies.[11] Thus the numbers were modified in 2002 in what the annual portfolio quality report described as a fine-tuning. The highest scores got diluted by reporting results on the basis of recent annual averages. There had been, said the quality controllers in 2002, a modest overestimation of portfolio improvement and so they modified their measure of 'riskiness' to encourage more candid reporting. There was an increase in the estimate of 'projects-at-risk',[12] mostly in Africa, and an adjustment in the 'realism index',[13] which was reduced from 80% to 72% to allow for the overestimation. It appeared that managers were gaming the system to show the results that they wanted.[14]

Thus, after the inexorable rise of entry quality from 1996 to 2001, the Compact years, in 2002, for the first time, an entry-quality reduction was recorded. This was reported by the controllers as resulting from 'vulnerability arising from the limited experience of many new frontline staff and gaps in management'. Still, the most recent quality scores show overall 90% acceptable ratings, with the major improvement in project supervision, as shown in Table 6.

The Bank's lending instruments that were claimed to be doing the best were the new type of adjustment loans, the PRSCs. However, the

---

[11] This was in 2002, which was the first year in which a large number of entry assessments (from 1996) could be matched to exit assessments.

[12] At risk means that the quality controllers consider that sustainability is in doubt.

[13] The realism index is the operational unit's estimate of risk in relation to the QAG estimate.

[14] The QAG's Annual Review of Portfolio Performance reported: '[W]ith staff and management adapting over time to the mechanism of the system the methodology has lost some of its heuristic value'.

Table 6. *Trends in quality of project design and implementation*

Region	Quality at entry %			Quality of supervision %		
	1997–1998	1999–2002	2003–2005	1997–1998	1999–2000	2001–2004
Africa	71	85	85	60	80	84
East Asia/Pacific	97	88	90	69	90	95
Europe/Central Asia	81	89	96	85	91	88
Latin America/ Caribbean	98	100	91	71	90	99
Middle East/ North Africa	63	96	78	71	95	82
South Asia	86	87	96	74	82	85
Bank-Wide	84	90	90	69	87	90

Source: QAG.

innovative products known as LILs (learning and innovation loans) and APLs, designed for flexibility and speed, were showing relatively poor results and not meeting their speed or flexibility requirements. Results for private sector loans were exhibiting contradictory behavior, with a reduction from 71% satisfactory in 1996–2000 to 61% satisfactory in 2001–2005, while their 'sustainability' (from 56% to 71%) and 'institutional development impact' (from 28% to 43%) went in the other direction.[15]

The at-risk projects were also showing inconsistencies that raised questions regarding the candor and reliability of reporting and managerial supervision. The QAG assessors reported that one-quarter of the at-risk projects were not being identified by the project managers. They recommended increasing the number of assessors to remedy this.

As can be seen in Figure 7, a rather lower percentage of projects overall were found to be sustainable, or to have substantial institutional

[15] Sustainability is defined as 'the likelihood that the project will maintain its results in the future' – that the benefits exceed the depreciation, operational, and maintenance costs. Institutional development is defined as the extent to which a project has improved an agency's or a country's ability to make effective use of its human and financial resources.

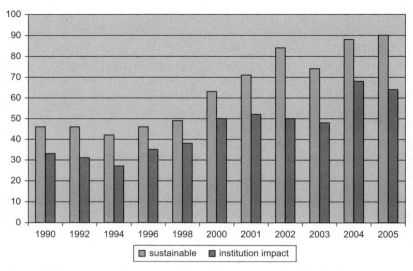

Figure 7. Percentage of projects with satisfactory sustainability and institutional impact.

development impact. Yet these indicators also showed a remarkable rise, with both doubling since the mid-1990s.[16]

Improvement was also claimed in processing. Over 1996 to 2000, gestation periods from concept to approval were claimed to have been reduced for all loans.[17] The reported cost of making loans also reportedly fell because of quicker processing, although this improvement was offset by the new fiduciary and safeguard responsibilities. There was also

---

[16] Project scores by sustainability and institutional development impact.

1990	1992	1994	1996	1998	2000	2001	2002	2003	2004	2005
46	46	42	46	49	63	71	84	74	88	90
33	31	27	35	38	50	52	50	48	68	64

[17] The time lag for project preparation (from the concept paper to the Board) was reduced from 24 months to 13.5 months, but rose in 2000 back to 15.4 months. In addition, several months were needed for the development of the concept, and for loan signing and project startup. The reduction in the more complicated and labor-intensive investment loans was less, from 26 months to 17 months, returning to 19.5 in 2000. Source: 'Refueling Current Business Activity', World Bank, 2001. Subsequent experience suggests further reversions.

a shakeout in the portfolio of lending projects and knowledge products that were not moving forward. An 'overhang' of more than 600 projects that were not likely to perform was duly shaken out in 1996 and 1997. These projects had already used up some $60 million in preparation costs, or more than a quarter of the total expenditure on loan preparation during the period. Over 1998 to 2000 the shakeouts continued. In terms of knowledge products, a large number of stranded economic reports were also dropped or removed from lists in 1998 and 1999 (more than the amount actually completed). Here the objective was better fulfilled as the cost incurred on dropped work fell significantly thereafter.

QUESTIONS ABOUT THE PERFORMANCE NUMBERS

The 2000 Meltzer Commission challenged the Bank's operational performance and effectiveness results. The commission's conclusions were themselves not unanimous, or highly researched, but they were influential with the U.S. Treasury. The commission focused on the relatively low sustainability and impact scores prior to 2000 and concluded that the OED's claims of success had 'low marks for credibility'. The Bank leapt to its own defense; it called the report unfair, saying that it distorted the results and misrepresented the evaluation methods, classifying all projects of low sustainability as failures while attributing improvements to outside factors. A large number of projects of uncertain sustainability, the OED said, could in fact turn out to be sustainable. And if they did not, then sustainability was, in any case, a poor indicator of performance because it was not a measure of economic efficiency – a project could be acceptable even if it was not sustainable.[18] The OED also objected that the commission had described it as an internal auditor, whereas it was in fact an independent unit reporting directly to the board, and that it was 'widely recognized as a leader in development evaluation'.

Was there in fact a reasonable basis to the commission's 'low marks for credibility' (even though the commission itself was only guessing)?

---

[18] Letter from R. Picciotto to Alan Meltzer dated March 1, 2000.

Prima facie there seemed to be such a basis. Let us look again at some of the figures.

How was it possible to explain the rapid rise in entry quality? The major increases recorded in the quality of project preparation and management each year from 1996[19] included the period in which the reorganization was most disruptive of morale and work programs. In 1997, as the reorganization took hold and staff morale dipped to its lowest point, the time spent in the field by operations staff fell significantly.[20] At the same time, recorded project preparation time fell and internal pressures, such as from the new time-consuming fiduciary and safeguard responsibilities, operational directives, and outside funding needs, worsened. The period 1999 to 2000 involved the flawed, if not chaotic, launch of the new information system when Michael Hammer had warned of a performance dip. These do not seem to be conditions in which better performance, let alone a major leap in performance, would be likely.

If such a rapid improvement did in fact happen, then, given the organizational problems being faced at the time, it would suggest that better projects came from worse management. In fact, as late as 2001, when the acute phase of the reforms was over, project supervision was still under severe pressure. The record performance of completed projects in 2005 applied to the average entry year of 1998, not only the year of major organizational disruption but also one prior to the absorption of new skills into the organization.

The quality of knowledge products – analytical and advisory work – was subject to the same constraints. As mentioned earlier, the period 1996 to 2002 was one in which the total analytical (ESW) output was very much reduced because of a severe lack of resources to undertake studies, so much so that output had to double over 2003–2004 to clear the backlog of basic reports. This was also hardly a situation conducive to rapidly increasing quality. Given the modest past performance and

---

[19] 'Supervision Quality. A QAG Assessment', World Bank, October 1999. Supervision quality of human resource projects alone was judged to have leapt from 56% satisfactory in 1997 to 81% satisfactory in 1998.

[20] That is, by about 25% compared to the annual average for the previous few years.

continuing questions, some members of the Bank's board, such as the executive director for India, later openly expressed doubts about the rapid rise in analytical report (or ESW) quality scores.[21]

Knowledge projects such as technical assistance loans similarly dramatically improved their entry quality by 2005, according to the QAG. Yet previously they had not performed well. Preparation of such projects was labor-intensive, and they required specialized design and high levels of local commitment, without which they were likely to fail. In 1992, the evaluators found that more than 50% of 'free-standing' technical assistance projects had not succeeded in their core objective of knowledge transfer. A task force tried to improve the success rate and launched a special institutional development fund. A 1994 report to the board said that institution-building technical assistance projects were seen as intrusive and faced resistance from the recipients.[22] A 1997 Quality Assurance Group (QAG) report continued to note poor performance and lack of interest in TA projects.[23] Many governments were reluctant to accept such projects. The Russian government, for example, complained about an excessive focus on foreign experts, which it thought both expensive and unnecessary.[24]

Processing efficiency was stated to have improved. However, while the average time needed to get a project to the board was reduced, the savings during the period in question was really because of a boom in fast-processed structural adjustment loans in Asia, and much of that from the cancellation of halted projects. As for the rest, it was often more a case of increasingly complex procedures and delays. The indications are that gestation periods lengthened again, even in the case of

---

[21] In April 2003, during a board discussion on the 'Strategic Update Paper'.

[22] 'Improving the Management of Technical Assistance for Institutional Development', Organizational Design staff, World Bank, August 1994.

[23] 'Reviews of Technical Assistance Loans in the World Bank', Internal Report, QAG, February 1997, cited in Rich, Bruce, 'The World Bank under James Wolfensohn', in Pincus, Jonathan R. and Jeffery A. Winters, *Reinventing the World Bank*, Cornell University Press, 2002. Despite the poor record, projects with large elements of technical assistance may have been looked on favorably by the Bank's quality overseers because they 'build institutions'. Technical assistance lending increased significantly despite poor past performance, and by the end of the 1990s there were more than 122 technical assistance loans in the portfolio.

[24] 'Russia – Country Assistance Evaluation', World Bank, 2002.

the so-called learning and innovation loans (LILs) that were designed for fast processing.[25]

The time lag between entry and exit raises a significant point. The average project life of about seven years[26] meant that up to 2004 the ratings of completed projects were not reflecting the organizational changes. If project entry quality is linked to project outcome performance, as it is considered to be, then with this implementation period it would follow that the improvements from 1996 to 2005 must have largely reflected projects designed and implemented over the period 1989 to 1998, which was either well before the reorganization had started or as it was starting.

If we assume that the trend in performance scores is approximately correct, then, taking into account the seven-year average time lag, a more simple and plausible story to be read from the time series of completed project scores is as follows. The decline in the performance of completed projects from a high (80%) in 1981 to a low (56%) in 1987 applied to those projects that entered the system on average seven years previously, that is, in 1974 to 1980. This decline reflected an overexpansion of lending to risky projects, like the RIDPs, during the McNamara period. The partial recovery followed by a renewed drop in scores over 1988 to 1994 then would reflect the projects that entered the system in 1981 to 1987. This was the time of the gradual rationalization of the organization under Clausen that was then cut short by Conable's disruptive reforms of 1987–1988. The performance improvement of 1995 to 2002 reflected projects entering the system between 1988 and 1995; this was when the institution was struggling back onto its feet again following the 1987–1988 disruption. Completed projects rose to a peak

---

[25] Learning and innovation loans (LILs), introduced in 1999 as small, quick loans for experimental and risky projects, were supposed to be fast (six- to nine-month processing and three to five years' implementation) and did not have to be approved by the board. After three years a review found that the average processing time had grown from seven months to seventeen months, with approvals slowing significantly, and this trend has continued. The Bank's corporate strategy paper for 2004–2006 still talked about the 'work under way' toward a more flexible set of lending products and streamlined processes.

[26] This average life has remained quite constant despite the advent of fast disbursing loans. In 2005, for example, the cohort of 'exiting' projects evaluated by the OED (IEG) had an average age of about seven years since approval.

of performance in 2002, and these projects were, on average, designed and launched in 1995, well before the start of the reorganization. In 2003–2004 performance receded slightly, suggesting once again that organizational disruption (in 1997) might have been responsible. The quick recovery to the record-setting 82% satisfactory outcomes in 2005 seems to contradict the story, but there was then a relapse to significantly below 80% in 2007, which would reaffirm problems connected with the reorganization.

If the significant exit performance improvement up to the early 2000s really did occur, then the next question is, why should the projects designed and launched in the 1990s by an organization supposedly in need of drastic reform show such significant increases in quality? It is not that the projects were rescued ex post by superior organization of supervision and management, because supervision capacity itself was under severe pressure during most of the reorganization period, from 1997–1998 onwards.[27] The leap in supervision quality claimed by the QAG after this does not square with its own later reports. The 2002 Annual Report on Portfolio Performance, for example, was saying that management was still spread too thin, with adverse effects on portfolio management. The report opined that the rapid turnover of front-line staff had resulted in a loss of institutional experience and 'some consequent increase of the Bank's vulnerability on the quality front'.[28]

Once again, the improvement in project outcomes from 1995 to 2002 was more likely caused by the gradual recovery from the major disruption of the 1987 reorganization. There was a link between organizational dislocation, breaks in accountability, and declines in the quality of project preparation and supervision. It turns out that the Wapenhans Report of 1992 would have been dealing with a crisis that had already passed since project entry quality was already apparently rebounding even if exit scores were still declining. Similarly, the 1990s

---

[27] In fact, Dollar and Svensson showed that the Bank's supervision effort had no significant effect on project performance in the case of structural adjustment programs, which is affected more by variables representing political stability. Dollar, D. and J. Svensson 'What Explains the Success or Failure of Structural Adjustment Programs?', draft, World Bank, 1997.

[28] 'Annual Review of Portfolio Performance', World Bank, 2002.

reorganization came after entry quality had largely recovered, and it had the effect of cutting out of the Bank much of the skills that had engineered the recovery.

REASONS FOR DOUBT ABOUT PERFORMANCE MEASURES

Any explanation of why performance changed is obscured if the performance estimates themselves are unreliable. The complexity of the Bank's projects, their long gestation periods, and the even longer time needed to measure their effects mean that projects are not like garments, cars, or mail delivery services where objective quality indicators can be easily defined and used. It is difficult and expensive to measure their quality. There are a number of reasons why performance measurement may have been flawed, and may have become increasingly so over the reorganization period.

First, the new types of assessments by the QAG were often based on desk work, and some of the good results from the late 1990s and beyond were based on scanty evaluations, for example, what were called 'rapid supervision assessments'. A sample of one in seven projects was taken by the QAG, examined on average over one and a half days using desk reviews and telephone interviews, and an assessment was made. The use of desk appraisal was also important in a more systemic way. In 1997, as part of the attempt to streamline the process of report production under the new information system, a new documentation process was introduced that included detailed templates, guide notes, and help desks, from concept through to completion. The QAG also provided its own guidance checklist of more than fifty issues, from concept through to implementation.[29]

The improvement in entry quality coincided with the introduction of the new documentation systems, which made written reports more comprehensive and better organized. The Bank is not alone, but is perhaps in a class of its own, in placing a high weight on the quality

---

[29] These include concept, approach, technical setup, economic rationale, safeguard policies, environment, information disclosure, participation, social impact, financial management, institutional capacity, implementation capacity, risk assessment, processing timetable, and internal review.

of the written word. The judgment about improved entry quality might have reflected better documentation. The quality controllers tended to confirm this when they noted that behavior changes improved the form more than the substance of portfolio quality as familiarity grew with the reporting system.[30] In 2005, a QAG report said that performance reporting was still subject to a lack of candor and introduced a new report form to try to improve it. Neither was paper documentation apparently reduced with the 'wired office'. In 1998–1999, the Bank's consumption of paper averaged a steady 160 tons a month, enough to use up more than 1,000 Southern Pine trees.[31]

Second, the Bank's projects, despite calls for simplification dating from the Wapenhans Report and before, grew increasingly complex and difficult to manage. Complexity is not consistent with quality on the ground. The IEG (OED) figures for what it calls 'demandingness, complexity and riskiness' showed a strong increase over the 1990s.[32] 'Complex' projects increased from 43% in the first part of the decade to 77% in 1999–2000. There was a constant disconnect between calls for simplicity and pressure for more sophistication. A management review in 2001 declared: '[C]reating, sharing, and applying the cutting edge technology necessary for poverty reduction remained a central element of the work program'.[33] But in developing countries what is often needed is not 'cutting edge' but 'common sense'. Overcomplexity, especially in relation to capacity to manage projects, remains now just as serious a problem.

[30] 'World Bank Operational Effectiveness; Preliminary Results from OED and QAG for Fiscal Year 2000–01', World Bank, February 13, 2002, p. 1.

[31] I am indebted to Ray Newbold of Louisiana Technical University for the following calculations. A six-inch diameter tree will have about 0.04 cord and a nine-inch tree about 0.10 cord of wood. A cord will produce something in the neighborhood of 1.25 tons of paper. So, 160 tons of paper would require 128 cords of wood. 128/.0.04 = 3200 six-inch trees, or 128/0.10 = 1280 nine-inch trees. About a third of the tonnage of paper will be from residual sawmill chips (lumber production) from trees used for other purposes, so consumption will range from 2134 new six-inch trees to 854 new nine-inch trees each month, plus an amount of tree 'waste' from elsewhere (say the equivalent of 20% additional full trees).

[32] 'Demandingness, Complexity and Riskiness of Evaluated Operations – Exit Year Groups 1990–94, 1995–98, 1999–00', OED World Bank, 2000.

[33] 'Retrospective Review of FY00 IBRD/IDA Work Programs and Budgets', World Bank, July 13, 2000, p. 9.

Third, Bank projects are increasingly not susceptible to quantitative assessment, and cost-benefit analysis has fallen into disuse.[34] The ERR measure has in the past been the Bank's principal indicator of economic viability. But it is only useful where costs and benefits are realistically quantifiable. 'Non-tradables' like health and education are relatively difficult to value, and the Bank's investment projects have been increasingly in such non-tradables. Those that do not get ERR ratings include credit lines to banks, social investments, agricultural research and extension, population and health, education, environment, public sector management, and multi-sector loans. But now even more, the Bank's projects are in areas where benefits cannot practically be quantified – that is, institution building and public sector reform. Knowledge products, like analytical studies, are the most difficult to measure of all. Caufield[35] quotes a Bank staffer from the early years of McNamara's diversification into social projects: '[W]ith a lot of this stuff it's very hard to say the project works or it doesn't work. The more we move into the social realm the harder it gets to have any kind of yardstick'. In the institution-building area the problem is greater.

For many projects, monitoring and evaluation (M&E) 'performance indicators' have in effect replaced a priori cost-benefit assessment. These indicators are intended to provide shortcut measures of the outcome and impact of projects based on variables such as the increase in institutional capacity, investment, output, and employment. Such indicators are currently being developed for foreign assistance programs worldwide, and the Bank regards itself as being in the lead in this endeavor. However in areas such as public sector governance and the rule of law, it may even be difficult to find meaningful partial indicators because of measurement and attribution problems. Furthermore, in

---

[34] The Wapenhans Report noted that economic analysis was not being effectively used. Report interviewees complained that pressure to deliver projects, work fragmentation, and administrative overload prevented proper appraisals even where they could be done. In the mid-1970s, the Bank assumed the lead on the design of economic analysis methodology, incorporating income distribution. However, the work was not adopted within the institution and largely forgotten outside academic circles.

[35] Caufield, Catherine, *Masters of Illusion – The World Bank and the Poverty of Nations*, Henry Holt, 1996, p. 102.

2005 the evaluators reported that monitoring and evaluation were very weak.[36] In contrast, the areas where quantitative ERRs are easiest to estimate are for goods-producing projects such as in industry, which is a sector that the Bank has withdrawn from almost completely.[37]

M&E is an inappropriate approach to measuring a project's worth. It is essentially a tool of management, not of economic appraisal, and the M&E project performance indicators are firstly based on partial outcomes,[38] and secondly do not generally factor in project costs. The failure to factor project preparation and supervision, both by the Bank and by the recipient government, into project management costs over the lifetime of a project, and compare them with expected benefits, is a curious gap in methodology that appears to assume that these costs are trivial. But for smaller, labor-intensive, institution-building projects, such costs are likely to be significant in relation to benefits. Furthermore, factoring in government costs would provide a critical indicator of when an excessive burden is being placed on government capacity, which is a regular and serious issue.

Quantitative assessments, while being used much less, are also not always reliable. The evaluators recalculate ERRs to produce RERRs in case of overoptimistic ex-ante estimates. For example, in 1991, when project quality was under special scrutiny for the Wapenhans Report, the RERRs for 120 completed projects were calculated at 16%, whereas the initial ERRs averaged 24%. But over 1995 to 2000, the revisions showed little difference. In 2000 average ERRs were 22%.[39] Since 1995 the worst returns have been in water supply and the best in telecommunications, transport, and mining, while agriculture, despite its bad previous performance, was estimated to be making 18 to 19% over 1995–2000. African projects returned results no worse than any others.

---

[36] In 'Improving the World Bank's Development Effectiveness: What Does Evaluation Show?', World Bank, IEG, October 2005. Monitoring and evaluation in the health, education, and urban sectors was found to be so weak that little was known of outcomes, and almost 40% of the lines of credit had no information on effects such as the repayment rates on bank loans.

[37] The first texts on cost-benefit analysis in developing countries, produced by UNIDO and the OECD, in fact focused on industrial products.

[38] Benefit indicators might include measures such as capacity development, morbidity decline, number of graduates, employment generation, and physical output change.

[39] 'OED Reach', World Bank, Spring 2000, no. 24.

In fact, the 1995–1998 ERRs calculated for completed projects in Africa were the best of all the regions.

The level of the achieved ERRs might be questioned on intuitive grounds. Thus, if in a particular country a 20% real return to investment was generally achievable, then, at likely investment rates in poorer regions, the real rate of economic growth would be of the order of 3 to 4% per annum. But real rates of growth recorded up to 2000 in some regions were substantially less than this. According to the Bank's world development indicators, in Eastern Europe and the former Soviet Union the average growth rate over 1990 to 2000 was minus 1.6% per annum. In Sub-Saharan Africa it was 1.6% in 1980 to 1990, rising to 2.4% in 1990 to 2000.[40] Yet in Africa the estimated long-run ERRs were around 20% on Bank projects while in Eastern Europe and the Former Soviet Union the 1990–2000 average RERR was no less than 26%, despite the negative GDP growth.[41]

Could such high returns have been achieved because the World Bank's projects had been shining beacons of light amidst darkness? Economic theory suggests that investments in developing economies could earn high returns because complementary factors of production like labor and land are in abundance and underutilized. If projects are carefully targeted to potentially high return areas, the good results might be plausible, but much Bank investment goes into difficult sectors where complementary inputs (such as management skills) are lacking, and are characterized by implementation problems and heavy transaction costs. The OED itself stated[42] that 'many activities take place in countries characterized by scarce human resources, weak infrastructure, and weak implementation capacities'. The Bank's projects have continuously shown high returns on paper, even in environments where development assistance otherwise seems to have failed. In fact, a recent evaluation report states that the high returns on individual projects have come despite the fact that overall country program results are unsatisfactory in 33% of the countries that the Bank lends to.[43]

---

[40] Source: World Bank, World Development Reports (2002 and others).

[41] It was after only 2000 that GDP growth rates worldwide increased substantially. Over 2000–2005, Sub-Saharan Africa averaged 4.2% and Eastern Europe and the former Soviet Union area 5.4%.

[42] 'OED Reach', World Bank, Spring 2000, op cit.

[43] From 'Improving the Bank's Development Effectiveness', op cit.

The fungibility of aid money also makes it less likely that high returns will accrue in poorly run economies. This is because, as research has found, aid money tends to increase government expenditure according to its average pattern of expenditure, and poor governments tend to spend money ineffectively. So aid tends to go to the same ineffective outlets.[44]

Thus, while increasingly the Bank's projects are not being quantitively assessed, those that are face assessment bias that may not be adjusted on a systematic basis by the evaluators.

As mentioned, there are indications that performance problems finally came into view with a sharp relapse in the percentage of projects deemed satisfactory by the evaluators, falling back from 83% in 2006 to 76% in 2007, a level more like that of the late 1990s (albeit still surprisingly high). Outcomes deteriorated particularly sharply in the area of 'poverty reduction', and also in 'environment', 'energy', 'education', and 'finance and private sector development'. This was partially offset by some reported gains. 'Social protection' and 'social development' projects, for example, were claimed to have risen close to 100% 'satisfactory'. The projects completed in 2006–2007 had an average start year of 2000, right in the middle of the reorganization. This dip would tend to reaffirm the hypothesis that the organization's problems were caused more by the organizational disruptions themselves than by the bad attitudes or incompetence of the workforce.

THE COUNTERFACTUAL: WHY DEVELOPMENT IMPACT
HAS BEEN WRONGLY MEASURED

The IEG reports on development effectiveness are often cautious. For example, the 2006 edition discussed realistically many of the problems facing development projects, albeit still claiming remarkable results. But generally there is undoubtedly an institutional tendency to optimism and a loss of memory about failures, and there is also fear of bad publicity, especially under the scrutiny of the U.S. Congress and

---

[44] Dollar, David and Lant Pritchett, '*Assessing Aid*' – *What Works, What Doesn't and Why*, World Bank and Oxford University Press, 1998. The net effect of an average dollar of aid has been to increase public investment by only the average of 29 cents.

increasingly other donor governments. However, there is also a significant and more technical reason for incorrect performance assessment. This is not a problem of measurement but a problem of how the benefits of an assistance project are defined, and it is an important reason for doubting the rapid and consistent improvement in performance measurements up to 2005.

To assess accurately a public assistance project's impact it is necessary to know what would have happened if there had been no project, that is, the 'counterfactual'. If there is no net additional economic activity compared to the counterfactual, then there is no basis for the expenditure of public money. Whereas it is relatively easy to define the 'additionality' of a new factory increasing exports, or a new bridge crossing a river, it is difficult to find it in a project whose aim is to build institutions, which is now the Bank's main focus. To find the additional gain often requires identification of some type of beneficiary 'control group',[45] which involves overcoming significant practical problems of survey sampling and data collection.[46] Expensive impact assessments using these techniques are carried out for a very small proportion of the Bank's projects. Between 1980 and 2005, the OED only carried out twenty-three of the most rigorous of such evaluations across six separate sectors out of its hundreds of completed projects because it did not have the resources and time, up to several hundred thousand dollars per full evaluation, to do this work.

The additionality question is a commonsense one. It simply asks what difference a project really makes to an economy. A Kenyan journalist made this point quite simply about one of the World Bank's

---

[45] 'Lessons and Practices', OED, World Bank, November 1997. The classic representation of the counterfactual is the control group used in trials of new drugs. This is the group that gets the placebo while a treatment group gets the real thing. However, it is not possible to administer a placebo to those who don't get the benefits of a development project (e.g., to assess a school lunch program you cannot give real food to one group and artificial food to another). It is necessary to 'construct' a counterfactual, usually after the event. The IEG constructs counterfactuals by observation, focus groups, and surveys.

[46] Matched samples may be difficult to identify and use, and errors in data may result from several causes, both theoretical and practical. The latter include the fact that those who receive and those who don't receive assistance have different motivations for answering questions, and poorly paid field workers often write down interviewees responses regardless of whether they make sense.

best-known and principal knowledge products; he wrote[47]: 'the Government this week launched the investment climate assessment . . . . Why was a heavily indebted country like Kenya taking a loan from the World Bank to have a team of researchers to gather information that we already know so well? . . . I wondered if the Government might not actually save us money by dusting off some of the old reports on the shelves and distributing them to the public for debate'.

There are many examples where additionality is dubious. For example, donors set up business development centers to assist local businesses, but the centers provide free services that undercut small local firms (e.g., accountants) who could also provide such help but are sidelined, to the detriment of local business growth. In one case, a Bank project that was rated 'highly satisfactory' assisted export businesses in Mauritius to hire foreign technical experts, but many of the firms were already hiring them while some others gained from free services, but the economy might have lost from the interference with the existing business networks. The country could possibly have done just as well without the assistance. In the Baltic region, another project rated 'very satisfactory' helped to restructure the local banking system after the breakup of the Soviet Union. But at that time the private financial market was already developing rapidly and could very likely have done it better alone. In another case, free assistance was being given to strengthen the capacity of a number of banks while at the time the same banks were willingly purchasing commercial consulting services from elsewhere. An institution-building project involved a $500 million loan in 1998 to guarantee lending to small businesses in Argentina, to strengthen the capital market and long-term lending. The project was considered exceptionally innovative and thus widely applauded. But even in relatively sophisticated Argentina there was little local understanding or buy-in.[48] It was cancelled less than halfway through its expected life.

Assessors are often more impressed by 'what the project did' rather than whether it 'made a difference'. The work on a particular project

---

[47] Odeng, Pete, in *The Nation* newspaper (Kenya), February 23, 2003.
[48] The government, like many others, preferred the simplicity of the traditional financial intermediary loans that the Bank has tried hard to phase out.

might well be of high quality, but high quality does not mean high impact – especially in a widely subsidized, aid-dependent project environment. It is necessary to take a step back to see what really happened on the ground.

The Argentinean example was an exception in that the OED evaluation recognized the problem. It reported as follows: '[T]he project ... created a direct Government intervention in the financial markets at a moment when the Government and Bank were pushing for an across-the-board withdrawal of the State from those markets'. 'For the Bank's cumbersome, market insensitive and goal-ridden operational style the challenge proved too great'. The evaluators opined that the additional activity generated was about zero, and the zero benefits were achieved at a significant cost in public money both from the Bank and the government of Argentina itself.

A recent example of the limits to institution-building additionality is an effort to set up 'public-private sector dialogue' in Africa and elsewhere. Costly international conferences have been held (to dialogue on how to dialogue), impressive communiqués issued, dedicated Web sites set up, and extensive literature produced, including a 200-page how-to-do-it manual put out by the Bank to approving reviews by the other donors.[49] The rationale for improving dialogue is fine in countries where the public sector has been dominant and the private sector viewed with suspicion. But it is unclear why external donor agencies are required to manage such a dialogue that *perforce* has to be demanded by private interests. Aid-funded dialogue bureaucracies are likely to fizzle out once assistance is stopped. In some cases the dialogue process stalls as it waits for outside funding, to meet hotel expenses for attendees. Even if some benefit can be extracted from such efforts, it is often doubtful whether they justify their cost.

These examples do not mean that cost-covering additionality is unlikely in general. The most likely situations where it might occur, if an intervention is effectively designed and implemented, are those in

---

[49] Herzberg, Benjamin and Andrew Wright, 'Public-Private Dialogue: The PPD Handbook: A Toolkit for Business Environment Reformers', World Bank, December 2006.

which the private sector has little involvement (does not develop the counterfactual). These opportunities arise where action by government is essential and unique, that is, in public goods such as development of the legal system and judiciary, and especially in global public goods like handling climate change or global health, where the counterfactual may well be lack of effective action by anyone, private or public. An example of the creation of a new global market that at the same time addressed issues of the environment is the series of carbon purchase funds that were initiated by the Bank's Prototype Carbon Fund in 1996.[50] Global information provision can also sometimes succeed in this respect. For example, the IFC's annual 'doing business' report, which provides an intercountry league table on ease of conducting business, has established a special role for itself and is taken quite seriously by governments that want to attract foreign investment. An important example in the current context is information related to financial stabilization strategy, implementation and management, and the appropriate international architecture to maintain long-term financial market stability, a public good largely under the responsibility of the IMF but assisted by the Bank.

It was only in 2004 that the Bank launched a Development Impact Evaluation Taskforce to extend its evaluations to account properly for these impact effects. The twenty-five years of development project outcomes set out in Figure 6 are virtually all based on partial evaluations. How could changes in project quality be inferred on this basis? It might be justifiable to base such an inference on trends even if the absolute numbers are wrong for one or more of the reasons outlined. But such an inference is problematic because the assessments have been applied in different ways to different parts of the assistance program.[51] More significantly, the diversification of Bank projects into institution-building may mean that the impact is now less easy to identify overall, and the above examples suggest that the counterfactual is more likely to get

---

[50] The Bank has been active in the development of the carbon market, first through the Prototype Carbon Fund to demonstrate how to cost-effectively achieve GHG reductions, and more recently through other funds such as the Community Development Carbon Fund (CDCF) and the Bio Carbon Fund (BioCF). Source: World Bank, www.carbonfinance.org.

[51] 'Improving the World Bank's Development Effectiveness: What Does the Record Show?', OED/IEG, World Bank, October 2005.

undervalued in institution-building projects. Some support for this comes from a report on capacity building in Africa.[52] The evaluators said that there were serious deficiencies in the diagnosis, design, and evaluation of capacity building projects.

Institution-building is difficult and slow, and outside interventions have great difficulty bringing about real change. The fact that a project appraisal contains a lot of institution-building content guarantees no more than good intentions; it does not guarantee better results. If the counterfactual has been undervalued in institution-building projects, and if these projects have comprised a rapidly increasing share of the portfolio over the past ten years, then the rate of improvement of the Bank's overall project performance would have been exaggerated

The questions about what was really achieved are not easy to ignore, and indeed Francois Bourguignon, the Bank's last chief economist, responsible for setting up the impact task force, wrote in a recent paper: '[M]uch (though not all) aid has been wasted on poorly conceived and executed projects and programs, often fettered by debatable conditionality'.[53] Further, 'meta-analysis of ninety-seven different studies on the impact of aid and growth, drawing on three different approaches used in the literature, concluded that at best there appears to be a small positive, but insignificant, impact of aid on growth'. There is no good reason to suppose that the Bank's own projects have not been part of the wastage referred to.

PROJECT QUALITY AND POLITICAL LENDING: SOME COUNTRY EXPERIENCES

Under Article 4, Section 10 of the IBRD Articles of Agreement, the Bank is expected to avoid political judgment in making loans. 'The Bank and its officers shall not interfere in the political affairs of any member; nor shall they be influenced in their decisions by the political character of the member or members concerned. Only economic considerations

[52] 'Capacity Building in Africa; an OED Evaluation of World Bank Support', World Bank, 2005.
[53] Bourguignon, Francois and Mark Sundberg, 'Aid Effectiveness – Opening the Black Box', World Bank, 2007, p. 1.

shall be relevant to their decisions, and these considerations shall be weighed impartially in order to achieve the purposes stated in Article 1'. But in the event, due to shareholder pressure, it has considerable difficulty avoiding politics. Large amounts of lending to countries like Zaire under Mobutu and the Philippines under Marcos were examples, as was the lack of lending to Chile and Vietnam in the 1970s.[54] Clearly, if the Bank's lending and advice are politically motivated, then the allocation of assistance will not be to the most productive outlets and aid effectiveness will be reduced. Could the improvement in effectiveness claimed by the Bank during the reorganization period be attributable to a reduced political influence on where its funds and advice went? Unfortunately the answer is probably no.

The Bank's differential treatment of the former Soviet states is one illustration of the background influence of politics. By the end of the reorganization period in 2002, at the top of the assistance tables to the former Soviet Union was Armenia, with about $200 of assistance per head of population from twenty-eight Bank loans and credits. Armenia's strategic isolation[55] made a relationship with the Bank a political imperative, regardless of local concerns about privatizing its utilities and selling its cognac distillery, and it agreed to a series of adjustment programs. Georgia held second place in the league table with $128 per head through twenty-eight loans. Russia and the Ukraine were the largest recipients, and on a per capita basis they were halfway down the list. Tajikistan had received $46 a head and seventeen loans. Uzbekistan had received $23 a head through twelve loans, mainly in the 1993–1998 period, when enthusiasm had not yet been dampened by obvious non-cooperation on reform. Turkmenistan received $20 a head and three loans. The three 'Stans' received these loans even before 9/11, when their strategic importance rose. At the bottom of the league came

---

[54] To name some famous cases, the Bank rejected loans to Poland in 1948, Egypt in 1956, Chile in 1973, and Vietnam in 1978 on political grounds, while approving loans to Zaire under Mobutu and the Philippines under Marcos. In the 2000s, the effort to make loans to, for example, Pakistan, Turkey, and Tajikistan, appear politically colored.

[55] Armenia was subject to an energy blockade from Azerbaijan, with whom it had a territorial dispute over the province of Nagorno-Karabakh, and difficulties with Turkey to the West and Georgia to the North.

Belarus, which had received $19 a head from four loans, or, since 1994, just $2 a head from only one loan, for its 10 million population neighboring Russia and the Ukraine.

The treatment of Armenia at the top of the assistance league and Belarus at the bottom were politically driven. Armenia was a tiny country that nevertheless had significant U.S. attention, partly because of its large, and relatively wealthy, Diaspora, living mainly around Los Angeles, and because of its potentially strategic location in the largely Muslim Caucasus. Belarus was a country with no American Diaspora and of no strategic interest to the United States since its neighbor, Russia, was the main concern.[56] While Armenia got a lot of attention, after a small initial effort in 1993–1994 Belarus was rejected for further Bank lending, in the company of 'rogue states' like Syria, Burma, or latterly Zimbabwe.

Ostensibly this rejection was because the government failed to apply market reforms, although perversely its state-controlled production and exports were doing well. Its posture offended both U.S. politicians[57] and IMF/Bank economists. Other governments, such as those of Ukraine and Uzbekistan, had at least had the courtesy to respond to Bank and IMF advice, even if they had little intention of heeding it. In the event, dogma won over common sense, and initial government hopes that the Bank would assist change by taking a 'seat at the table' came to naught. Instead, top-level requests for assistance were rejected whether they were for its old state enterprises or its new private enterprises. Armenia got its loan to finance new enterprises despite its very weak banks while Belarus's version of the same loan was blocked because the

[56] Belarus has had a history of a similarly traumatic nature to that of Armenia. Both countries are highly vulnerable to energy boycotts. Armenia lost much of its historic land and was in dispute with Azerbaijan over part of what was left, and its Diaspora had been subject to mass killings under the Ottoman Empire. Belarus had been a victim of constant foreign invasions. During the Second World War it lost one-third of its population. It surrendered its nuclear weapons. It was the main victim of the Chernobyl nuclear accident, which contaminated one-fifth of its territory.

[57] U.S. displeasure at Belarus' leader originated in the inadvertent but unexplained shooting down of a U.S. air balloonist in 1994. Then, in 1998, the diplomatic corps was told to move to residences away from the presidential compound. Warnings (e.g., of pollution from a poultry farm) went unheeded and finally ditches were dug across their driveways. These were filled in again, but too late. The Western ambassadors withdrew, citing breach of the Vienna Convention.

government wanted to restore some of its diluted bank holdings. From then on Belarus received the 'tough-love treatment'.[58] This treatment continued for a long time. A Bank project to alleviate the effects of the Chernobyl disaster finally got funded in 2006, by which time the Children-of-Chernobyl were already grown up. The United States was the single no-vote.[59]

There have been more important examples of politically influenced lending and political refusal to lend than the case of these two small former Soviet republics. Russia itself is a significant example, and outside the former Soviet Union there are many others. Politics does influence project decisions, in breach of Article 4, Section 10 of the Bank's Articles of Agreement. The important point is that political lending does not require a reorganization to fight poverty, nor is it consistent with the objective of increasing development project quality. If lending is influenced by political decisions, then the development assistance approach and the structure and strategy of the assistance organization are largely irrelevant and the quality of development assistance projects is beside the point. The reorganization period did not in principle change the role of political lending despite its heavily publicized commitment to effectiveness, and post-reorganization the issue remains central. A current $500 million Iraq assistance program approved under Wolfowitz' presidency is a prime example. As has been demonstrated by the severe problems of the U.S. reconstruction efforts

---

[58] Belarus was a country featured at a Bank workshop in 1998 entitled: 'Tough Love; Should the Bank Lend to Non-Reforming Countries?' 'Tough love' from the United States has continued for many years. Congress, with the vocal support of Sen. McCain and Condi Rice, found time in the midst of urgent world business to pass the 2004 Belarus Democracy Act to punish 'Europe's last dictator'. The 2008 State of the Union address featured Belarus alongside Zimbabwe on the Bush list of undesirables. In 2008, the United States all but severed relations over a political detainee. If reforms arrive, they will, however, be more due to Russian economic pressures than Bank or IMF conditions, or political sanctions.

[59] The $50 million Post-Chernobyl Recovery Project was approved in April 2006, twenty years after the accident. The Bank stated that the project, to provide cleaner energy, 'would change people's lives for the better in the contaminated zones'. The loan submission to the board was delayed for several months by Paul Wolfowitz, and the U.S. executive director was the lone vote against the project because it was not 'humanitarian'.

in Iraq, development assistance in a war zone is least likely to have sustainability or institutional impact, or to justify economically the international public resources spent.

EVALUATION INDEPENDENCE

While the Bank's project performance measures can be questioned on technical grounds and on grounds of political influence, a further concern is the independence of the evaluation function. Did the reorganization make any difference to this?

The Meltzer Commission was up front in claiming that the evaluators were not sufficiently independent of the Bank to bring enough pressure on performance. Adam Lerrick, in one of his frequent letters to the *Financial Times* on March 6, 2002, called for a triennial independent audit of the Bank's activities, asserting that self-policing involved a conflict of interest. Pieter Stek, chairman of the Board Committee on Development Effectiveness (CODE), wrote a rebuttal that the CODE was actively monitoring the IEG.[60] At the same time, the Bank's newsletter[61] asserted that not only the OED, which formally reports to the board, but even the QAG, which reports to the top management, was independent.

Despite the rebuttals there were in fact links between the evaluators and the operational units that could be regarded as questionable. First, there was the 'revolving door' whereby Bank staff could move from operations to evaluation and back as part of their career progression. But in addition there were areas of formal collaboration. Evaluators' draft reports were shared with the management, who prepared a formal 'management response', after which a joint position was agreed on for presentation to the CODE. Eight weeks before a planned CODE meeting a 'ledger of OED recommendations and management response' was

---

[60] *Financial Times*, March 12, 2002. Stek responded to a charge of being passive, but not to that of lack of evaluation independence. He wrote: '[F]ar from being passive, the Board oversees the independent evaluation function through a standing committee on development effectiveness. This committee meets twice a month to review all the main OED products and reports to the full Board, thereby ensuring that evaluation findings and recommendations are acted on by the World Bank management'.

[61] *Banks World*, March 2002.

presented to the board, almost always a highly polished and heavily 'cleared' document. The QAG and the OED also made joint presentations, such as the announcement of the latest operational performance scores. In fact, it was not only Meltzer who called for a truly independent agency, but also the Gurria–Volcker commission, whose conclusions were friendlier to the Bank.[62]

The existence of a link between operations and evaluation does not mean that the IEG has not made tough and candid assessments of Bank work. The outgoing director general of the OED, Bob Picciotto, a forty-year veteran of the Bank, in an interview in October 2002 spoke of the need for courage, in order to be able to 'speak truth to power'. For example, in 1999, an OED report[63] downgraded thirty years of the Bank's work in Indonesia, making special reference to the failure of senior managers to heed warnings of financial sector collapse. It wrote of a reluctance to offend a major borrower, a refusal to address corruption, and a dysfunctional internal culture that punished staff for identifying problems that could slow down lending, all of which contributed to the 'myth of the Indonesian miracle'. Some staff 'feared the potential negative impact on their opportunities that might result from challenging the mainstream thinking'. Another example of OED directness was the Argentina 'backstop facility' referred to above. A report on the Bank's global programs such as the Global Environmental Facility came up with a long list of criticisms. A 2002 evaluation of assistance to Russia was bluntly critical, especially on the early phase of assistance. The 2005 report on African capacity building was equally so. A 2007 IEG report on agricultural lending to Africa paints a thoroughly dismal picture of inadequate attention to the sector.

The indications are that the IEG findings for 2007 have called a halt to the twelve-year run-up in 'quality'. Perhaps this is due to hard-headed realism, and perhaps because the credibility of the previous claims is increasingly shaky. But, in any case, a reality check is indicated.

There is no doubt that the OED has assumed an independent posture from time to time. The evaluators have the right intentions, and at

---

[62] Report of a Blue Ribbon Commission chaired by Paul Volcker and Jose Angel Gurria, April 26, 2001. Carnegie Endowment for International Peace.
[63] 'Indonesia Country Assistance Note', OED, World Bank, February 4, 1999.

certain times when under scrutiny they have been aggressive. But in the longer run the issue is not one of good intentions but objective interests. It is about the location of the evaluation function within an organization, and what that implies over time, including the times when focus has shifted away from evaluation to other matters. Conflict of interest is not a matter of intentions but of objective facts.

The links between the evaluators and the managers, information overload and difficulty in identifying clear criteria of failure, tend to prevent evaluators from taking an independent stand. Critical positions might get bogged down in detailed reviews and explanations. Outside pressures and the nature of the management–board relationship encourage management to send as far as possible unchallengeable documents to the board. These are the same dynamics that push the institution into providing defensive performance numbers to the outside world rather than explain that development problems are large and need dedication rather than oversight distractions and scores.

THE ORGANIZATION AND COST OF THE QUALITY INFRASTRUCTURE

The quality of the Bank's products is closely monitored. The Donor's Evaluation Cooperation Group has stated that the Bank's evaluation methods are 'closest to best practice among MDBs'.[64] As one vice president put it, '[T]he Bank invests heavily in independent evaluation, and its Operations Evaluation Department is unique among development institutions in the scale and scope of its work'.[65] What have been the scale and cost of these quality control structures?

The introduction of the Inspection Panel in 1993 was only the start of a rapid expansion of evaluation infrastructure that took place during the 1990s. Currently, the infrastructure includes, in addition to the QAG and the IEG, an operational policy group (OPCS) that makes product assessments and controls a network of quality management

---

[64] 'Development Effectiveness at the WB; What Is the Score?', OED Reach, World Bank, Spring 2000.
[65] 'Managing for Quality and Development Effectiveness', World Bank OED, January 10, 2000.

units within the operational regions, especially Africa; an internal audit group that has responsibilities for assessing operational risk; and a department of institutional integrity that acts in effect as a parallel internal auditor focusing on allegations of corruption.

Each different organ of control provides its own specialized performance assessment process.[66] The QAG has entry, supervision, and advisory input reviews. The IEG process starts with self-evaluation by operational units,[67] followed by an IEG review of the initial evaluation and then a joint submission by the OED and the operations unit to the board sub-committee (CODE). Then, for 25% of completed projects, usually those that are large, innovative, or controversial, there is a performance audit after one to three years, which involves a brief field visit. Finally, for about 5% of the projects, impact evaluations are done, three to ten years after completion.

The quality infrastructure uses the services of about 700 full- and part-time professional assessors altogether. Of this total the IEG has nearly 200 staff. The QAG has some 35 and it calls on 300 others including consultants to work part-time. A third network, the OPCS, has groups of people across the Bank responsible for monitoring project preparation, and quality units in each region. The inspection panel has three inspectors and other support staff. The internal audit department has about forty-five staff. The most recently formed Department of Institutional Integrity had fifty-six in 2006, and as a result of its status elevation it is likely to perhaps double in size.

---

[66] For example, the QAG publishes an 'Annual Report on Portfolio Performance' that monitors quality-at-entry (QAE) (aspects of design) and quality-of-supervision (QOS) (how projects are being managed); its project-at-risk measures look at generalized risk indicators. The QAG's entry evaluations are carried out using about fifty criteria over nine areas of assessment. Project-at-risk measures are based on a twelve-point rating. Low scores on three criteria or more means 'at risk'. It is too expensive for the QAG to look at all projects, so a sample of around 10% is taken. The IEG looks at post-project outcomes of projects at the country, theme, sector, and project levels. It publishes the 'Annual Review of Development Effectiveness'.

[67] 'Evaluating Development Outcomes. OED Lessons and Practices', World Bank, July 1997, describes the process as 'embedded in self-evaluation'. One of the results of the Wapenhans Report was to change the name from 'project completion reports' to 'implementation completion reports' on the grounds that the former signified that the project was ended when the loan was repaid, when in fact it was usually still operating.

While not part of the reorganization, the latest addition, the new anti-corruption bureaucracy, will be a significant extension of the watchdog cadre that grew up during the 1990s. Apart from its enlarged core unit, it will be loaded with an external advisory board to watch over the watchdogs, and a consulting unit to show how assistance should avoid being corrupted. A managing director would be responsible for action plans on corruption cases. The number of staff and the budget assigned to the department even *before* the new proposals were already much greater than the combined staff and budget of the same units in the AfDB, ADB, EBRD, IDB, and IMF, while its caseload was smaller.[68] It is therefore to be expected that this new addition to the back line will be significant.

Thus a group of assessors equal in number to nearly 20% of the professional staff conducts checks, while the latter has its own self-checking responsibility. Whereas for the first half of its existence the Bank had no formal evaluation organ (the OED was formed in 1973), in the second half it incorporated an extraordinary burden of quality control but one whose value added is doubtful.

The QAG was originally set up with a sunset provision, to close down when it had done its work of upgrading the Bank's projects. But in 2001, at the end of the reorganization period, the QAG chief was in favor of continuing. He reported that a focus group session had come out against the sunset idea on the grounds that the gains were fragile, because new types of projects needed new approaches, and because a 'credible system for holding staff and managers accountable for how they do their jobs is essential to effective management'. The cautionary note on the gains, which was in fact very appropriate, was in contrast to the previous five years of celebration of quality increase.

During the period of the reorganization the costs of all the watchdog organs rose steadily[69] while at the same time the operational budget was falling. Formal control and review by 'the 700' is however only the exposed part of the evaluation iceberg. The costs are multiplied by the regular process of operations self-evaluation, supervision and

---

[68] Data from Volcker Commission report on the Department of Institutional Integrity, Appendix A, Table 1. The report focused mainly on borrower corruption but also devoted two chapters to internal investigation.

[69] From $18 million in 1997 to $26 million in 2002, and above $30 million in 2006.

completion reports, heavy cross-checking and review of documentation needed before a project goes to the board, the time spent responding to the quality controllers, and the time spent by the internal advisers (e.g., the networks) acting as quality advisers. Fiduciary compliance alone is estimated to add 6% to administrative costs. Thus it seems likely that the combined effort comprises more than 20% of staff time. More than 20% of administrative costs would mean that the total cost of the Bank's quality industry and its affiliates would amount to more than $400 million per annum.

The evaluation burden has expanded further since 2004 as a result of the Development Impact Evaluation Taskforce, which has spawned monitoring and evaluation units around the organization. To support such initiatives, just before Wolfensohn's term expired, an OECD forum in March 2005 issued the 'Paris Declaration on Aid Effectiveness' in which most foreign assistance agencies committed themselves to a so-called 'statement of resolve', which included a 'practical, action-ori-entated roadmap to improve the quality of aid and its impact on development' through 'ownership, alignment, harmonization, managing for results, and mutual accountability'.[70] The introduction of the new, expanded program of development impact evaluations that responded to the Paris Declaration will add further to the direct costs but not necessarily to benefits of the Bank's operations.

QUALITY CONTROL AND ORGANIZATIONAL EFFECTIVENESS

In 1992 a report to the board, responding to the pressure to create the inspection panel, found that internal supervision, reporting, audit, and evaluation facilities in the Bank were quite adequate in comparison with other organizations, such as the USAID, CIDA, and KfW, and that an internal inspection panel would have little added value. The setup of the panel was opposed by many top staffers including Ernie Stern, operations chief, and as a result it was set up to focus outside the organization on

---

[70] 'The conclusions of a conference in September 2008 at the third anniversary of the Paris declaration admitted to lack of progress on this statement of resolve'.

complaints that the Bank had failed to follow its own operational poli-cies.[71] Following the inspection panel, the additional control capacity cre-ated in the following years was not based on a pre-determined plan but proliferated within the organization largely because of external pressures.

Given its imperfect origins, is it possible that the organizational structure put in place by the Bank to improve quality control actually compromises quality? Organizational re-engineering texts such as that of Hammer and Champy,[72] describe how the organization of large firms can deteriorate. To deal with evolving dysfunction they have to return to first principles and identify the 'end-to-end' business processes needed for effectiveness. Hammer wrote that 'a lot of work goes on in organizations that does not add value to the company's product or service'. 'One signal of value-subtracting work' they said, 'is excessive checking and control . . . . Problems are caught not when they actually happen but only much later in the process, requiring more than one step to be redone'.

How would the setup of quality control actually reduce quality? The answer to this is largely in terms of its effects on incentives. The result of heavy checking and control is, for example, likely to be a change in the behavior of operational management. First, operational management will simply have less time to spend on operational issues, including the design and implementation of good programs, while expected to spend more time on examining ways of improving quality. Second, it may have less incentive to ensure quality because of an expectation that the controllers will catch problems in time. Third, it may take precautions against being exposed, or delayed, by the controls and become less innovative, or manipulate the controls through better formal prepara-tion and drafting of documents.

---

[71] See Fox, Jonathan, 'The World Bank Inspection Panel and the Limits of Account-ability', in Pincus and Winters, eds., op cit. In the first years of its existence the panel handled seventeen cases, the most controversial being the Arun lll dam in 1993 and the Western China Poverty Reduction Project in 2000, the first of which was cancelled under activist pressure, one of Wolfensohn's early actions, and the second withdrawn by the government of China. The panel was ultimately set up to provide an early warning to the Bank's management of outside opposition – 'to prevent surprises'.

[72] Hammer, Michael and James Champy, *Reengineering the Corporation; a Manifesto for the Business Revolution*, Harperbusiness, 2001.

Regarding the first possibility, the proliferation of checking and sur-
veillance agents tends to increase the inward-looking, bureaucratic
response to real situations. In 2001, the QAG chief agreed that with
the large number of evaluation entities 'it is not surprising that some
task managers feel besieged, especially in the current budget environment',[73] although at the same time, he asserted, '(we) are consulting
regularly to minimize any overlaps and to maximize synergies'. But the
QAG report for 2005 noted no improvement. It said that staff already
overloaded with mandates think that the focus on monitoring and
evaluation will take away resources from preparing good projects,
and it is inconsistent with the continuing emphasis on annual delivery
targets. 'Approximately one-third of those interviewed had virtually no
understanding of the Results Agenda' said the QAG. 'Many viewed it as
a vague concept that involved high-level meetings with no linkages to
improving results at the project level'. 'Staff also expressed confusion'
said the report, 'about the complexity of terminology associated with
changes in lending and supervision guidelines that are intended to
increase the results focus in operations'.

Regarding the second possibility, the dilution of direct-line management responsibility and the shrinkage of operational managers' time to
deal with operational problems may have created a tendency to defer to
a benign quality controller as an extra resource for getting projects
through the system.

Regarding the third possibility, the QAG reported a tendency to game
the system by selecting projects that avoided time-consuming safeguard
observances while also taking advantage of the guide notes and help
desk facilities to improve the form rather than the substance of projects.

Ex post evaluation (by IEG) has a more neutral effect on behavior
than entry evaluation because it does not generally interfere with current organizational transactions, only with completion assessments.
Nevertheless, it causes much time to be spent negotiating outcome
scores, or agreed positions on past problems, and thus also crowding
out operational management time.

---

[73] Interview with Prem Garg: 'Bank Portfolio Healthiest in Two Decades', *Bank's World Today*, March 13, 2001.

Thus, even apart from what it costs, it may be dysfunctional for an organization to spend a significant proportion of its time 'looking over its shoulder'. The issue is whether several hundred formal quality controllers and part-time helpers, coupled with the extensive informal quality control activities expected from usually reluctant project staff, can perform a value-added role, especially recalling that the proliferation of quality control was largely because of outside pressure. The Bank operated for its first twenty-five years without any formal project evaluation. Heavy injections of quality control and evaluation may be part of the problem but not part of the solution, and the question could be whether returning responsibility back to operations, to restore the integrity of the basic process, as Michael Hammer puts it, would not be the best strategy. There is a potential conflict between efficient organizational performance and the diversion of extensive resources by the organization into checking its own progress.

THE REFORM OF QUALITY: A CONCLUSION

Four points have been made in this chapter. First, the Bank claimed significant improvement in operational effectiveness as a result of the reorganization, but re-interpretation of the performance measures suggests that they were flawed and provided grounds for doubt about the extent of improvement.

Second, to the extent that there was some performance improvement during the reorganization, the origins most likely date back to the recovery period following the last reorganization in 1987. The probable causal link between periods of organizational disruption and dips in quality (in 1987–1988 and possibly also in 1998–2001) is inconsistent with the argument that quality was a function of the level of employee skills.

Third, the causes of possibly flawed performance assessments are a combination of technical and organizational factors. A key factor is the inadequate approach to the evaluation of impact, which may have resulted in exaggerated estimates of improvement. The lack of independence of the evaluation infrastructure in the longer run must also have affected measured performance.

Finally, the resources used and the bureaucratic weight of the quality control and integrity checking infrastructure itself is likely to have reduced effectiveness because it has distorted incentives and displaced organizational effort by distracting the operational managers of the Bank from operational work – design, preparation, implementation, and management of programs.

Can an organization run properly when it is expending a major proportion of its resources second-guessing its own performance? The answer from management theory is 'no' and the evidence set out would support this conclusion. From the point of view of corporate effectiveness, the evaluation infrastructure would need to be dismantled or very much rationalized so that the weight of responsibility for 'project quality' can be returned to the operational managers, subject to performance criteria on which they have to deliver.

The Bank of course requires operations quality control just as any effective organization. But data on the broader lessons of development assistance evaluation are a global public good needed to improve future assistance worldwide. As such, assistance evaluation is not necessarily the role of one particular organization but may be better located in a separate international evaluation body, leaving the Bank and other organizations to focus on improving their operations.

What can then be said of the reorganization period's initiatives to improve project and knowledge quality? Like many of the reforms, they were haphazard and without adequate forethought, largely under outside pressure, and the claimed improvements are highly questionable. There is at least a likelihood that the quality control infrastructure has not added value and that it is part of the waste of resources involved in the Bank's back-line organization. Whereas in the wider financial sector currently the charge is one of inadequate regulation, in the case of the Bank and other development finance agencies a re-examination of the whole purpose of the heavy watchdog culture is needed.

8

Financing the Reorganization

The finances of the Bank came under a number of pressures during the reorganization period. First of all, the Strategic Compact itself set aside some $570 million for the Bank's reorganization over three years, including $420 million for re-engineering (less $170 million in expected savings) and $150 million for redundancies. At the same time the re-organization period saw a rise followed by a steep decline in total lending that has been maintained since, a shift in the structure of lending away from income-generating large loans to small, loss-making knowledge products, and finally an increase in administrative costs. Prima facie these changes would have been expected to create pressures on the Bank's net income, on its financial sustainability, and on its operational independence. How far was the Bank able to manage these pressures?

LENDING FALTERS

A potential decline in IBRD lending, due partly to high *transaction costs*, was one of the principal concerns aired in the Strategic Compact. As shown in Figure 8, a plateauing in lending volume occurred in 1996, and this was the source of the Compact's concern. But the onset of the Asian economic crisis for a time obscured the problem, as the growth of new lending approved by the IBRD recovered and rose to a record in

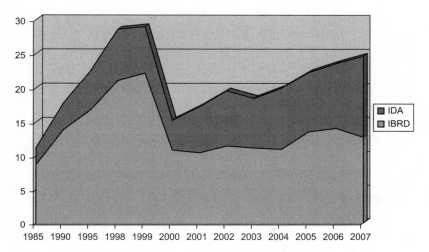

Figure 8. Annual IBRD lending and IDA credits and grants ($ billion).

1999 of $22 billion.[1] Thus the Compact was agreed on, by chance, just prior to a peak in lending.

During the reminder of the reorganization period after 1999, IBRD lending was sharply reduced, running at half the peak level, and it has recovered only slightly since.[2] Total lending in 2000 was back down to less than 50% of the allowed lending ceiling, the level at which the last capital increase was approved. IDA lending and grants rose to

---

[1] IBRD loan and IDA credit and grant commitments ($ billion)

	1985	1990	1995	1998	1999	2000	2001	2002	2003	2004	2005	2006	2007
IBRD	8.7	13.9	16.8	21.1	22.2	10.9	10.5	11.5	11.2	11.0	13.6	14.1	12.8
IDA	2.5	3.9	5.7	7.5	6.8	4.4	6.8	8.1	7.3	9.0	8.7	9.5	11.9
Total	11.2	17.8	22.5	28.6	29.0	15.3	17.3	19.6	18.5	20.0	22.3	23.6	24.7

Source: World Bank Annual Reports.

[2] The Asian crisis loans provided in 1998 and 1999 have now been partly prepaid. As a result, over 2001 to 2007 the average IBRD net lending amount was minus $6 billion a year. The negative position is likely to continue unless there is a sustained recovery in total lending. If we count the repayments as well (that is, the total net transfers), then most regions of the world are paying back to the Bank every year more than they are receiving.

compensate for this after 2003.[3] While the initial concern expressed in the Strategic Compact was overtaken by the record lending of 1998–1999, the sharp reduction at the end of the Strategic Compact period was a reminder of the potential financial sustainability problem of a long-term decline in lending leading to a corresponding decline in loan income.

FINANCIAL PROFITABILITY

Financial profitability is a more important issue for the IBRD than for IDA. First, it raises its money from the financial market and therefore needs to remain financially sound, and, second, it has historically been the largest part of the Bank Group and has provided the financial underpinning, which has included making transfers to the IDA. The IDA, on the other hand, is largely donor funded and thus not answerable to the market but to the aid policies of its owners. Consequently, the long-term financial independence and sustainability of the Bank mean looking particularly at the IBRD.

As shown in Table 7, the IBRD has turned a comfortable if modest nominal profit (net operating income) almost every year of its existence (averaging between $1 and $2 billion per annum). The return on its equity has fluctuated around 5%, which is comparable with the other international financial institutions, although recently the IFC and the EBRD have been making higher profits.[4] The IBRD's profitability is supported by the fact that it does not pay dividends to its shareholder governments and this allows it some freedom to either accumulate funds or operate at a lower gross rate of return than the private sector. The amount of this funding cost advantage is higher the greater the

---

[3] IDA grants were introduced in 2003. The donors agreed on a partial switch to grants that now comprise about 20% of the total financing, averaging around $2 billion a year since 2003. The total IDA outstandings were reduced significantly from 2006 under the MDRI debt reduction program, but have since remained slightly higher than the outstanding IBRD loans.

[4] See Hurst, Christopher and Eric Peree, 'Only a mid-life crisis? The future for IFIs in an integrated world, EIB Papers', *European Investment Bank* 3(2): 24, 1998. Returns on equity in private banks were significantly higher than for the World Bank over 1992–1996.

Table 7. *IBRD income and expenditure (US$ billions)*

	1997	1998	1999	2000	2001	2002	2003	2004	2005	2006	2007
Income (net): loans	1.36	0.74	0.80	1.03	0.99	1.96	2.15	1.61	1.12	0.91	1.05
Income: investment	0.87	1.46	1.44	1.59	1.54	0.74	0.42	0.30	0.63	1.06	1.17
Other income (net)	−0.17	0.16	0.50	0.15	0.17	0.08	0.03	0.05	0.09	0.11	0.06
Less admin costs		0.71	0.87	0.97	0.95	0.88	0.88	0.88	0.93	1.02	1.06	1.07
Operating income	1.35	1.49	1.77	1.82	1.82	1.90	1.72	1.03	0.82	1.02	1.21
Less loss provisions	0.06	0.25	0.25	−0.17	0.68	−0.02	−1.30	−0.67	−0.50	−0.72	−0.45
Net oper. income	1.29	1.24	1.52	1.99	1.14	1.92	3.02	1.70	1.32	1.74	1.66

Source: Annual Reports.

ratio of equity capital to lending.[5] This helps the IBRD to subsidize its lending and undercut private interest rates, or to absorb higher overhead costs, or to do both.[6]

Looking back over ten years since the start of the Strategic Compact, net income has been in positive territory throughout. In some years income from lending alone has dropped below $1 billion, less than 1% of assets, but declines have always been offset by income from investments[7] and/or from a reduction of provisions for loan losses. The investment income has been earned on the IBRD's relatively high liquid asset holdings, which have provided it with a degree of operational independence.

Nevertheless, over 1998 to 2001 average loan income fell significantly, prior to the arrival of the increased revenue associated with the Asian crisis loans. Of some concern was the fact that the level of net loan income after deducting administrative costs, as shown in Table 7, became negative in 1998 and 1999. There was concern that lending was no longer making a contribution to the Bank's profits. In 1999,

[5] When it is up against its allowed lending ceiling (so that its equity/debt ratio is at its minimum level) the average cost advantage is quite small (equal to around 1.5%, or 150 basis points) while just after a sizeable increase in paid-in capital, such as in 1988, it could be quite large.
[6] Another useful advantage was that the IBRD could borrow from other central banks. In 1973, for example, this amounted to nearly half of all borrowing.
[7] The split between loan income and investment income has fluctuated according to factors like the total amount of lending, the fees and margin on loans, and the changes in interest rates on investments.

Table 8. *IBRD and IDA administrative costs (US$ billion)*[a]

1996	1997	1998	1999	2000	2001	2002	2003	2004	2005	2006	2007
1.17	1.15	1.26	1.49	1.49	1.41	1.53	1.51	1.7	1.92	2.01	2.04

[a] Excluding development grant.

at a strategy seminar, a financial director surprised the top managers with a presentation showing them that the Bank's lending profit margin was in danger. Up to that time only a few of the twenty-six vice presidents were aware that the Bank's lending activities were losing money. However, from 2002, loan income recovered significantly because of the servicing of the crisis loans and declines in borrowing rates compared to lending rates.

However, despite the intermittent negative return on lending (once again in 2006 and 2007 loan income after administrative costs fell into negative territory) there was in fact no stress on the profit margin during the reorganization, or since, because of the offsetting contribution of investment income. The year 2003 saw a record net income of $3 billion, and subsequent levels have been safely above US$ 1 billion. The costs of the reorganization period and beyond were thus covered without difficulty, even though the compensating movements of lending and investment income have sometimes appeared fortuitous.

RISING OVERHEAD COSTS

Despite the generally satisfactory net income situation, an important goal of the reorganization was to control administrative costs through higher productivity in delivering its loans and advice. Did this happen?

As shown in Table 8, the administrative costs of the IBRD and IDA[8] together rose continuously up to the middle years of the Strategic Compact and then fell back in 2001, in compliance with the deal made between the president and the board. After 2001, however, costs resumed growth

---

[8] There are a variety of definitions of administrative cost used. This one is based on what the Bank calls its gross administrative budget, but excluding the cost of its development grant facility and before counting fee income. Other measures put the administrative cost ratio at a higher level, surpassing 10%.

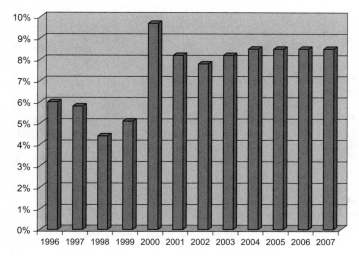

Figure 9. IBRD and IDA administrative cost burden.

at a relatively rapid pace of 8% per annum over the next four years to 2005. By 2006 they surpassed $2 billion.

A gauge of cost efficiency is the ratio of administrative costs to lending over the longer run, since lending reflects the level of effort applied, to loans and also to an extent to knowledge products if there is a relation between activities in either product. As can be seen from Figure 9, the ratio has shown considerable fluctuation. Its fall in 1998–1999 resulted mainly from the surge in lending while the rise in the cost ratio over 2000–2001 reflected the fallback in lending. Since 2004 the ratio has been steady at 8.5%. This level appears to be showing a higher sustained level than was occurring pre-reorganization.

These results suggest that the reorganization period did not create savings in process cost or increases in operating productivity in the longer term.[9] At the same time, administrative costs have not yet risen

---

[9] Productivity measures are in fact difficult to define. The 1996 report of the Task Force on Multilateral Development Banks commented that a lack of efficiency yardsticks 'makes it all the more important that the Boards and management remain alert to the dangers of letting costs, e.g., staffing costs – get out of hand ... the scale of their operations must not be allowed to inhibit ... expeditious decision-making'. In *Serving a Changing World, Report of the Task Force on Multilateral Development Banks*, IMF/World Bank Development Committee, 1996, p. 20.

Table 9. *IBRD balance sheet (US$ billions)*

	1999	2000	2001	2002	2003	2004	2005	2006	2007
Assets									
Disbursed loans	117.2	120.1	118.9	121.6	116.2	109.6	104.4	103.0	97.8
Cash and investments	31.0	25.6	24.9	25.3	29.8	32.9	27.9	26.4	23.8
Swaps receivables	79.0	78.5	75.1	76.7	81.3	83.0	85.9	78.4	81.4
Other (net)	7.2	7.7	7.9	9.3	7.0	6.9	6.8	6.8	6.9
Less loss provisions	−3.6	−3.4	−4.0	−5.1	−4.0	−3.5	−3.0	−2.3	−1.9
Total	230.8	228.5	222.8	227.8	230.3	228.9	222.0	212.3	208.0
Liabilities									
Borrowings	115.7	110.4	106.8	110.3	108.5	108.1	101.3	95.8	87.8
Swaps payables	82.0	82.6	79.5	78.6	77.5	80.2	77.7	74.9	75.2
Other liabilities	5.1	6.2	6.9	6.5	6.4	5.1	4.5	5.1	5.1
Equity (cap + reserves)	28.0	29.3	29.6	32.3	37.9	35.5	38.5	36.5	39.9
Total	230.8	228.5	222.8	227.7	230.3	228.9	222.0	212.3	208.0

Source: Annual Reports.

to the level where overall profitability is likely to be significantly impacted.

ASSETS AND LIABILITIES

Does the IBRD balance sheet show any adverse financial effects from the reorganization?

As shown in Table 9, on the assets side, lending grew throughout the period and peaked at $122 billion in 2002. At the same time the provisions for losses were a very low percentage of the assets because of the highly secure nature of the IBRD's loans. The 2002 provisions rose temporarily to 4% of the outstanding loans, but they were not in any sense threatening. Since 2002 they have fallen substantially every year. Cash and investments rose steadily and exceeded the required levels.[10]

On the liabilities side, the peculiarities and strength of the IBRD's capital structure were discussed in Chapter 1. Currently, only $11.6

---

[10] Cash and investments rose temporarily as a result of prepayments, but there has been a rundown in this item since 2004 through a sharp fall in borrowing, in order to bring liquidity down to the level required by the operating rules. The swap entries do not represent the IBRD's main business but coverage of risks from currency and interest rate changes. These items are excluded from some versions of the balance sheet.

billion (6%) of the total subscribed capital is paid-in.[11] This means that the subscribing member governments contribute only a small amount of actual cash while the rest, up to the value of total outstanding loans, is promised. The IBRD is thus protected against insolvency. Total paid-in capital plus reserves (US$ 39.9 billion) plus callable capital in 2007 came to US$ 218 billion, which is the current lending ceiling. The IBRD's equity position, at nearly 40% of outstanding loans, is historically strong and very strong by international banking standards.

The strength of the balance sheet is reflected in the fact that the equity to loan ratio, the main performance measure, was strong and steadily increasing throughout the reorganization period. As in the case of its operating income, the IBRD's balance sheet was not materially affected by the reorganization. The Bank's owners were secure in the assumption that the capital base of the institution was too strong to be significantly affected by a $570 million gross investment in reorganization and redundancies, spread out over several years, while the potentially adverse effects on profits of the knowledge bank were not as yet manifest. It was this fundamentally strong position that was an underpinning of the apparently relaxed attitude toward the reorganization itself. The Bank's financial protections allowed significant freedom of action for organizational adventures.

FINANCIAL PROTECTIONS

The IBRD's profitability is protected *inter alia* by its tax-free status and its free equity financing, and its solvency is guaranteed by its capital structure. But in addition to these it has numerous other protections that underpinned the costs of the reorganization.

The most important additional safeguard is that, under its Articles of Agreement, borrowing governments guarantee repayment of the Bank's loans.[12] These guarantees mean that, at least in principle, the institution

---

[11] Of this total $6.9 billion has been paid in convertible currency by twenty-two OECD Development Assistance Committee countries of the United States, Canada, Western Europe, Japan, Australia, and New Zealand. The United States has paid $2 billion of this amount.

[12] Article 3, Section 4 states that all borrowings by non-government sources will be guaranteed by the government or an acceptable agency, and that otherwise borrowings are through the government, which by implication gives its guarantee.

does not need to worry about the absolute or relative riskiness of each borrower country.[13]

Under the general loan conditions there is also the 'negative pledge agreement' whereby government and public sector borrowers agree not to pledge assets as security to any other lender without first obtaining the IBRD's agreement and/or providing it equal security. The negative pledge requirement is a powerful, and also somewhat controversial, form of protection.[14] Gavin and Rodrik wrote: '[T]here is something more than a little schizophrenic about an agency that preempts potential private lenders because they are allegedly too risk averse (a main rationale for Bank lending), then demands that its loans should be senior to any other, thereby shifting most of the risk on to private investors'.[15] Securing IBRD loans to increase the risk for private loans potentially reduces private investment.

A senior status for the Bank's loans has also been accepted by other official donors, who have at times forgiven their own borrowers' debts to protect the Bank's loan recovery record. Between 1990 and 1995, for example, US$ 4 billion worth of bilateral aid was used to pay off debts, mainly of Guyana, Nicaragua, Cameroon, Peru, and Haiti to multilateral agencies, of which those of the Bank and Fund were the largest.[16] Using a procedure called the 'fifth dimension', soft IDA money has also been used to pay off harder IBRD loans, thus allowing IBRD loans funded by the private sector seniority over IDA loans funded by donors.

---

[13] Lending terms are broadly the same for all borrowers, regardless of each country's track record (such as previous or potential defaults on bonds).

[14] The negative pledge caused trouble in the case of the very first loan – to France. The French government accused the Bank of infringing on its sovereignty but agreed to go ahead because it was persuaded that weakening of the rule would adversely affect future Bank lending. The rules were partly amended in 1993, in the case of Russian oil and gas producers who wanted U.S. Eximbank loans. The amendments were limited to pledges of up to eighteen months' worth of payments on long-term loans to mainly privately owned export enterprises.

[15] Gavin, M. and D. Rodrik, 'The World Bank in Historical Perspective', *American Economic Review* 85(2), 1995.

[16] Cited in Caufield, Catherine, *Masters of Illusion – The World Bank and the Poverty of Nations*, Henry Holt, 1996. Caufield writes: '[T]he Bank's excellent repayment record owes a great deal to the sacrifices of its rich members. In 1992 alone they reduced or forgave US$10 billion worth of debt owed to them by 40 developing countries . . .'.

Table 10. *Debt of countries with payments overdue*
($ million) in 2007

	IBRD	IDA
Cote D'Ivoire	473	1859
Liberia	152	109
Myanmar	–	776
Somalia	–	437
Sudan	–	1277
Togo	–	701
Zimbabwe	445	504
Total	1070	5663
% of outstanding loans	1.1%	5.5%

Source: Annual Report.

A further protection arises through the IBRD's large cash holdings. The cash to loan ratio increased to record levels as a result of prepayments on Asian crisis loans and remains at 25% of loans, well above the prudential minimum of about $18 billion.[17] Investment income from the cash reserve over 1998 to 2001 covered part of the administrative costs and would do so again if interest rates went back up to the average levels of the past. The IBRD could in principle operate for a long time like a foundation or a think tank, spending the income from an endowment. This has been a further important source of its operational independence and it is still seen as a vehicle for retaining independence.

As a result of its financial protection the IBRD has rarely faced crises or even difficulties from delinquent borrowers. As Table 10 shows, currently only about 1% of its total disbursed loans are in arrears, from just three countries: Cote D'Ivoire, Liberia, and Zimbabwe.[18] Arrears to the IDA were larger but still modest, with nearly 5.5% of its loans outstanding, from seven countries.

Argentina threatened to go into arrears briefly in 2002, but this was averted. The share of IBRD non-accrual debt has only once reached 4%,

---

[17] The minimum is now set at the highest six months of debt service obligations plus one half of the projected net loan disbursements for the year. The maximum is set at 50% above this level. In 2005 the level was just under the maximum.

[18] Since the first case (Nicaragua) some seventeen countries have fallen into arrears at some time or another to the IBRD, but of these fourteen were back in eligible status by 2007.

and that was in 1989, when Peru went into default. Over the past few years the arrears rate has fallen to the lowest level in decades and the Bank has been able to reduce its provisions proportionately.

RISKS, STRESS TESTS, AND THE DOOMSDAY SCENARIO

The confidence of the IBRD's lenders (the bondholders) is critical to its financial sustainability because this is a determinant of the rates at which it can lend. The bondholders are mainly interested in its loan repayment record and its guaranteed capital as their security, rather than its current profits. However, one major default could create the need to set aside provisions and reduce or eliminate profits in any one year, drawing adverse attention and conceivably affecting the Bank's credit rating. There is thus an element of insecurity, and a continuing concern, largely because of the relatively thin net income margin. There is a sense in fact that the IBRD might at times be skating on thin ice. For example, there was a brief alarm in 1997 when projections showed the potential reduction in income from lending, as a result of which the IBRD lending spread was raised to 0.75% from 0.5%, and a front-end fee of 1% was re-introduced. In that instance the projection was wrong as it could not foresee the Asian crisis.

Every year the management provides to the board a report on its uses of net income. 'Stress tests' are conducted to determine the Bank's ability to continue expanding lending in the face of a 'non-accrual shock',[19] which would reduce its equity capital. The equity to loans ratio measures how large a default could be tolerated. The most sensitive potential problem is country risk and loan concentration. Currently, the IBRD has a single borrower exposure limit of $14.5 billion per country (15% of the current loan amount).[20] A group of eight countries (China, India, Brazil, Turkey, Indonesia, Russia, Colombia, and Argentina) account for some 60% of the outstanding loans.

---

[19] The size of the hypothetical shock is determined by a portfolio risk analysis, which covers 95% of the possible outcomes – i.e., all but extreme cases. The test is whether under the supposed shock the Bank will maintain adequate equity capital to cover a loan growth of 3% per annum.

[20] The exposure limit is based on the lower of 10% of its total authorized capital and reserves and a risk measurement based on income.

The concentration risk is however low. Only China is close to the limit. The Bank's paid-in capital and reserves have been large enough to absorb 100% of the losses on the three largest borrowers simultaneously, and it is almost inconceivable that any of these major borrowers would default permanently on all its debts. So the chances of an insolvency threat (resulting in a need for a capital call) are minute. However, the loan concentration increases the potential for a large provision against losses that would affect annual book profits.[21]

The loss provision's potential effect on annual profits is illustrated by Argentina, which in 2002 had $9 billion outstanding to the IBRD and went briefly into debt service arrears of $792 million. If this amount had been deducted, current income would have been reduced by about half. Fortunately the arrears were cleared within weeks. In 2001 a general increase in risk and overdue payments by Zimbabwe and Cote D'Ivoire resulted in provisions of US$ 676 million, which cut profits by 37% for the year.[22] This created a situation where the Bank could not meet its stress-test growth target.[23] The net operating income of the Bank fell to $1.14 billion, the lowest level for many years. However, this temporary reduction did not create significant difficulties for the IBRD's longer term profitability. Projections are that net operating income will continue to come in at well over $1 billion a year for the foreseeable future.

The worst case scenario is a combination of adverse factors all acting together – low lending and interest rates (such as occurred in 2005), significantly increased loan loss provisions (such as in 2001), special payments (e.g., to the pension fund), and increased administrative cost, in any one year. Even in such a situation, however, the effect on the solvency of the IBRD would still be negligible since its equity is so strong, provided that its owners and clients are perceived to be prepared to honor their guarantees. The IBRD has never come close to the doomsday event, a solvency crisis needing a major call on its uncalled capital. If its callable capital was to be

---

[21] The rules on provisioning require that all the loans to a country are generally placed in non-accrual status if any payments are more than six months overdue. At such a time all unpaid interest and other charges accrued on loans outstanding are deducted from the IBRD's current income.

[22] See World Bank Annual Report, 2001, p. 36.

[23] It could only meet 1.6% growth compared to the stress test growth rate of 3%.

seriously weakened by repudiation by some of its major shareholders, its solvency might become precarious. But the chances of this happening are about the same as the chance of a breakup of the UN. Certainly the board of directors was safe in the assurance that reorganization costs would not make a dent in its solvency.

The more realistic lesser doomsday scenario might require a small amount of capital to be called and paid-in by member governments. The major impact of this would most likely be on the IBRD's autonomy. Considering the lengthy battles over the last two capital increases and all the recent IDA appropriations (e.g., in 1994, when the United States came within an ace of repudiating an international commitment), calling on the U.S. government for a significant proportion of its US$ 30 billion callable contribution could mobilize irresistible political opposition. The U.S. callable capital is committed under international agreement, and under the existing legislation the U.S. Treasury could release $7.6 billion without congressional approval. Congress has authorized the rest but not appropriated it, meaning that it would be possible to stall the release of further funds, and this is where the maximum punishment could be meted out.

Meeting the U.S. obligations on callable capital would not be the same as bailing out the IBRD (that is, it has no parallel to the 2008 Wall Street bank rescues) since the capital is committed as part of its initial agreed financing. The taxpaying public might not of course either understand or accept the distinction in practice, but they would probably be comfortable that the maximum exposure of the United States to the IBRD is far below the level of funding committed to support the U.S. banking system. This suggests a further reason why the Bank's solvency would not be threatened.

The level of the IBRD's equity in 2007 was in fact significantly above the highest projected requirement taking into account a partial doomsday event. The excess amount the IBRD has described as a 'risk capital buffer'. The existence of this buffer, that is to say capital in excess of foreseeable long-term requirements, has started to lead to some impatience among shareholders, and calls for a reduction that could involve some form of dividend payment or further transfers from net income. Such an event could create problems in terms of a reduction in the investment income that the IBRD has had to rely on for its profits in four out of the last ten years. But it is unlikely that the shareholders would take a step that seriously reduced income sources unless they wished to phase out the institution. In fact, shareholder signals have been mixed since they also seem favorable to allowing the IBRD to retain equity and invest it in higher risk and return assets, which would potentially increase its financial independence.[24]

Once again, therefore, the long-term strength of the IBRD's finances meant that the reorganization was able to pursue its multiple initiatives almost entirely free of concern about their financial implications. This strength will be sustained provided no exceptional shareholder demands arise.

MELTZER AND THE POLITICS OF BANK FINANCE

Other political agendas among its main shareholders could in principle reverse the years of build-up of the financial edifice. In 2000 the Meltzer Commission proposals could have drastically affected the financial future of the Bank if the United States had in fact been able to get them implemented. The principal recommendations were for the IBRD to phase out lending to middle income countries (with more than $4,000 per capita) or those with investment-grade international bond ratings, over five years, and to reduce or eliminate official assistance to countries with more than $2,500 in per capita income. This would mostly apply to Eastern Europe, and a number of countries in East Asia, the Caribbean and Latin America, and Turkey. Regional development banks, said the commission, should assume responsibility for their regions and the Bank should provide advice to them, while its direct assistance would focus only on Africa, Europe, and the Middle East until their regional banks took over. Its callable capital would be reallocated to the regional banks in line with the declining Bank portfolio.

The principal effect of these proposals would be a major downsizing of IBRD assets, liabilities, and capacity. The Bank would end up with a

---

[24] The diversification of IBRD investments into higher risk assets was one of the initiatives attributable to Robert Zoellick after assuming the presidency.

small loan portfolio. With reduced leverage the incentive to borrow and seek advice from the Bank would correspondingly shrink, and the global knowledge capacity would become less relevant.

The Bank not surprisingly objected to most of the proposals.[25] It objected to cutting lending to middle income countries on the grounds that such lending in fact could be used to leverage policy advice in richer countries, subsidize smaller loans to poorer countries, and help to finance the IDA. Another commission, Volcker-Gurria, agreed with the Bank.[26] Other commentators also dismissed parts of the Meltzer Report. For example, Nancy Birdsall, a former senior manager,[27] pointed out that even middle income countries such as Brazil, Mexico, and South Africa cannot always get long-term loans, especially counter-cyclical loans. However, the 9/11 terrorist attacks put IBRD downsizing on the back burner as the U.S. administration was now faced with the need for stronger global governance institutions.

Meltzer had proposals for the IDA as well, that grants payable to service providers should replace loans, and that all claims against the HIPC countries should be written off, subject to effective economic strategies. The United States tried to push through a proposal for 50% IDA grant financing, but the final agreement reduced this to around 20%, for social development projects, largely because the European shareholders suspected that the U.S. agenda was really to close the Bank. A broader move toward grants would have significantly reduced the long-term funding of the IDA, 50% of which consists of loan fees and repayments. Without an extra provision to close this gap, maintenance of IDA lending would have also put more pressure on the IBRD to step up transfers, which would eat into the IBRD's net income just at the time when its income sources were to be cut.

The Meltzer proposals indeed seemed to imply a long-term intention to close the Bank down, accentuating the thin ice that the Bank potentially skates on. The most carefully crafted financial protections are thus

---

[25] Letter from Wolfensohn to Professor Meltzer, dated February 28, 2000.

[26] Report of a Blue Ribbon Commission chaired by Paul Volcker and Jose Angel Gurria, April 26, 2001.

[27] Birdsall, Nancy, 'The World Bank of the Future: Victim, Villain, Global Credit Union', Carnegie Endowment for International Peace, April 13, 2000.

potentially hostage to politics and ideology. However, the Bank escaped this challenge, along with the financial pressures, and operated with impunity throughout the reorganization.

THE FINANCIAL IMPACT OF THE SHIFT TO KNOWLEDGE AND INSTITUTION BUILDING

Reduced lending and higher administration costs did not create problems for the IBRD's financial performance during the reorganization period. However, the shift from large infrastructure and policy-based loans toward institution-building, typically based on smaller, technical assistance–type loans and advisory services, might mean an increased vulnerability in the long term. In the past the contribution of different products to the Bank's profitability was not widely known or regarded as a significant issue. The Bank's infrastructure chief at a 'Corporate Day' in 2000 surprised participants with a presentation showing that the debate about knowledge services was ignoring the bottom line, and that infrastructure projects underpinned the banks earnings. Eighty percent of the staff outside the infrastructure sector, he reported, produced only 20% of the Bank's net income.

From the 1990s the average size of a loan from the Bank has fallen from about $90 million to about $80 million. With the largest loans average processing and management costs could be less than 1% of the loan value, compared to net income on the loan of 0.5 to 0.75% of loan value per annum. But, at the other extreme, small, labor-intensive loans, usually related to knowledge and capacity-building, may cost between 5 and 20% of the loan value, and yield an operating loss to the institution.

The potential vulnerability created by the switch to knowledge products is increased because the Bank's procedures do not require direct comparison of the administrative costs and revenues of each of its loans, so managers do not have guidelines on how much can be spent on a particular project consistent with profitability.[28] The cost of preparing

---

[28] The Bank spends about $400,000 to 500,000 on loan preparation, and altogether more than $1.5 million on preparation and management over the life of a typical project. The average direct costs of producing a formal advisory report are around $150,000, while the total including an overhead factor would be nearly US$400,000.

and managing a loan is intended to be covered, on average, by the margin between lending rates and funding cost, or in the case of IDA by an administration fee, so the financial income from a project has never been an issue of concern. However, from a corporate standpoint, the profit margin on a loan is important and it varies greatly, with small institution-building projects being expensive in relation to loan size.

A way to pay for the shift from loans to knowledge services would be to charge fees. The Bank has earned service fee income, recently running at around $200 million per annum, but most of the fees are for managing trust funds, pensions, and providing services to other institutions of the Bank Group and outside (e.g., asset management services to central banks). Only a tiny amount, around $5 million per annum, has been revenue received for direct country advisory work, in places such as Saudi Arabia and the Gulf States, a minute fraction of the IBRD's administrative costs. Thus the Bank does not have a ready market for fee-based knowledge services. Even if front-end fees, such as were introduced in 1998 to cover preparation costs, were regarded as fee income, they would still cover less than a fifth of the value of the IBRD's administrative costs, and in any case they are not payment for advice per se.

What could happen if the trend to small projects continued? Could the IBRD convert itself, in the case of serious deficits in loan income, into a foundation funded by an endowment? The yield on its liquid assets would need to be high enough to pay for rising administrative costs and preserve the real value of its reserves.[29] Otherwise, the real value of assets would fall steadily, year by year. This combination of factors would result in the gradual decline of the institution, or its transformation into a UN-style agency, or a fund similar to the IDA. The knowledge bank idea clearly creates some potential for this scenario. However, current trends suggest that large-scale lending will recover.

---

[29] There was a fall in interest rates on liquid assets from over 4% in 2001–2002 to 3%, which reduced investment income to the lowest level since the 1980s. Further falls in interest rates in 2002–2004 brought the average yield down from 3.2% to 1.8%, reducing investment income further.

IMPLICATIONS OF FINANCIAL STABILITY

The basic financial model has stood the test of time. Whereas current profitability may be at risk in abnormal circumstances, solvency and liquidity are not in danger in any feasible scenario unless shareholder action changes the underlying parameters. Because of the gold-plating of the Bank's finances, especially through the shareholder guarantees and the sovereign borrower guarantees, the model easily weathered the storm of the reorganization and forecasts of doom have proved wrong, even with the unplanned switch to knowledge products.

The system provided the stability and the financial underpinning needed to sustain, and pay for, the adventurism of the Strategic Compact. The solidity of the Bank's finances has, however, been both a blessing and a curse, on the one hand helping to preserve an institution in the face of outside threats, and on the other allowing it a loosely defined corporate strategy, high overheads, and expensive agencies of governance. This is a situation with potential for 'moral hazard' – whereby protection encourages more risky behavior – and it is an underlying factor in the loose management of the reform program.

9

Why Did the Reforms Fail?

RECENT THOUGHTS ON REORGANIZATION

In the 1980s and 1990s, corporate re-engineering was a significant factor in corporate America, but many of its advocates revised their ideas. Michael Hammer, perhaps the tsar of all organizational reformers, in the second edition of *Reengineering the Corporation*[1] wrote: '[P]erhaps predictably, reengineering quickly became a bandwagon that everyone tried to jump on; but, problematically not everyone knew precisely what it was he or she was getting involved in'. 'Give me re-engineering and give it to me fast' was the command from many uninformed chief executives. This was a situation ripe for disaster. Re-engineering came to be viewed as an easy panacea that the CEO can simply delegate.[2] John Kotter said, later on: '[T]he perception that large organizations are filled with recalcitrant middle managers who resist all change is not only unfair but untrue'.[3]

Second thoughts were already abroad as the Bank launched its own re-engineering revolution, but public organizations and their overseers tend to follow rather than lead with regard to ideas about corporate efficiency, effectiveness, and change, and the Bank was a follower.

[1] Hammer, Michael and James Champy, *Reengineering the Corporation; a Manifesto for the Business Revolution*, Harper Collins, 2001.
[2] The organization theorist, Charles Handy, said in a similar vein: '[O]ne cannot eliminate bureaucracy by decimation, by firing people or cutting inputs, or by top down demands for reform'. Charles Handy, *Understanding Organizations*, Penguin, 1983.
[3] Kotter, John P., 'Leading Change; Why Transformation Efforts Fail', *Harvard Business Review on Change*, 1998.

WHAT WENT WRONG?

There were serious problems in nearly all the dimensions of the Bank's reorganization program. The re-engineering of the organization was semi-chaotic, poorly designed and managed, and had to be partially reversed, largely failing to meet its objectives of increasing the efficiency of skill usage and only partly increasing focus at the country level. The re-skilling of the workforce was a failure in that it was poorly conceived, did not accurately forecast skill needs, and cut out of the organization existing skills that were needed. The shift in the Bank's product line moved ahead but in an opportunistic manner without a clear strategy, and it was not pro-poor. Nor was the Bank's comparative advantage determined between the new knowledge bank and the old lending bank. The claimed large increase in quality of the Banks products was questionable and the quality control infrastructure was not properly planned and is at risk of being dysfunctional. The information systems were poorly implemented. The partial merger of the Bank and the IFC was not properly thought through and was largely reversed. The finance area managed to avoid major disruption because it was not a central part of the reforms, and indeed the strength of the Bank's finances provided an underpinning for its adventures elsewhere.

Modest achievements (such as further decentralization, the exploitation of information technology, the introduction of participatory approaches, the strengthening of issue advocacy, and the diversification of financial products) were outweighed by the mistakes due to simultaneous, badly planned change in many areas at once – the *redefinition of objectives* toward the knowledge bank, the *matrix*, the *networks*, the *internal market*, the *task charging system*, the *decentralization*, the *budget cuts*, the *redundancies*, the *skill mix restructuring*, the *de-layering and re-grading*, the new *information system*, and the *budgeting system*. In a recent management book,[4] Gary Prusak, a corporate consultant and one of the Bank's change advisers, echoed the view that many corporate re-engineerings took on too much change at once. He thought that

---

[4] Davenport, Thomas H., Laurence Prusak, and H. James Wilson, *What's the Big Idea? Creating and Capitalizing on the Best New Management Thinking?*, Harvard Business School Press, April 2003.

approaches that worked but were not dramatic should be better persevered with. Such a view applied, par excellence, at the Bank.

How could such a deplorable process have been allowed to proceed?

Is Bank Assistance to Developing Countries Doomed to Ineffectiveness?

The question raised at the start of this study was whether successful aid for development is possible. If the concept of external aid is flawed, then the reorganization of an aid institution will never succeed in delivering high-quality projects and successful poverty alleviation. If, for example, development necessitates the mobilization of internal capacity – cultural, social, and economic – and not external aid, then the efforts of external agencies, especially those subject to external agendas, are wasted. Thus the Bank, and other institutions that are particularly driven by such agendas, are simply not the right vehicles. However, as we argued before, aid-pessimism at this depth ignores, amongst other things, external assistance successes that have occurred, and it also ignores the widely justifiable and enormous task of producing global public goods that has increasingly featured in the Bank's assistance efforts. Thus, this is an extremist position that may be reasonably set aside in preference for our focus on the organizational factors.

Was it the Weak and Obstructionist Management and Staff?

The main premise of the 1990s reforms, and those that preceded and succeeded them, has been that there were deficiencies in the workforce – that is, lack of the right skills, lack of innovativeness, inappropriate attitudes, and, latterly, possibly even corrupt behavior. In addition, managers were not interested in managing, or they were not sufficiently engaged that they could successfully implement reforms. Claire Short, the British minister of overseas development, famously warned in September 2001 of the employee fifth column of 'reactionary forces at work' that were trying to undermine the excellence of Wolfensohn's re-organizational initiatives.

The inadequacies of the reform process could indeed be regarded as the direct responsibility of the management and staff. Once the Strategic Compact had been approved by the board of executive directors, responsibility was passed rapidly down the chain of command. Thus the failures of the management matrix and strategic staffing were to an extent failures by senior managers whose jobs it was to put together the detailed designs and implement them. The middle management and rank-and-file staff in their turn were those whose skills, team spirit, and cooperation were needed to make the new systems work, but who were at times resentful, mistrustful, or unable to work as teams, or they were inadequately innovative.

However, while management and staff cannot be absolved from responsibility, for many reasons they are not likely to be the principal actors in the failure of the reforms. Perhaps one of the most suggestive pieces of evidence for this is that major dips in quality seem to be associated with organizational disruption, while rising quality seems to have been associated with stability, when the employees of the institution have been able to operate in a more rational and coherent work environment. Thus organizational disruptions damaged performance by placing unreasonable pressures on management and employees. As regards the rank-and-file, tests prior to the reorganization revealed results-driven personalities quite appropriate to dealing with a complex environment. It was more the institution that imposed certain behavior than individuals determining institutional behavior, and the new environment imposed further, exceptional demands on its individual members that constrained their ability to deliver results.

One illustration of the constraints on coherent operations management is the need to raise funds. The Bank states that 'trust funds are key vehicles for leveraging the World Bank's resources toward pursuing its core objectives of poverty reduction and sustainable growth, and achieving the Millennium Development Goals'.[5] Currently it holds about $11 billion in trust.[6] A special department handles

[5] 'Trust Fund Annual Report', World Bank, 2006.
[6] In 6,000 separate trust fund accounts, of which about 900 are active programs.

thousands of applications a year and its costs are only partially covered.[7] Most of the funds are specialized,[8] but a proportion, around $400 million, equivalent to about 20% of administrative costs, is for mainstream work such as loan preparation.[9] In 1996 the task force on multilateral development banks warned about the dysfunctional growth of outside funding of Bank operations.[10] A significant part of project officers' time is spent raising operational funds to do their work, and many of the funds are also managed from outside by recipient governments even though the actual work is coordinated by the Bank, while the complex oversight needs create a potential for mismanagement.[11]

The pressures on the management and staff were also applied within a perverse incentive environment. The employees could not act both as first responders and policy negotiators. Simplification was urged but not rewarded. Team-building was the aim, but the matrix emasculated the teams. The information bureaucracy impeded the flow of information. Time recording prevented efficient use of time. De-layering did not increase accountability and discouraged hard work. Projects were to be simplified but became relentlessly more complicated. Improved quality was urged but time had to be diverted to fund raising and intensifying controls.

---

[7] Costs are 10 to 15% of the fund value for the smaller funds.

[8] For debt reduction, health, the environment, consultancy services, and other needs.

[9] Of these, the Japanese PHRD fund is the largest single fund. One source of operational funding, the Consultant Trust Fund (CTF), supported by twenty-six donor countries, expanded from $2 million in 1986 to a peak of $75 million in 1998 in support of more than 1,000 activities, before falling back to about $50 million per annum because of freezing of some funds when incidences of fraud were discovered.

[10] *Serving a Changing World, Report of the Task Force on Multilateral Development Banks*, IMF/World Bank Development Committee, 1996, p. 21. The report stated: '[W]hen too many conditions are attached these trust funds can complicate the application of institutional priorities'.

[11] In 2000 three employees were fired and the Bank had to reimburse about $450,000 to Sweden and bar seven Swedish firms, one Dutch firm, and two individuals from future business. An international conference with donors in Paris in January 2002 started to try to rationalize the system, and the Bank introduced new rules after strenuous efforts to simplify, streamline, and integrate just one part of the trust fund system, the small funds provided by bilateral agencies.

While middle management and staff have to share some responsibility for the failure of reform, they were essentially passive within a system of unreasonable burdens that distracted attention from the important work, and flawed strategic judgments made elsewhere, responding to rather than initiating the changes.

Unworkable Ideas and Management Fads?

A second possible explanation is that the new systems were inherently unworkable, being based on ill-thought-out ideas of an ephemeral nature, or management fads.

The Bank's Staff Association thought that this was the case, that the Bank was adopting changes not because they were a proper fit for the Bank but because other organizations were currently attempting them.[12] A small group of reformers who spoke mainly to each other and treated outside views with increasing skepticism became locked into decisions that had been endorsed at the top and were difficult to reverse without damage to careers. In other words, a degree of 'group-think' had set in.[13] Managers were not prepared to risk opposing the direction taken. Wolfensohn also seemed anxious to be part of, or a key player in, a global business reform movement. The drive to new ideas became to some extent an end in itself. But many of the ideas had been adopted and discarded elsewhere.

The Economist in 1992[14] reported that 75% of those companies downsizing found that financial performance did not increase, and 67% found no improvement in productivity. Likewise, a study conducted by McKinsey and Company found that two-thirds of the thirty

---

[12] Staff Association newsletter, June–July 2001.

[13] The phenomenon of 'groupthink' occurs in closed or exclusive teams. Groupthink leads to poor judgment and bad decisions under peer pressure to conform, supported by the perception of safety in numbers and the implicit rejection of uninitiated outsiders. Group pressures lead to a deterioration of 'mental efficiency, reality testing, and moral judgment' (p. 9). A group is especially vulnerable to groupthink when its members are similar in background, when the group is insulated from outside opinions, and when there are no clear rules for decision making. See Janis, Irving L., *Victims of Groupthink*, Houghton Mifflin, 1972.

[14] 'The Cracks in Quality', *The Economist*, April 18, 1992, pp. 67–68; and 'The Straining of Quality', *The Economist*, January 14, 1995, pp. 55–56.

total quality management programs it examined had stalled or fallen short of yielding meaningful improvements.[15] Many of the other ideas of the 1980s met a similar fate. A survey carried out in 1988 showed that 90% of Fortune 500 companies had adopted the quality circles approach in the early 1980s, but had abandoned them by 1987.[16] The total quality management movement similarly reached its peak in 1993 and thereafter declined. Business process re-engineering cases rose from almost zero in 1992 to a peak in 1995 and fell rapidly back over the next five years. Prusak characterized Hammer's book on re-engineering as 'extravagant claims unsupported by fact'.[17]

The organizational change ideas generated in the 1980s and 1990s by the business school and consulting sectors[18] were partly new and partly just restatements of old ideas. Eileen Shapiro, a noted management consultant, was a skeptical observer of the restructuring efforts in the private sector. In 1996 she wrote: '[Y]ou can if you wish flatten your pyramid, become a horizontal organization, and eliminate hierarchy from your company. You can empower your people . . . commit to total customer satisfaction, open your environment and transform your culture. You can do the vision thing, write a mission statement, and put together a strategic plan. You can . . . shift your paradigms and become a learning organization. You can devote to total quality management. Or you can re-engineer your corporation. By themselves these ideas may be perfectly reasonable – doing them all at once in a shallow or

[15] *The Wall Street Journal* ran several reports on the issue. For example: '"Total Quality Is Termed Only Partial Success' (October 1991) cited the McKinsey study of 30 quality programs and studies of 584 companies by Ernst & Young and the American Quality Foundation. In May 1992, under the title 'Quality Programs Show Shoddy Results', it cited an ADL survey of 500 manufacturing and service companies. An article in July 1993 was entitled 'Many Companies Try Management Fads, Only to See Them Flop'.

[16] The life cycle of management ideas has been researched by L. J. Ponzi and M. Koenig. For example, see 'Knowledge Management: Another Management Fad?', *Information Research* 8(1), October 2002.

[17] Davenport, Thomas H., Laurence Prusak, and H. James Wilson, *What's the Big Idea? Creating and Capitalizing on the Best New Management Thinking*, Harvard Business School Press, April 2003, p. 107.

[18] Davenport, Prusak, and Wilson identified 680 separate books on change management, plus thousands of articles. Management authors often bewailed their rapid obsolescence (reflected in low second-hand prices on EBay) compared to textbooks in economics, sociology, and psychology. Davenport et al. measured the popularity of an idea by a 'bibliometric estimate' based on citations in professional journals.

vacuous manner is the problem'.[19] These doubts were already being aired in the industry before the Bank's reorganization started. There was an advantage in being able to see what had become of some of the earlier efforts, but that advantage was not used.

An Inherently Unmanageable Institution?

It is not easy to run public organizations, and to an extent the causes of the failure of the Bank's reforms were inherent in the nature of public organizations.

Public organization effectiveness has been specially studied within the broad body of organizational theory.[20] Such organizations produce diverse products and services, but they also have certain common features that distinguish them from private organizations. They face regulations, political pressures, and oversight authorities, and they are expected to meet relatively high expectations of transparency and accountability. They also often face multiple and ambiguous goals. The need for political endorsement leads to more complexity and outside interference. Processes are more formal and standardized, and they tend to be behind the curve in implementing change, obliged to use ideas borrowed from outside. Many of the difficulties are inherent and cannot be eradicated, only negotiated with. So effectiveness is always going to be a difficult target.

The Bank faces multiple and ambiguous goals, multiple principals, and imperfect instruments. Among its difficulties may be confusion between the role of an 'action' and a 'political' organization.[21] While as an action type it must deal in operational solutions, efficiency, and deadlines, as a political type it must set norms, air issues, discuss, and cooperate. Improper alignment of an action organization with advocacy work, or a political organization with operations, is likely to be dysfunctional. So there may be some justification in the conclusion that the

---

[19] Eileen Shapiro, *Fad-Surfing in the Boardroom*, Perseus, 1996.

[20] See, e.g., Rainey, Hal. G, *Understanding and Managing Public Organizations*, Jossey-Bass, 1997 and 2003. Rainey, of the University of Georgia, and others have conducted research into high-performance public organizations.

[21] See Bergeson, Helge and Leiv Lunde, eds., *Dinosaurs or Dynamos?: The United Nations and the World Bank at the Turn of the Century*, Earthscan, 2000.

reforms could never meet high expectations, and that possibly they achieved an adequate result given this constraint.

The history of public organization theory in the United States has in fact been largely a story of dysfunction. Just as the Bank came under critical scrutiny, the Reagan presidency saw a broad attack from conservatives on the U.S. public sector as wasteful and dysfunctional. In 1989 the Volcker Commission[22] reported a crisis in the U.S. public service. This led eventually to the 'Reinventing Government' initiative, or National Performance Review, launched in 1993. It proposed a 12% cut in federal staff over five years. The inspiration for this initiative was the idea of an 'entrepreneurial government'. Osborne and Gaebler, the authors of an influential book on government,[23] believed that there was too much centralization, too many standardized rules and processes, and too little flexibility. Reinvention lay in turning government workers loose to do what they knew how to do best. 'The *people* who work in government are not the problem' they said; 'the *systems* in which they work are the problem'.

The lack of a clear prescription makes it is necessary to be circumspect in deciding whether the Bank and other public organizations are or are not effective. It cannot be held to the same standards as a private corporation, and it has to be expected that there would be problems and complications as it negotiates its way through the maze of conflicting pressures and objectives usually put in place by those who criticize its inability to act effectively.

However, to agree that public organizations are difficult to manage does not imply that they cannot be improved. Certain basic

---

[22] 'Leadership for America; Rebuilding the Public Service', The Report of The National Commission on the Public Service, Washington, DC, 1989.

[23] Osborne, David and Ted Gaebler, *Reinventing Government: How the Entrepreneurial Spirit Is Transforming the Public Sector*, Addison-Wesley, 1992. This was a guidance text for the reinventing government initiative. The authors proclaimed ten user-friendly principles for successful change: steering rather than rowing; empowering instead of merely delivering services; encouraging competition rather than monopoly; a focus on missions more than rules; funding outcomes rather than inputs; focusing on the needs of customers, not the bureaucracy; concentrating on earning, not just spending; investing in preventing problems rather than seeking to cure them; decentralizing authority; and leveraging the marketplace instead of creating public programs.

requirements need to be met: The public organization needs a set of objectives that are as clear as possible, good leadership, aligned capacity, and a work environment that provides defined and understood tasks. This is the ideal. Is there any reason to conclude that the 1990s reforms of the Bank could not have reasonably achieved these basic expectations? If it is reasonable to suppose that they could have been met, then it cannot be concluded that, simply because the Bank was a public organization, little could be done. Hence this is not a good explanation for the results.

Top Management Was Out of the Picture?

Another explanation for the reform failure lies with those responsible for managing the institution's strategy and direction – that is, the top layer of management. The managing directors seemed to have distanced themselves from the implementation of the reorganization and passed responsibility down the hierarchy. They were not interested in the Cost Effectiveness Review. The president himself seemed to utter warnings and exhortations while he concerned himself with high-profile external public events rather than delivering successful internal changes. Internal dissatisfaction with leadership performance developed through the organization period and peaked in 2001, the year of the 'MENA letter'. In response to the criticism he finally set up a formal management committee composed of the managing directors, Ramphela Mamphele, Jeffrey Goldstein, Peter Woicke, and Shengman Zhang. One of their tasks was to head up strategy in the main operational areas. However, the managing directors were notable in having almost no operational experience at that time with which to pronounce on strategy in the Bank, as the MENA letter had opined.

The strategy process was in fact a good illustration of weak implementation of organizational change at the top. The process was introduced by Wolfensohn, with monthly 'Corporate Days' and an annual 'strategic forum' (or 'implementation forum') normally attended by the president and top management. The principal strategy document considered by the annual forum was the 'Strategic Framework Paper', which led into a shorter 'Strategic Directions Paper', which was later renamed the 'Strategy Update Paper'. The strategy papers were discussed at the board in March and April each year. To one top manager the new system was at first a revelation, effectively replacing the informal one-on-one discussions that past presidents had had with top management. But it was not delivered properly. Instead of systematic documents integrating the areas of strategy – that is, the intended *outputs* an organization will deliver, the types of *inputs* that it will use, and its required *organizational structure*,[24] the strategy papers were more vehicles for rhetorical statements about progress. It was unclear what role they were supposed to play.

The 'Strategy Update Paper' produced in 2001 at the most acute final phase of the reorganization stated: '[T]he past year has seen significant improvement in our management procedures with the management committee and in management-staff cohesion', and 'the management committee is working to ensure that corporate priorities are aligned with country programs and tradeoffs are managed'. It went on: '[W]e would reaffirm the centrality of the CAS (country assistance strategy) as the unit of account for the Bank's business, focusing on reducing poverty and promoting sustainable development; recognize that the CAS process involves the selection of sectoral and economic priorities from Bank economic and sector strategy and instrument menus, subject to agreed performance standards; require strict adherence to specific safeguard policies that relate third party risks and business policies; and, establish credible systems for compliance monitoring which are linked to institutional policy-making functions and individual performance evaluations. At the same time we would establish just-in-time resolutions procedures ... whereby staff can get quick hearings and decisions on the interpretation of policy' (p. 17).

The strategic framework was described by one internal skeptic as 'confused, meaningless and stuffed with every cliché that has been uttered in the last two years. ... With all these good things we are going to do it is not clear how we will organize to do them (especially given

---

[24] See Collis, David and Cynthia Montgomerie, 'Creating Corporate Advantage', in *On Corporate Strategy*, Harvard Business Review (paperback), 1999.

the underlying theme of doing it all cheaply)'. Another wrote: 'I believe that it is about time that senior management tried to connect to reality; or is this something that middle management is trying to avert at all costs by producing such strange documents?'

Another Strategy Update[25] was a complicated account of current developments, seemed to confuse means and ends, and constantly restated objectives rather than analyzing choices. 'Teams from across the Bank' stated the paper, 'are working to increase the impact of capacity enhancement components embedded in CASs, ESW (economic and sector work), and projects, and also to enhance the impact of dedicated skills building, knowledge sharing and capacity enhancement activities', to produce an 'integrated package of development services'. Furthermore, it claimed that it 'enabled the Bank to identify a series of cross-cutting issues that needed to be addressed to remove institutional impediments to implementation'. To put all this together, it explained, 'cross-cutting teams of managers brainstormed to map recommendations and to assemble road maps and timetables to tackle these questions: building on work already under way'.

The board had difficulties in understanding the paper.[26] Despite its standard expressions of 'welcome', 'full support', 'commendation', and references to 'excellent presentation', the directors said that they could not find anything on a number of important issues, such as the trade-off between lending and knowledge services, the decline of lending alongside the scaling up of output, the rationale for the selected (seven) areas of focus, and the problems of the matrix management system. There was doubt expressed about the true value of the analytical studies. There were also questions about how finance was being allocated, the cost effectiveness of each outcome in relation to its financial allocation, the savings resulting from the elimination of activities, fewer loans, and cost sharing by countries. There were questions about the income projections in relation to administrative costs. These issues were all the bread and butter of corporate strategy.

[25] 'Strategy Update Paper', World Bank, 2004–2006, p. 10.
[26] April 2003 discussion of the 2004–2006 Strategic Update Paper.

The errant corporate strategy process was one illustration of a leadership and top management that were insufficiently engaged in, and had inadequate understanding of, the difficult issues of reforming a complex, large-scale organization with multiple objectives. The disorganization of the top management is a further explanation for the failure of the reorganization to achieve its aims.

Governance – The Absent Presence in the Reorganization

There are thus a number of partial explanations for the failure of the reforms. Some, such as the capacity of management, are proximate explanations and some, such as the inherent unmanageability of an organization as complex as the Bank, are more fundamental and long term. However, there is one issue that has not been addressed and which was not addressed as part of the Strategic Compact proposals or during the reorganization itself. This was the role of the principals of the organization, that is, the board of executive directors that was a party to the Strategic Compact. Where was the board of directors, the stewards of the Bank, while the flawed process unfolded?

Part II of this study has looked at the organizational changes that took place within the diagnostic boundaries set by the Strategic Compact. In setting the boundaries, the Compact effectively excluded a dimension of the Bank's organization system and thereby limited the diagnosis and proposed solutions. Part III of the study goes outside these boundaries and looks at the way the Bank is run from a broader perspective, to see how far such a perspective can provide better explanations. This broader perspective involves the organs of governance of the institution, that is, its board and its leadership.

Responsibility for the reorganization belonged to those who were putting on the pressure or channeling the pressure for the Bank to make changes. Responsibility for failures of the process must also at least partly lie with those same entities. The implication of the association between the 1987 disruption and the decline in product quality, and the possibly similar association between the 1990s reforms and the most recent drop in quality, and from simple observation, is that outside pressure, including shareholder pressure, could have a significant adverse effect on internal quality. If the top management were disengaged, then the board was even more so. The semi-annual progress reports to the board were not used as opportunities to systematically re-engage with the reorganization's progress and new resource requirements. An element of the board, albeit a small one, thought that the chaos that ensued during the reorganization was quite a justifiable way of shaking the institution out of its presumed complacency. How far the stewards, that is, the principals, could be held to account for the reform failures is clearly of considerable importance.

PART III

TOWARD REAL REFORM: THE GOVERNANCE AGENDA

10

The Governors and the Directors

SHOULD GOVERNANCE HAVE BEEN
A PART OF THE REORGANIZATION?

The extent of the deficiencies of the reorganization raises questions about the stewardship of the Bank. Should the governors and the directors have exercised greater control over events? To what extent were they responsible for the missteps? To what extent were their actions consistent with their fiduciary obligations? What are the implications of the style of governance for getting the organization on to a satisfactory path toward effectiveness?

The Strategic Compact was drawn up between the president and the board of executive directors. As we have seen, it was not a carefully planned initiative, but originated as a way of getting the board to increase the budget and was then broadened out into a reform program. Within this reform program, the critical dimension that was not 'on the table' was governance itself. Understandably, the Compact did not require its signatories to subject themselves to its discipline. Neither the board of directors nor its secretariat was expected to change processes or to reduce expenditure. In fact, the life of the board seemed to remain unaffected by the churning that was taking place in the organization over which it had oversight, despite the fact that the board members worked every day in the same building as the people over whom they had responsibility.

The fact that the Strategic Compact did not address the Bank's own governance meant that it was, rather, looking down inside the organization to identify the problems and find the solutions, that is, looking to the organization's management and employees – structure, capacities, and attitudes. In so doing it avoided issues that were at that time very much on the Bank's own agenda, and very topical in the institutional economics that the Bank was increasingly espousing to formulate its own vision of development.

One question that institutional economics asks is how the relationship of principals (owners) and agents (management) can be aligned for maximum organizational effectiveness – for example, how to ensure the right structure and the right information for shareholders to get effective oversight of the managers. To reduce 'agency costs', the objectives, incentives, and information of both owners and managers need to be aligned, and this is more difficult when an organization is subject to multiple principals with differing political and economic agendas, and if shareholders are democratic governments, then their own agendas can change.[1] In such cases the best structure may not be identifiable, but instead there may be a need to continually redefine it.

The Bank has a strong corporate governance advisory capacity with numerous specialists advising on how to structure organizations. In particular, it has advised on the governance of public organizations. A relatively early example was a paper by R. Muir and J. Saba.[2] 'Clarifying the relationship between State Enterprise managers and owners', they wrote, 'is one of the most fundamental issues for the State as owner of the corporation to address'. 'The key issue is how the shareholders – the principals – can achieve efficiency, profitability and accountability while also permitting the managers – the agent – the necessary degree of autonomy to operate the corporation in a competitive market environment'. The authors were referring to enterprises, not to development organizations, but much of what they said has general application. Another Bank paper stressed symmetry of information to prevent management taking advantage of their position to set agendas and standards

---

[1] See Spiller, P. T., 'Politicians, Interest Groups, and Regulators; a Multiple Principles Agency Theory of Regulation, or "Let Them Be Bribed"', *Journal of Law and Economics* 33: 65–101, 1990.

[2] Muir, R. and J. Saba, 'Improving State Enterprise Performance', World Bank Technical Paper 306, 1995, Chapter 2.

that are to their own advantage. Non-availability of information, it stated, creates dysfunctional behavior on both sides.[3]

The issue of corporate governance assumed a place of sufficient importance in the Bank's agenda following the Asian economic crisis that a special Memorandum of Understanding was signed between the heads of the Bank and the OECD in June 1999.[4] Although it was referring mainly to private organizations, some of its assertions are of relevance here. Annex 4 of the memorandum, for example, states that 'a board's ability to successfully discharge its fiduciary obligations hinges upon having a core group of professionally acclaimed independent directors'. They should be 'of sufficient caliber that their views will carry significant weight on the board regardless of whether or not the chairman is an elective or nominative director'.[5] Effectiveness also depends on the quality of information. Key information is often obscured by agenda papers that are either too thin or strategically too voluminous. To avoid asymmetries of information and difficulties of monitoring, board members and audit committees should be well versed in areas such as business law, accounting, marketing, finance, or production, and should interact with the company's chief financial officers. Furthermore, the acid test of the balance of any board, it said, is whether it can, when the chips are down, stand up to the CEO and, if necessary, replace him.

It is not surprising that the reform agreement between the Bank's board of directors and the chief executive did not focus on reform of the signatories themselves, since the agreement presupposed that the problems lay elsewhere. But, given the long-term nature of the Bank's organizational difficulties, and the importance of regular re-definition of the governance arrangements of a complex public organization, the fact that a major reform exercise ignored this key aspect of organizational effectiveness suggests that it could only provide a partial solution, at best. Serious reform would need to consider this critical factor.

[3] Shirley, Mary and L. Xu, 'The Empirical Effects of Performance Contracts', Policy Research Working Paper No. 1919, World Bank, May 1998.

[4] 'Corporate Governance – A Framework for Implementation', Bank/OECD Memorandum of Understanding, World Bank, June 1999.

[5] Ibid., pp. 29–30.

THE BANK'S SYSTEM OF GOVERNANCE

Following on from the introduction to the Bank's governance in Chapter 1, Figure 10 shows the way the Bank's governance, in its broadest interpretation, is structured. It includes various categories of shareholders and borrowers, debt holders, outside groups, and client governments that also have a stake. The system involves multiple stakeholders and multiple objectives. This is complicated further by the lack of general unanimity on what constitutes a good 'development product'.

The board of executive directors, which is the central organ of governance, is located between the top management and the board of governors, who are heads of parent ministries representing shareholder countries. This is nominally a two-tier system in which a supervisory board monitors a management board. However, it is unlike the two-tier system that is well established in some European countries because there is no clear separation of powers. Instead, the Bank's governors have delegated most of their powers back to the directors, while frequently the top management consults directly with the governors, especially the U.S. Treasury. Furthermore, the nature of the Bank as a

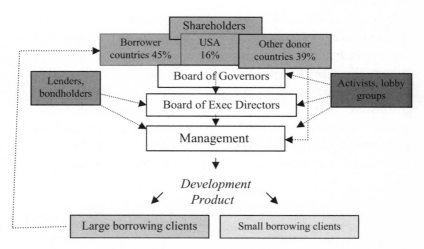

Figure 10. The governance structure of the Bank.

mutual association means that some of its clients themselves have influence over the oversight bodies.

Figure 10 shows the voting share distribution of the IBRD. The IDA's distribution is slightly different, but the overall architecture of oversight applies to both. The multiple objectives of the Bank as a whole are also reflected in de facto oversight by the bondholders and the political activists. The Bank, and especially the IBRD, therefore has partly private and partly public oversight, and tries to match the private good (protecting commercial lending interests) with the public good (developing the world) and special interests (e.g., the foreign and domestic policies of powerful shareholders). The position of the board of directors in these circumstances is confused and becomes vulnerable to the demands of one or a group of powerful shareholders or political interests with a determined agenda, or multiple and conflicting agendas.

The principals represent different interest blocks, and within each block there are sub-blocks. The 'part 1' donor countries, including the United States, are the principal shareholders. The influence and special interests of the United States have given it the informal position of a 'G1'. The United States holds 16% of the shares while the other donor countries hold 39%. Thus the donor countries altogether hold 55%, and out of this group, five countries, the G5 (United States, UK, Japan, France, and Germany), hold 37% and have their own directors on the board. The U.S. shareholding has fallen steadily over time as it has reduced its financial commitment, but it has obtained a proportionate reduction in the percent of votes required to maintain a veto power over constitutional changes.

The other shareholders, the 'part 2 countries' with 45% of the shares (partly unpaid and not taken up[6]), combine the roles of both owners and clients. The block is divided into at least two sub-blocks (large and small) because major borrowers such as China, India, and Turkey have greater influence over the Bank's policies (dotted line in Figure 10) than minor clients such as Zambia, Nepal, or Nicaragua. The latter are

---

[6]   Unpaid subscriptions result in the actual votes of the 'part 2' countries being below their actual entitlement.

hard-pressed to have their interests addressed unless special interests are involved, as in the cases of Kosovo, Bosnia, East Timor, and the West Bank. Those small borrowers that are poor, non-strategic, and the target of unfavorable major shareholder attention are at a special disadvantage.

Shareholder voting power has since the foundation of the Bank been based on, first, a 'basic vote' and, second, a quota based on GDP, the level of reserves and foreign trade levels. Currently seven smaller European countries with 3% of the world GDP hold about the same voting power as seven Asian countries with 24% of the world GDP, measured according to purchasing power. On this measure the OECD countries as a whole hold 62% of the votes with 52% of the world GDP. For several years discussions have ensued on how to extend the 'voice' of the poorer and disenfranchised shareholders and to redistribute votes.

Another block is the lenders. The views of the lending community have been paramount from the start. However, the stringent requirements originally imposed by the lenders have relaxed over time, and if the IDA expands relative to the IBRD, this will in the long run reduce the influence of the lenders and increase that of the shareholders. In the meantime, however, a triple-A IBRD bond rating remains essential.

Finally, there are the independent NGO activist groups. While their power is informal, they may be regarded as a 'principal' in that, since the 1980s, they have gained increasing leverage over the main shareholders, especially the United States, in setting the development agenda. NGO influence is essentially U.S.-based (e.g., such groups as the Sierra Club and Jubilee 2000). Some NGOs tend to be self-selected, and this has started to lead to increasing demands for accountability of the NGOs themselves, and a possible waning of influence as some issues, like the Bank's environmental accountability, have been partly addressed.[7]

The IBRD faces complex governance. If it rid itself of the pressures of satisfying its lenders, it might have a better chance of aligning its

---

[7]   Larry Summers, the U.S. Treasury secretary under Bill Clinton, thought that the Bank, having striven to accommodate the critics, was being excessively influenced by unelected groups.

interests with its shareholders, critics, and clients. If it aligned itself more with the interests of the lenders, it would get some insulation from the demands of political oversight, but then it would pay the price of more complex objectives. If it aligned itself too closely with the political interests of its major shareholders, it might risk detaching itself from the ideal of assistance to clients in most need and run into opposition from the NGOs. If it aligns itself too closely with the borrowers, it risks upsetting major shareholder agendas. If it focuses on its own survival as an institution, it incurs the opposition of all.

Scandizzo at the EIB wrote similarly[8]:'[L]ack of definition of shareholder rights on one side and covert vesting of rights on to management and "key" shareholders on the other, may have helped to free the organization from the encumbrance of multilateral controls and costly active monitoring. At the same time lower monitoring costs may be more than counterbalanced by high costs of lobbying, public relations and the management of periodic reorganizations and related bureaucratic crises'.

With such unclear arrangements effective action by the principals is constrained and would justify regular reviews of the governance arrangements to ensure the continuing effectiveness of the institution.

EXTERNAL PRESSURE: THE ROLE OF THE U.S. SHAREHOLDER

The influence of 'G1' has been critical to the way the Bank has been run since its foundation. Increasingly over time this influence has been difficult for the institution to sustain. Catherine Gwin, in the Bank's official history, wrote that the U.S. pursuit of objectives was driven more by short-term foreign or domestic political imperatives than by concern for the effectiveness of Bank operations. She wrote that U.S. pressure 'caused the Bank to wage a constant fight for its autonomy, as a result of which its leadership and staff have developed a protective

---

8   Scandizzo, Pasquale, 'The Purpose, Management and Governance of the IFIs: A Case Study in Ambiguity', EIB Papers, European Investment Bank, 3(2).

shell of beliefs and practices that, while insulating the Bank from U.S. pressures, has hindered its effective functioning'.[9]

Another observer, Robert Wade, noted that its location in Washington exposed it to the force of American political culture.[10] Americans, more than citizens of other prosperous democracies, he wrote, distrust political power; are fearful of centralized government; are contemptuous of bureaucracy; and seek to fragment, divide, and control it, thus tending to eclipse concerns to improve administrative capacity. American political culture, he added, supports an adversarial and rule-bound system with little discretion for regulators and an assumption that compliance depends on penalties. Any signal of displeasure by the U.S. executive director 'has an almost palpable impact on the Bank leadership and its staff, whether the signal is a complaint or a request for information'.[11]

The United States was supportive in the first two decades of the Bank's existence, and it also supported the founding of the IFC and the IDA. Its concern at that time was sharing the burden rather than exerting control or limiting funds. However, during McNamara's presidency support waned because of objections to the Bank's expansion. During the Nixon and Carter presidencies it fluctuated according to the demands of U.S. assistance strategy, and then from 1980 the Reagan administration adopted an oppositional attitude. As David Stockman, Reagan's budget director, explained it later: '[T]he international aid bureaucracy was turning third world countries into quagmires of self imposed inefficiency and burying them beneath mountainous external debts'[12] The U.S. concern now was to limit the size of the Bank, to enforce transparency, and to avoid loans to politically unacceptable countries, while in the 1980s the

---

[9] Gwin, Catherine, 'US Relations with the World Bank 1945–92', in Kapur, Devesh, J. Lewis, and R. Webb, *The World Bank: Its First Half Century*, Brookings, 1997.

[10] Wade, Robert, 'Showdown at the World Bank', *New Left Review*, Jan./Feb. 2001.

[11] Ibid., p. 8. This was also the view of Harvard Professor of Government James Wilson: 'Americans always entertain the suspicion that the Government is doing something mischievous behind their backs and greet with outrage any indications that important decisions were made in a way that excluded any affected interest – no matter how marginal'. Wilson, James Q., *Bureaucracy – What Government Agencies Do and Why They Do It*, Basic Books, 1989, p. 304.

[12] Stockman, David, *The Triumph of Politics; How the Reagan Revolution Failed*, Harper & Row, 1986.

U.S. Congress became increasingly sensitive to its environmental lobby groups, and the U.S. director in 1986 voted against a project for the first time on environmental grounds.[13]

U.S. hostility was diluted as the Bank became important to attempts to deal with the Latin American debt crisis – through the 1985 Baker Plan and the subsequent 1988 Brady Plan to restructure private debt. This change of attitude, combined with the supposed success of the 1987 reorganization, led it to agree to the 1988 IBRD capital increase, but this was once again a temporary truce. The United States had argued at Bretton Woods against permitting the Bank to lend directly to the private sector, but it reversed policy and tried to use the 1991 IFC capital increase negotiations to force a change in the Articles regarding private sector lending. In 1994 Congress was taken over by the Republicans, Jesse Helms became chair of the Senate foreign relations committee, and the third-year payment under the already agreed upon IDA 10 replenishment was withheld.[14] Despite lobbying by the White House and private businesses, the final payment was about half of the commitment. The thirteenth replenishment of IDA talks almost reached a deadlock over aid policy and the use of grants, emanating from the Meltzer Commission report. The insistence of the United States on linking aid to performance was also opposed by donors who doubted the feasibility of judging foreign assistance on short-term results.[15]

One of the most notable ways that U.S. power has been imposed is through its informal mandate to select the president, a mandate that has often been used more to meet the demands of U.S. domestic politics and less to ensure merit. The succession to Clausen was a case in point. Barber Conable was a newly retired Republican congressman, well respected[16] but with no experience of development issues and no knowledge of or interest in the Bank. He reluctantly accepted the job when agreement could not be reached over anybody else and the U.S.

---

[13] Robert Kasten and David Obey held more than twenty hearings on the environmental and social impacts of Bank projects and its apparent abuses and errors. Caufield, Catherine, *Masters of Illusion*, Henry Holt, 1996, p. 172.

[14] The U.S. share of IDA 10 was $3.75 billion out of $18 billion.

[15] See, for example, 'Developments Over IDA Fund Replenishments. Poor Nations Get Wrong Signals', *World Bank Press Review*, January 23, 2002.

[16] He was regarded as an able chairman of the House Ways and Means Committee,

administration feared that further delay would result in their forfeiting the selection role. Yet Conable himself became a victim of the hard-line U.S. attitude, and he did not stand for a second term partly because of his disillusionment with his erstwhile friends in the Republican Party. Just after he stepped down in 1991 he said: '[H]ere we are in the US . . . the nation that created the Marshall Plan, that provided key leadership in creating the Bretton Woods institutions . . . Yet even knowledgeable Americans don't know what the World Bank is'.[17] The subsequent presidential appointments of Preston and Wolfensohn were not politically partisan, but the use of the Bank president's office as an instrument of patronage was taken to a new level by George W. Bush, who appointed not one but two political allies to the role.

While the United States did not find it important to select the Bank president on merit, its attitude was different in the case of the European selection of the head of the IMF. In this respect the IMF succession in 2000 that brought in Horst Kohler came after the United States opposed the first European nominee, Caio Koch-Weser, a former Bank managing director, precisely on grounds of insufficient merit.[18] That is, it seemed that the United States had no difficulty in ignoring merit in selecting the head of the Bank but blocked European proposals to appoint a generally well-qualified candidate under the European's IMF selection mandate.

Finally, the United States has been foremost in pushing its own policies regarding favored and disfavored country lending. While it cannot veto loans (though it has voted against more than 100), it can bring influence to bear on other shareholders and the office of the president can promote, delay, or prevent the submission of a loan to the board. Wolfowitz, for example, secured reluctant board approval for a $500 million Bank program in Iraq.

The U.S. attitude toward the Bank reflects a general American prejudice against vaguely defined international welfare handouts, while most are unaware that the U.S. foreign aid contribution has been the lowest in terms of GDP of any rich country. Even if the 50% planned boost in assistance through the Millennium Challenge Fund set up in 2002 actually

---

[17] Cited in Kapur, Lewis et al., op cit., p. 1202.
[18] A behind-the-scenes battle was waged by Larry Summers, former Bank Chief Economist and at that time at the U.S. Treasury.

occurred, the proportion would still remain at the lowest end of the range. The U.S. contribution to the Bank has comprised actual paid-in cash to the IBRD of $2.6 billion; callable capital (unpaid) of $30 billion; and cash contributed to the IDA of about $30 billion over sixty years. The amount paid in cash by the United States to the Bank over sixty years is a small fraction of the amount paid annually to U.S. farmers in agricultural subsidies, while the cost of two Virginia State transport projects (the Woodrow Wilson bridge and the Springfield interchange) is larger than the entire U.S. cash contribution to the IBRD since its foundation.

The Meltzer Commission[19] made a higher estimate of the costs to the U.S. taxpayer of $3.45 billion per annum, consisting of forgone interest on paid-in capital, the annualized cost of IDA subscriptions, the interest cost of retained earnings, and a compensation for risk of $1.39 billion per annum.[20] The allowance for risk was dubious since the Bank has never faced significant arrears, but even so the total annual cost is tiny by comparison with the tax breaks on U.S. agriculture, and the United States meanwhile also gains from the presence of the Bank in Washington in terms of foreign and economic policy leverage, increased export markets, and procurement contracts. The Meltzer Commission embodied the U.S. campaign to cast adrift its unwanted offspring. Its report had four dissenting members and the Bank dismissed virtually all the proposals. Nevertheless, it was taken seriously in some quarters. Republican Chairman Jim Saxton, of the Joint Economic Committee of Congress, was a Meltzer ally. 'The highest priority of public aid policy' he stated, 'should be the implementation of effective strategies to combat poverty, not the interests of the managers of a failing bureaucracy'.[21] Paul O'Neill, then treasury secretary, tried, unsuccessfully, to get Wolfensohn removed.[22]

---

[19] Report of the International Financial Institutions Advisory Commission (IFIAC), 2000, p. 43, Table 3–5.

[20] The assumption made for the value of risk exposure on U.S. callable capital is based on one-half of the market valuation of the average risk premium over five years on emerging market sovereign debt.

[21] Public Statement issued by Joint Economic Committee of Congress in January 2002.

[22] O'Neill did not approve of the way the Bank was being run (in contrast to his own leadership at Alcoa Aluminum). But Wolfensohn was steps ahead of O'Neill's somewhat unsophisticated assault, enlisting the support of Condeleeza Rice, an occasional musical partner. These events are recounted in Sebastian Mallaby, *The World's Banker: A Story of Failed States, Financial Crises, and the Wealth and Poverty of Nations*, Penguin, 2004.

In the, albeit unlikely, doomsday financial scenario member
countries might be called on to bail out the Bank through their callable
capital. Could the United States renege on its capital commitment? As
explained, current legislation allows the Treasury secretary to order
the release of up to $7.6 billion without congressional approval. The
remaining $22.3 billion has been authorized by Congress but not
appropriated, so further congressional action would be required even
though the total commitment is recognized (in an opinion of the
Treasury chief counsel) to be an obligation of the U.S. government.
The uncertainty about the $22.3 billion is an implicit if very distant
concern, brought more to the fore by action like the refusal by
Congress to appropriate the agreed-upon IDA contributions. The
probability is that, in the doomsday scenario, unlikely as it may be,
Congress would appropriate the funds, but at a heavy political cost to
the institution.

Just as the U.S. position changed when it needed the Bank's help
with the Latin American debt crisis, it changed, even more so, with the
war in Iraq. The administration now needed to maintain meaningful
avenues of international access and the Bank was an important avenue. The history of its relations with the Bank has been dictated by
such fluctuating interests, complicating an already complex situation.
U.S. political interference in Bank lending has been in conflict both
with the Bank's Founding Articles, which the United States largely
wrote, and with its demands for increased aid effectiveness. Its
demands for extra layers of oversight and quality control have been
in conflict with the need for organizational efficiency. Its instinct for
root-and-branch organizational shakeups has been in conflict with the
aims of increasing development effectiveness. The U.S. dominance of
the Bank's governance, through its host status, veto power, and diplomatic leverage, has made it a major factor in the Bank's governance
conundrum.

THE CHARACTER OF GOVERNANCE

The board of executive directors has been delegated power by the
governors over nearly all decisions while the governors retain exclusive

power only over membership, capital increases, strategic associations with other international organizations, allocation of net income, and closure of the Bank. Despite its broad de facto powers, as mentioned, the executive board was, however, early on effectively removed from authority over day-to-day operations, including the origination of projects, while the powers delegated to it by the governors came to be used only in a reactive way, deferring to management's judgment. As a result, the Bank's two-tier governance structure essentially consists of two boards that are both non-executive.

While it is de facto non-executive, the executive board nevertheless adheres to its role in the founding Articles, insofar as it 'shall function in continuous session at the principal office of the Bank and shall meet as often as the business of the Bank may require'. With the exception of the U.S. office, directors and their staff not only have their offices within the Bank, but they are also on the Bank's regular payroll.[23] Thus they are in a position of being *de iure* executive, *de facto* supervisory, and at the same time paid as though they are on the staff of the organization they are supervising.

The board of governors, in the form of the development committee, meets only twice a year to discuss development policy and long-term strategic direction. The board of directors meets on average twice a week while during the remainder of the time the directors' offices track the Bank's activities. The 24 directors have their own staff of about 160 plus 65 in support, and a corporate secretariat of a further 100 staff provided by the Bank to keep them informed. Each director's office has an alternate and a group of advisers (up to nine in the largest office, for Francophone Africa). The corporate secretariat is supposed to provide policy support to the board; advice to management and staff to ensure that only quality products reach the board; and a key role in building closer cooperation between the board, shareholders, and management. It has to 'facilitate board members' understanding of, and *support for*, the Bank groups strategic agenda' (my italics) and it is responsible for drafting the board's annual work program.

---

[23] Executive directors currently receive a salary of US$212,000 per annum net of tax, equivalent to a Bank internal director.

The board has several committees, for audit, budget, personnel, and administration.[24] There is also the committee on development effectiveness (CODE) set up in 1995 that oversees the IEG. CODE has its own sub-committee responsible for looking at strategy papers, country assessments, evaluations, and organization structure. It is the most important committee from the point of view of corporate strategy and development policy. With its own sub-committee it has in the past had considerable influence, but this waxes and wanes with the personalities involved, playing the role at one time almost of a third layer of governance and at other times a board appendage.

Board directors are predominantly from the civil service, with some from political and academic backgrounds. Among their advisory staff the pattern has been the same. The only director appointed frequently from a non-public background is from the United States. In 2006 Herman Wijffels, a former private banker, became the Dutch representative, but this was unusual. Out of the total 2002 intake of twelve new Executive Directors, just one had a substantial private sector background, as a consultant mostly to the international financial institutions, and only one had extensive private sector experience independent of the IFIs, in the coffee industry. Of those appointed at the end of 2000, all had purely or largely civil service backgrounds, and a handful had experience in academia, consulting, and banking (usually central banking). Almost none had any experience at all of corporate management in large-scale organizations. Going back to 1992, the intake was essentially the same. There has been a lack of experience in board activity as it is generally understood in the corporate world – corporate strategy or planning, finance policy, capital investment decisions, governance, management systems, re-organization, administration, and personnel policy.

The directors' position is further circumscribed because of factors such as their short tenure. Most directors are formally appointed for a two-year term, and the average, including a few long-term incumbents, has been about three years. In the case of the constituency chairs, that is,

---

[24] To enhance its relevance, the name of this committee was changed from the CODAM to the COGAM, where DAM had stood for 'Directors Administrative Matters'. GAM stood for 'Governance and Administrative Matters'.

the country group directorates, a high turnover is encouraged because, in some groups, countries wait in line for their turn to assume the directorial role.

THE INFORMATION PUZZLE

Among the key issues in effective corporate governance are good communication and information symmetry, both between the board and management and between the board and the shareholders. But while asymmetric information always strengthens the management vis-à-vis the shareholders, the problem is particularly acute in the case of public organizations like the Bank, where differing interests among the shareholders and the difficulty in linking outcomes to specific actions by the organization further strengthen the management's position. Asymmetric information does not mean lack of information going to the principals. It can also mean too much. Information overloads can do the same thing as information blackouts.

The information flow to the Bank's owners has never been regarded as satisfactory despite the large secretarial capacity put in place to inform them. The Meltzer Committee and the U.S. Treasury continually called for 'more transparency', as have the NGO activists. For example, in 2002 the Bank Information Center, an activist group, issued a briefing note on the so-called 'democratic deficit'[25] in which it demanded the opening up of board meetings to the public. A large group of NGOs wrote to the vice president for operations policy asking for open board discussions and a provision of quality assurance information to the board. In 2006 the same activist groups[26] were complaining that the Bank selectively disclosed information it deemed in the public interest, and that good governance with enforceable transparency mechanisms should apply not only to borrowers, but also to the World Bank itself.

One of those who particularly looked at the board/management information flow was Moises Naim, a former director and now editor

---

[25] 'Development Bank Transparency, 'Issues and Opportunities for 2002–03 – Promoting the Public's Right to Know', Bank Information Center, March 2002.

[26] The groups were the Bank Information Centre (BIC), CEE Bankwatch Network, Jubilee USA Network, Government Accountability Project (GAP), and CRBM.

of the journal *Foreign Policy*. The problem he described was one of information overload rather than information deficit: '[A] divided Board of overwhelmed executives many of whom cannot afford to irritate the Bank's management and usually leave by the time they begin to be more effective, is no match' he wrote, 'for the usually brilliant group of professionals with decades of experience at the Bank'.[27] Sometimes information does not flow within the board entities themselves. The link between the CODE and the board has, for example, sometimes not been strong largely because the time required to attend committees has discouraged interest. This has left the CODE at times to pursue its own agenda, sometimes acting as a third layer of governance supplementing both boards.

The information overload problem originated during McNamara's presidency, when the practice arose of keeping the board quiet by swamping it with reading.[28] Kapur writes that the ability to sail loans past the board smoothly became a mark of success, and there was a premium on the quality and meticulous thoroughness of documentation.[29] The number of documents going to the board rose from about 300 annually in the 1950s to more than 1,000 in the 1970s, and another fourfold by 2002. In January 2002, the Russian Director, Bugrov, at his farewell reception said that the sheer volume of reading for the board was so time consuming that it caused the loss of professional edge, while the rapid turnover among the board membership – with roughly one-third leaving every two years, made it even more difficult to handle the volume of information. Similarly, a memo from one director in November 2003[30] complained that the board was drowned in so many

---

[27] Naim, Moises, 'From Supplicants to Shareholders; Developing Countries and the World Bank', in G.K. Helleiner, ed., *The International Monetary and Financial System: Developing-Country Perspectives,* Palgrave Macmillan, 1995.

[28] Michael Irvin in the Cato Institute newsletter (1990) cited a remark made by a vice president (Robert Picciotto) in May 1989, namely, that the board should get the 'mushroom treatment': '[K]eep it in the dark; feed it garbage'. Picciotto went on to be director general of the OED, in constant contact with the board.

[29] Kapur, Lewis et al., op cit,. p. 1183.

[30] The board director was Per Kurowski. He also wrote: '[W]e are drowned in too many written and spoken words about too many topics so that our power, as a body, is completely diluted to such an extent that we could easily qualify as the most expensive rubber stamp in mankind's history'.

written and spoken words about so many topics that its power was completely diluted. Regarding a significant current Board policy concern, to increase the 'voice' of underrepresented member countries, he said this: 'It really doesn't matter if you are a Pavarotti if you have to sing in Madison Square Garden during a Knick's match ... because you will not be heard anyhow ... Our Board's acoustics are so bad that ... in reality, no one has a voice'.

At the start of each year the board is presented by the corporate secretariat with its work program for the year. That is, the program is drafted by the Bank, not by the executive director's own staff. The typical work program overview memorandum alone is a densely packed, polished document that reads like a smaller version of the Bank's corporate strategy papers and does not provide much room or time for questions. Each month it is backed up by a crowded calendar of events. In 2005 it was decided to assist the complex process by introducing a 'Strategic Overview Tool' and 'Quarterly Strategic Reviews' of the board's work program so as to monitor its progress in relation to strategy. The Strategic Review itself was to be monitored by the directors assisted by the corporate secretariat.

Some directors seem to appreciate the set menu of activities, but others see it as an intrusion. Some (for example, within the G5 countries) take a proactive role, supported by specialized staff at home and in Washington. But many of those who are either less well supported or less dedicated regard it as a convenience to be able to take a reactive role, responding to the already demanding agenda. For those whose tenure is so short that they cannot hope to establish a considered independent posture, to simply go with the flow is the most feasible course of action. The board has been described as a parliament rather than an executive body, and some members are apparently satisfied with that characterization.

Fifty to 100 documents a week are presented to the board, including loan and guarantee appraisals, country strategy and policy papers, HIPC reports, internal policy papers, annual reports, administrative and process matters, action plans, oral briefings on special issues, committee reports, nominations, agreements, audits, and OED and other performance reviews. Of these, as many as forty substantive and

sometimes lengthy, complex, and specialized papers have to be ana-
lyzed, reviewed, and for which policy positions might have to be worked
out.[31] In addition, board committees themselves are very time consuming and interest in them is constrained by this. In fact, the CODE
subcommittee responsible for studying evaluation reports has much
fewer resources to do it than those available in the Bank, unless it makes
liberal use of capacity in home governments. Once the work bandwagon
is rolling there is little time or leverage for fundamental questions.

Apart from the question of the adequacy of information there is also
the question of what is done with the information when it is received.
An extreme characterization of this was from Bruce Rich, the environmentalist and well-known Bank adversary: 'The octopus-like bureaucracy' he claimed, 'emits an immense ink cloud of reports that for twenty
years have identified the same problems, but the reports like all their
predecessors have no lasting operational consequences . . . . The executive board is mollified, since the turnover rate and lack of institutional
memory and continuity is high'.[32]

The follow-up on reports to the board is typically non-substantive.
Out of numerous possible examples, let us revisit the January 2000
board discussion on a series of major evaluation reports on development effectiveness. The report of the meeting starts: '[T]he Directors
welcomed the clarity, comprehensiveness and candor of the three
reports and commended the authors. They also expressed satisfaction
that solid progress had been made in improving the quality and effectiveness of the Bank's operations. They commended the president, his
management team and Bank staff for the achievements while emphasiz-
ing that there is no room for complacency . . . . Several Directors

---

[31] Board workflow is a frequent topic. See also Woods, Ngaire, 'Making the IMF and
World Bank More Accountable', in *Reforming the Governance of the IMF and the
World Bank*, Ariel Buira, ed., Anthem Press, 2005, p. 154; Kapur, Devesh, 'From
Shareholders to Stakeholders – The Changing Anatomy of Governance of the World
Bank', in Jonathan R. Pincus and Jeffery A. Winters, *Reinventing the World Bank*,
Cornell University Press, 2002; and Catherine Caufield, *Masters of Illusion*, Henry
Holt, 1996, p. 237, who wrote: '[F]or many years management fed information to the
Board sparingly; today the directors have access to any document in the Bank. The
trick is that in order to ask for a document it is necessary to know of its existence'.
[32] Rich, Bruce, 'The World Bank under James Wolfensohn', in Jonathan R. Pincus and
Jeffery A. Winters, *Reinventing the World Bank*, Cornell University Press, 2002, p. 53.

expressed appreciation that management had made a concerted effort to prepare a draft program to address the areas of weakness . . . '. Instead of this polite and largely meaningless bromide, drafted by the corporate secretariat itself, the report would have been more usable as a management tool if it had been written more in the following style: 'Mr. A asked the management to clarify X . . . Mr. B expressed doubt about the estimates on Y which he thought had distorted the decision . . . and asked for a review . . . Ms. C asked the management to justify their decision on Z . . . in terms of long term strategy. Ms. D remarked that a first rate analysis of . . . had been done, but further research on A was needed on . . . Subject to the following reviews and clarifications the Board agreed . . . . A further meeting on the revisions will be held on. . . .'

While the board's supervisory, rather than management-oriented, approach prevents it from taking effective steps to remedy the situation, information overload encourages the perverse demands for more transparency and more reviews or task forces even in the face of streams of information.

THE DIPLOMATIC QUID PRO QUO

The information overload is partly due to the unusual character of the board – management relationship. In 1946, as mentioned in Chapter 1, the first president, Meyer, resigned after only six months, having had continual disputes over what he saw as excessive interference by the U.S. director. This event had a major effect on the type, volume, and quality of communication between the board and the management thenceforth. For this reason and others, the board retreated into a reactive role, leaving substantive operational actions to the management.

The acquiescence by the board in its ceremonial function has resulted in an unwillingness to handle substantive issues. In 1999, for example, during the most acute phase of the reorganization, the nine members of CODE met about three times a month. They considered more than 100 OED/IEG reports, studies, and presentations, and they 'fully endorsed' the management's quality improvement messages. CODE's subcommittee had twelve members meeting once a month. The overall posture in their report to the CODE was similarly polite. The report says that the subcommittee 'welcomed', 'was pleased', 'reviewed and commended', and was 'impressed'. Among recommendations they suggested 'that efforts should be redoubled'; there was 'some room for refinement'; the issue 'will continue to require careful attention'; and, finally, they note the challenges ahead. These are the customary responses. The response to the reports on aid effectiveness of January 2000 followed the rule of the 'three C's'. The directors welcomed their 'clarity, comprehensiveness and candor' and 'commended' (a fourth) the authors and the Bank, while noting a fifth, that there was no room for 'complacency'.

The board has never turned down a loan submission. Behind-the-scenes negotiation often occurs before loans reach the board, especially for loans to countries that are sensitive from the G5 or G1 viewpoint, and this is part of the unwritten understanding whereby the board defers to management on one level in return for management's deferral to the board on another. This accommodation has resulted in some poor decisions, a classic case being the approval of the Polonoroeste project in Brazil.[33] Still, it would be wrong to suggest that the directors have never exercised their muscle, or their expertise.

The board as a whole has exercised its opposition to the growth of administrative costs, which triggered the 1987 reorganization, and created budgetary showdowns that led to the 1997 Compact, both examples of getting tough. The board tried hard to manage the chief executive and in 2001, the final year of the Strategic Compact, held the organization to such budget stringency that the core operational work was, as I have shown, significantly reduced and 12% of the employees had to leave. Smaller scale positions have been taken against the 2000 Development Gateway and a 2001 faith-based initiative. The HIPC initiative involved a lot of supporting input from the board. The restart of infrastructure financing was partly the result of a strong position taken in 2003 by the directors representing India and China. The governors stood up to the president when, at the 2006 Annual Meetings, Wolfowitz encountered

[33] As reported by the OED in 1990. Over 1981 to 1983, the board unanimously approved more than $400 million for the project. At the initial approval several directors congratulated the Bank staff and Brazilian authorities 'for their conception and design ... their truly integrated nature and the comprehensive approach to development they represented ...'. The project was halted after lengthy outside protests, in 1985.

strong opposition to the scale and intentions of his anti-corruption program.

There were also a lot of questions in the board about the 2004–2006 corporate strategy document (the Strategic Update Paper). These covered financial sustainability, lending, administrative costs, and the matrix. But the questions revealed frustration. One director said: '[F]or over three years we have been calling for an analysis of this issue of great strategic importance to the Bank and its future as a lending institution as well as the relationship between the lending activities of the Bank and its financial strength'.

The frustration of the director, however, was symptomatic more of the weakness than the strength of the arrangements. In a properly functioning board senior directors do not spend three years making the same speech about the need to do something. They reach down into the management and get the answers or they get the internal directors to do it for them, or they fire the CEO.

In 2002 an informal survey of the board advisory staff took place as a part of the research for this study. One member of an executive director's office made the following statement: '[T]here are numerous cases where members of the Board oppose something that they don't like. That's natural. But we have to understand that rejecting or even opposing a project at this level (the Board) means deeply embarrassing top management and the work they have done. In a sound institution like the World Bank severe criticism like that just doesn't seem logical. Sometimes an executive director would rather remain silent than to criticize a colleague from the Bank'. Another response was: '[Y]es, management tries to keep the board at a distance and it is a smart move. As soon as you provide the Board with all the information you inevitably have people from the board asking questions, picking on the process and generally trying to get involved'. And finally a third: '[Y]es, the Board is a little distant from top management, but we have to take into account that the Bank is a very unique and complex organization and a lot of interests and egos are working together there'. These views, aired by members of the board of executive director's very own internal advisory staff, and not by the Bank's corporate secretariat staff, reflect the extent to which 'oversight' can be misunderstood.

In 2004 the Bank's summary of a consultant study on board effectiveness suggested gently that the Executive Directors should discuss among
themselves what they mean by enhancing board effectiveness. They
should consider the need to carry out self-assessments and to ensure
that previous committee recommendations have not been lost. They
should consider how to strengthen corporate governance. They 'may
wish to anticipate' the requirements on the appropriate mix of skills and
knowledge base of the Bank by initiating preparation of their own
description/profile of their functions. The Bank itself, and even the
consultants to the Bank, appear to want to avoid upsetting the executive
directors. The mutual deference of the management and the directors is
a quid pro quo arrangement which commits one of the cardinal sins of
corporate governance. It is non-transparent, collusive, and it is definitely not 'executive'.

The management/board ritual dance is formalized by numerous rules
for staff approaching the board. For example, the steps for submitting a
document are laid down in a five-page circular dealing with who should
receive what, who should clear, who should be copied, who should process, who should sign, when are the various stages of the process to be
done, and where exactly on which page various references and salutations
should be placed. There is a three-page 'FAQ' setting out common mistakes. There is a note on attendance at meetings that says, *inter alia,*
'presenters will be told the approximate times for their items and should
stand by during the day to come to the board room immediately when
called. . . . Should the meeting go on into the afternoon staff will be tele-
phoned and told the board is breaking for lunch – they should not leave
their offices until called'. The ritual lends itself to anxiety on both sides,
but particularly so for the staff since the meeting might be the culmination
of two or three years' work and has the character of a thesis defense.

The quid pro quo is supported by the executive directors' diplomatic
status.[34] The body of directors is coordinated by a 'dean', as in the case
of the Washington Diplomatic Corps. Their suites of offices are located
close to those of the president and managing directors, and their

---

[34] Some are diplomats, while others and all their staff (except for the United States) have
the G4 official visa.

activities are looked after by their large secretariat. They have received special logistical facilities.[35] Special treatment in turn presumes diplomatic behavior, discretion, and a corresponding deference-in-turn toward the management in dealing with Bank issues.

The quid pro quo may break down when national interests intrude on board decisions, and then there is a conflict between the roles of director and quasi-ambassador. In his farewell speech of October 31, 2002, the departing head of the CODE, Pieter Stek, gently took the United States to task for advancing its special interests outside the Bank's normal channels. He spoke of the inability of some chairs to wear two hats, but merely the one in which they represent the views of their authorities. 'The existence of a resident Board', he said 'is only justified if we act as the officers of the Bank we are held to be by the Articles' He went on to address Wolfensohn: '[Y]ou were wholly justified in calling for a Board that in its supervisory role is not a corpus alienum governed by different objectives and characterized by single-hatted mental and moral aloofness'. The coded and nuanced language spelled out the ceremonial character of oversight. But the problem is more complicated than the two hats because the role of the director's hat alone is unclear.

Does semi-diplomatic status interfere with the autonomy of board judgment? There are several reasons why this might be the case. Diplomats tend to feel that they have to behave with caution, and to avoid aggressive postures that might in the end be wrong and expose their government to embarrassment. Second, their status in the United States is for many a major 'perk' that they are for the most part not inclined to endanger by arousing controversy and possible bad feedback at home. Third, some feel themselves to be appointed as wise persons whose job is to cajole, negotiate, and advise on high policy, not to involve themselves in the cut and thrust of corporate affairs. They may not feel the need to have technical capacity and are either indifferent to or overawed by the flow of information, and finally they may in any event feel

---

[35] An example of this was the exception made for the directors when a new Bank head office was constructed. At the request of some directors, a special smoking lounge was constructed with its own ventilation system while in the rest of the Bank smokers had generally to go out into the street.

justified in not getting involved in the details. The inadequate definition of the role of board directors is reflected in the comment of Ngaire Woods, a leading observer of Bank and IMF governance: '[M]ost directors live in a grey zone, based in Washington, DC, paid by the Bank, and neither instructed by nor accountable to most of the membership of the Bank'.[36]

THE BOARD AND THE WOLFOWITZ AFFAIR

In March 2007, 'In the Loop', a *Washington Post* gossip column penned by Al Kamen, ran a short story called 'Where the Money Is', about the fate of Paul Wolfowitz' personal friend, Shaha Riza, who had been obliged to leave the Bank to avoid a conflict of interest vis-à-vis her new boss. This triggered a scandal that heavily engaged the Bank's board and provided it with an opportunity to step out of its usual reactive posture and assume a directorial function. Was it able to do so?

On Wolfowitz' instructions Riza had been seconded to Bush's former assistant, Karen Hughes' Public Diplomacy Unit in the State Department, working with Liz Cheney (the vice president's daughter). The secondment was at a high Bank-paid salary with all but guaranteed reentry at a senior level and as such broke the Bank's rules,[37] as well as possibly the State Department's rules.[38] The Bank's Staff Association reacted adversely and the employees publicly protested the perceived conflict between the president's public posture on corruption and his private activities They had numerous reasons to be unhappy about Wolfowitz' appointment, starting with his central role in the Iraq war and continuing with the apparent selectivity and insensitivity of his assault on corruption in poor countries, and his appointment of several

---

[36] Woods, Ngaire. 'The Battle for the Bank', in *Rescuing the Word Bank, A CGD Working Group Report*, Nancy Birdsall, ed., Center For Global Development, 2006.

[37] The final committee report on this affair agreed that Wolfowitz had not been given clear advice by the Board's Ethics Committee on how to deal precisely with Shaha Riza's employment, but that any doubt he may have had did not excuse the issuing of instructions that breached staff rules, and it did require that he should have consulted the Bank's legal counsel, which he had not done.

[38] Riza was a foreign national (a British citizen of Libyan birth); see Blumenthal, Sidney, 'Wolfowitz's Girlfriend Problem', *The Village News*, April 19, 2007.

former Republican administration officials to oversee the staff themselves, and whose tactics had already led to the departure of several top Bank officials.[39]

Wolfowitz faced public demands to resign, even from his deputy, Graeme Wheeler, from other senior managers, and from major media outlets such as the *Financial Times*. The shareholders faced a crisis at the April 2007 Annual Meetings, whereupon the governors shifted responsibility to the board, even though issues concerning presidential appointments were among the few responsibilities that they still retained. An ad hoc committee was set up to deal with the situation, which over the next five weeks was buffeted by the media, the staff, Wolfowitz, his lawyer Bob Bennett,[40] the governors, and the NGOs. Finally Wolfowitz's chief adviser, Robyn Cleveland, intercepted three board directors[41] to seek a compromise, without the knowledge of the board committee. The compromise was maneuvered through the board and Wolfowitz announced his resignation on May 17 with the partial exoneration that he had demanded in order to depart, as he saw it, with honor.[42]

At first sight the resolution of the Wolfowitz affair could be construed as indicating a board revitalized. However, this was not the case. The prime movers in the affair were, first, the media (prodded by anonymous tip-offs from the Bank) and, second, the Bank staff itself, responding initially to the *Washington Post*'s revelations, and then to

---

[39] Among the internal watchdogs was the head of the Department of Institutional Integrity, Suzanne Rich Folsom, a Republican loyalist although appointed previously by Wolfensohn to strengthen relations with the U.S. administration. She was given by Wolfowitz a second title of counselor to the president, creating a dual role that turned out itself to involve a conflict of interest. The top managers that left included Shengman Zhang, who took a job at CitiCorp.

[40] Bennett's presence antagonized the directors because it transformed an internal administrative enquiry into a quasi-legal battle in which terms like 'smear campaign' and 'circus' were publicly bandied about, and countercharges made to sway outside opinion. The hiring of a high-profile lawyer reflected Wolfowitz's apparent tendency to 'ride roughshod' over opposition, and it probably sealed his fate.

[41] The directors approached were from the UK, Canada, and Mexico.

[42] The exoneration was a statement from the board accepting that Wolfowitz had acted ethically and in good faith (contrary to its previous findings) and an agreement that he remain in office for six weeks, allowing time to carry out further functions such as a planned farewell trip to Africa. When board members went to discuss the final terms they found that he had left his chief adviser, Cleveland, to deal with them.

further leaks to the Government Accountability Project and other media. The governors shifted responsibility to the board itself. The board was the last on this list to take up the issue, would almost certainly not have taken it up independently, and ultimately contradicted its own ethics findings with a compromise generated outside the agreed enquiry process.[43]

PRESSURE TO REFORM AND EFFORTS TO REFORM GOVERNANCE

The problems of the Bank's governance have been aired for a long time, by outsiders and insiders, and by the directors themselves. Moises Naim was the director responsible for preparing the 1992 Report of the Ad Hoc Committee on Board Procedures.[44] After two years, he wrote, this led to some minor changes that 'fell very short of the more drastic revamping needed to adjust the Board to the circumstances faced by the Bank'.[45] He claimed that the caliber of the directors had fallen as the role of the board became more that of a rubber stamp agency, as they were increasingly captured by their parent bureaucracies, and as the post became seen as a choice career move for long-serving civil servants. Short tenure and increasing complexity of the work were serious issues. 'In the two or three years that most directors stay at the Bank', he wrote, 'it is impossible, even for the few that have a good prior understanding of the institution, to master the overwhelming array of complex issues on which they are supposed to develop an independent opinion'.

The MDB report of 1996,[46] now forgotten, recommended that change start at the top. Boards needed members of stature and the right

---

[43] The unlikelihood of the board dealing with the case on its own was evidenced by the fact that the Ethics Committee had in 2006 refused to deal further with the issue after receiving an anonymous e-mail from a 'John Smith', presumably a member of the Bank's personnel department, detailing the terms of Shaha Riza's departure. The side negotiation that secured a compromise satisfactory to Wolfowtiz was also a form of insider deal.

[44] Naim, Moses, 'Report of the Ad Hoc Committee on Board Procedures', World Bank 1992.

[45] Naim, Moses, 'From Supplicants to Shareholders; Developing Countries and the World Bank', in G. K. Helleiner, ed., op cit., 1996, p. 293.

[46] 'Serving a Changing World, Report of the Task Force on Multilateral Development Banks', 1996, op cit.

experience, and rather than detailed loan monitoring, they should be concerned with strategic guidance, process reform, structures for efficiency, portfolio quality, and Bank performance. Evaluation reports should be issued to the president and OED (IEG), they recommended, without clearance.

A former vice president of the Bank, Josef Ritzen, was briefer and more scathing. The board is 'a wishy washy contraption of a more than sixty year old agreement. It is also a waste of talent and money, without contributing to a democratic form of representation'.[47] Most recently, in his concern to defend Paul Wolfowitz in his ethics problem, Robert Holland, who had been acting as U.S. director, attacked the member governments, the board, the staff, and seemingly himself all at the same time. Apart from his ritual annoyance over staff salaries, numbers, and tenure, he also accused the board of being unwieldy, parochial, overpaid, self-interested, and ineffective.[48]

There have been no less than nine formal reviews of board procedures since the foundation of the bank, five of which occurred between 1988 and 2005, on average one every three years, or about one for each cohort of the new executive directors. The timing suggests that the reviews have been more in the nature of an orientation briefing than a serious attempt at reform. The reviews were largely concerned with process – the format of reports and meetings and the shift of board business to strategy rather than project approvals. The board delegated certain less significant project approvals to management[49] and streamlined the procedures for others.[50]

The 2003 Toure report made a series of recommendations. The board once again tried to change itself through process – better documents, more focused discussions, and time limits for interventions. Project presentation was restricted to four minutes. Directors who filed written statements could only speak for three minutes, and should make new

[47] Ritzen, Jozef, *A Chance for the World Bank,* Anthem, 2005, p. 98.
[48] Holland, Robert B., 'The Real World Bank Scandal – Why the Bureaucracy Wants to Oust Paul Wolfowitz', WSJ.com, April 20, 2007.
[49] It delegates decisions on PPFs, LILs, and APLs (unless a meeting is requested).
[50] These procedures apply to routine operations, i.e., except SALs, HPIC, deviations from CAS, innovative and complex projects, lessons to be learned, and large projects. It also reviews one a year for all borrowers, and it reviews all guarantees.

points. It was 'recommended' that the president engage in discussions on strategy and risks at regular monthly dinners. Board papers should be well written and avoid advocacy. The board also adopted measures on etiquette (no unpleasant surprises).

Following the previous Toure report, the following reform action events took place: a 'retreat' (March 2004), a 'follow-up' (April 2004), a memorandum on chairmanship (June 2004), a board discussion to draft an 'action matrix' (August 2004), the establishment of a small working group (August 2004), and a document called 'Board Effectiveness; a Road Map' (December 2004) presented at the induction course for new directors. For a 'lunch' (December 2004) a note was provided by the general counsel on the legal framework for the discussion of corporate governance. There were then further formal discussions in March and May 2005, and a 'lunch' in July 2005. This series of social events and presentations over 15 months should not be mistaken for action on the substantive issues.

The small working group made recommendations on the work program, the agenda, the preparation of meetings, and the conduct of meetings, but left alone as outside its remit the terms of reference of committees, and the evaluation work of the board and its committees for attention 'in due course'. It called finally for a 'culture of transparency and constructive dialogue based on mutual respect and trust'.

In November 2005, two years after the 2003 Toure report, another paper on board effectiveness was issued. The recommendations approved in it included initiatives such as changes in lead times for documents, criteria for timing of agenda items, clarifications of procedures, refinements to documents, and procedures for board intervention. It proposed introducing the strategic overview tool to clarify timelines and set out issues. Once again it was about process.

In January 2007, as a result of the acrimonious Annual Meeting that occurred in Singapore in 2006, the board was goaded briefly, as it had been from time to time in the past, into assuming an effective oversight role. Emboldened or annoyed by the experience of the Singapore debate on an anti-corruption policy that appeared little related to wider conceptions of economic development, the budget committee objected to the annual budget proposals, charging that they lacked a coherent vision, strategy, or framework in which to assess choices or results. According to Fox News, which received the leaked board paper,[51] France's alternate board director took the lead, backed by the representative from Switzerland. They dismissed the management paper as a lost opportunity. Some asked for a 'real strategy' to be provided in time for the IDA 15 replenishment negotiations. However, the board's action may have been motivated more by its poor relationship with the incumbent president than by a change in its fundamental role, and this was resolved unexpectedly a few months later by the president's resignation.

The most substantive recent reform move focused not on organizational effectiveness but on the fairness of board representation of the poorer countries, known as the Voice initiative. It has been on the development committee agenda for five years. During this time, numerous analyses have been conducted of options for amending voting representation, but the measures actually taken have been peripheral – for secondment programs for poorer country policy-makers; learning programs for the directors' staff; an analytical trust fund to strengthen directors' offices; an increase in staff resources for the African directors[52]; and longer tenure by directors. While this initiative did not address the effectiveness of governance, it has taken up extensive board and secretariat time without clear resolution.

The effectiveness proposals that have been made have met varying fates. The proposal for longer directorial tenure was adopted, but only informally, because otherwise it would require a change in the Articles. Shorter tenures are in any case still favored in some multiple constituencies where countries have to wait for their chance for a seat. The original idea to increase board seats was finally adopted with the addition of one. The proposal for additional senior advisers to the directors and enhanced staff resources in other offices was also adopted. But the sum total of all action taken so far has been modest, and the critical area of the board's role in an effective organization not seriously looked at. The 2007 Development Committee paper[53] stated: '[A] first evaluation

---

[51] Behar, Richard, 'Wolfowitz vs. the World Bank Board: It's Trench Warfare', Fox-News.com, January 31, 2007.

[52] One proposal would have placed an IMF official as an adviser on the staff of an African director, despite the apparent conflict of interest.

[53] 'Voice and Participation of Developing and Transitional Countries in Decision Making at the World Bank – Options Paper', World Bank, October 11, 2007, p. 5.

of the implementation of Board effectiveness concluded that much progress had been made in improving Board efficiency'. On the other hand, the results of a board self-evaluation survey conducted in October 2006 suggested that more work was needed in strategic priority setting, senior manager and board roles regarding policy, the board's oversight function, and the follow-up on and evaluation of the implementation of the decisions made by the board. 'Board effectiveness' is one of thirteen areas listed in the survey report's 'action matrix' and it is also one of the few with no deadlines.

WHAT IS THE COST OF GOVERNANCE?

Board and corporate secretariat costs were excluded from the Strategic Compact agreement and were therefore not subject to its formal limitations, rising, albeit not greatly, over the period while total administrative expenses for the institution were being held down. Thus, during the reorganization period the total staff of both the board of directors and the corporate secretariat rose while the operations of the Bank were being downsized. As a result, its cost as a percentage of the total administrative budget rose between 1997 and 2001. Adding in the IEG and the Inspection Panel, the total costs of governance-related expenditure rose further. By 2005, more than $100 million per annum was being spent on the board, its committees, its staff, and the monitoring organs that reported directly to it. The total number of people involved in this industry was about 500, almost entirely paid for by the Bank.

In addition to the direct cost to the Bank, the governance function makes use of support offices in parent ministries, especially among the G5 nations, including the U.S. Treasury, the British Treasury and Department for International Development, and comparable German, French, and Japanese agencies, and also within most other OECD governments and single country holders of board seats. Average staff involved directly or indirectly in the oversight of World Bank business in OECD Governments varies, but might be around five full-time equivalent individuals. In the case of the UK, several officials oversee Bank business, but other sector specialists are brought in to review particular issues and projects. These act in effect as the advisory secretariat for the governor, but they are not accounted for within the costs of governance of the Bank. While their duties are general, not just oversight of the Bank, almost all 185 member countries have at least one official tracking what the Bank is doing, and the OECD donors and the large borrower countries (e.g., China, India, and Brazil) all have significant numbers involved. It might be supposed that altogether at least 500 officials outside the Bank have the equivalent of a full-time oversight role. This number added to the internal staff would bring the total to at least 1,000.

The availability of expertise to the board, less as it is than the Bank's, is diluted because the board is structured on the basis of geographical constituencies rather than specialist professional functions. So, the same information on projects and policies is needed by twenty-four different offices. That is, the 200 or so staff of the executive directors duplicate each other's work twenty-four times to provide information to their home governments, a situation that would not occur within the corporate sector, and which is wasteful. If executive board directors represented functions rather than constituencies, then much of the information flow could be filtered into specialist channels where it could be absorbed by specialists, considerably reducing costs and increasing effectiveness.

But the numbers cited do not reflect the true level of effort involved in overseeing of the Bank's activities. The informal understandings between the board and management on their relative roles lead to large amounts of work on behalf of the board in preparing and perfecting documentation, that is, in maintaining the unchallengeability of the Bank's documents. The documentation includes statutory corporate reports, analytical papers, project appraisals, presidents' reports, sector studies, policy papers, issues papers, country strategy papers, completion reports, sector strategy papers, answers, briefs, and the regional and Bank-wide portfolio reports. Work is expanded to provide the required polished appraisal and analytical documents or to otherwise meet the perceived or created demands of the board, or simply to maintain a distance by preempting questions. This process crowds out time for the design and implementation of projects and has a cost not only internally but also developmentally.

It may be reasonably guessed that the 'culture of perfection' leading to the burden of excessive time spent preparing documentation at all stages of the project cycle and in the corporate area takes up at least 20% of operational staff time, or the equivalent of more than 1,000 professional jobs, aside from the regular process of supervision and quality checking. The total of full-time equivalent jobs created by the special needs of the Bank's governance structure would then amount to 2,000, or more.

Thus, if we take the cost of governance as including the board of governors and Development Committee and their staffs in their home countries, the board of directors and their staff in Washington, the corporate secretariat, the OED, and the Inspection Panel, a total of $150 to $200 million per annum including overheads is probably spent on the board, supporting the board, reporting to the board, or second-guessing the board. The hidden costs within the institution itself probably cost an equivalent sum, or more. It is likely, therefore, that on a conservative calculation the costs associated with the Bank's governance system, both inside and outside the institution, approach $400 million per annum, or a sum equivalent to well over 15% of total administration costs. This sum is significant in terms of the investment resources of many poorer developing countries.

This expenditure of resources on oversight has failed, even so, to address the institutional transparency demands from both official sources such as the U.S. Treasury and unofficial sources such as the NGO activist groups. Clearly it is a wasteful system providing the wrong type of information to the wrong audience. If transparency is still inadequate even with this level of oversight, then it suggests dysfunctionality in the institution's governance. Reverting to the concepts of Michael Hammer, the question is whether this oversight activity is part of the Bank's basic process needs. Prima facie, if, at a minimum, 2,000 jobs have to be created in order to support the oversight of another 8,000 (9,000 with IFC and MIGA), or 5,000 professionals, and yet oversight is still inadequate, then the oversight process looks distinctly inadequate. The dysfunctionality of the oversight process has its counterpart in the dysfunctionality of the quality control and evaluation process, part of which also reports directly to the board.

WHAT IS EFFECTIVE BANK GOVERNANCE?

It is now accepted that good boards can add value to and poor boards can subtract value from organizations, and that they are a critical part of the overall picture. Their membership, size, composition, expertise, experience, and functioning are important. The experience with companies such as Enron in the United States in 2001 and 2002[54] re-emphasized this. During the last twenty years, along with the wave of reorganizations, board governance has become a major issue within the private sector as advanced economies have transitioned into new technology areas, and as developing economies have struggled with the development of the rule of law. In the early 1990s, boards of a number of major U.S. companies (e.g., General Motors, IBM, and Westinghouse) were restructured as a result of shareholders taking power – particularly major institutional shareholders such as pension funds (e.g., the California pension system CALPERS).

The debate about how to improve boards in the United States and Britain has been about their own model, the unitary board, which is also used in countries such as France and Italy. The other main model is the two-tier 'continental' model (used in Germany, Holland, Belgium, and eastern European countries such as Hungary, Poland, and the Ukraine).[55] Under the two-tier system, the supervisory board is non-executive and appointed by the owner, while the management board is executive and nominated by the supervisory board, on its own or jointly with the owner. A third model is the Japanese one, which is characterized by reciprocal board membership between firms doing business with each other.[56]

---

[54] Experience with Enron, Global Crossing, WorldCom, Adelphia, and other major firms that were found, or were suspected, to have hidden from their boards significant data about their performance.

[55] For an analysis see 'Comparative Study of Corporate Governance Codes Relevant to the European Union and Its Member States', European Commission, January 2002.

[56] There is a lively debate on the pros and cons of each model. As seen from the United States and UK, there are problems with the two-tier model because of possible conflict and excessive management leverage, while a unitary board is simpler. But information flow, rights and responsibilities, size, and personalities are probably as important as formal structure. (See Pannier, Dominique, ed., 'Corporate Governance of Public Enterprises in Transitional Economies', World Bank Technical Paper no. 323, May 1996, p. 17.)

Discussion in the United States has focused on moving toward open relationships between CEOs and boards, and to end the polarization encouraged by tight, formal control, or the cooption of shareholders by management. There have also been proposals to separate the role of the chairman from that of the CEO. The power of audit committees has increased as the watchdog of good governance and the fiduciary responsibilities of directors reaffirmed. Another component of the discussion has been about the need for outside versus inside directors, to create the right balance of understanding and perspective.[57]

A book by Ram Charan was used during the reorganization period as a kind of guidance text for the Bank's own board members.[58] The author urged firms to 'unlock the value of your Board'. 'The true potential of a Board' he wrote, 'lies in its ability to help management solve problems, seize opportunities, and make the corporation perform better than it otherwise would . . .. The board's wisdom and judgment is a valuable managerial resource for any CEO'. He cites General Motors in the 1980s under President Roger Smith, where a reconstruction of the board and a reformed, open, and interactive management–board relationship allowed a critical change of focus in marketing. The median size of boards fell from fourteen in 1972 to twelve in 1989, and outside directors were increasingly brought in. Some board subcommittees (such as the Bell Atlantic audit committee) worked as internal advisers on best practice. 'Each director' said Charan, 'should have something important to contribute and should be able to function well in a group of equals'.[59] The bottom line, according to the highly respected Citicorp chairman, John Reed, was that 'a good board will stop you from doing dumb things'. Increasingly boards were recast as proactive strategists rather than reactive rubber-stamps for powerful CEOs.

The dean of the Bank's board made a statement about the contribution of individual directors at the farewell cocktail party for outgoing directors in October 2002: '[S]ome of us have a lot of experience in development issues' he said. 'Instead of going out and looking for

---

[57] Both the revised combined code of the UK and the revised French principles of corporate governance, of 2003, strengthen the presence of independent directors.
[58] Charan, Ram, *Boards at Work*, Jossey-Bass, 1998.
[59] Ibid., p. 241.

experts, staff could find people here who would give them insights on development issues'. However, this seems to have been an isolated plea. More characteristically, the board requested, and received, a small-scale version of the Harvard executive retraining program provided to the Bank's management, so that the directors could obtain some understanding of what management was learning. The implication was that the expertise of the board was not wider than that of the Bank's management. Instead of being able to provide objective advice to the managers on development issues, the directors generally have to defer to them, while in terms of organizational know-how they have little to offer. This lack of a continuous, relevant, expert outside perspective on organizational dynamics is one of the key problems of the governance of the Bank.

Important as it is, reform of the Bank's governance however goes well beyond directorial expertise. It needs a systemic solution that clarifies the relative power and responsibilities of the two boards, governors, and executive directors, and the top management, both in relation to each other and in relation to outside entities that bring influence to bear.

The two-tier concept of a policy (supervisory) board and a management board is appropriate to an organization such as the Bank, but not as currently structured with confused hierarchy and responsibilities. While Western corporates have increasingly looked for non-executive outside directors to counterbalance insider power, the Bank has effectively only outside directors, even though its board directors are technically 'inside'. The existing executive directors, despite the fact that they walk the corridors, are, de facto, neither inside nor executive. Inside directors such as finance, operations, and strategy chiefs, along with the president, working alongside experienced and expert outsiders could be part of a solution to the effective direction of the Bank. Directorial expertise also requires sourcing outside the civil service and public sectors. Thus two key changes could include the introduction of directors, first, from inside the organization and, second, from the private sector.

If the Bank is to be an effective public organization in the twenty-first century, then the nature of the governance model needs to be changed. So far the efforts of several decades have been largely confined to small

changes in process. The pressure applied on the Bank's client governments for rapid institutional development has not been paralleled by
institutional change within the Bank itself. As a senior manager recently
said, with admirable but misplaced modesty, '[W]e have seen the problem and it is us'. But this statement seems to be more appropriate from
the governance overseers themselves, and there has been no apparent
realization on their part.

The recent Voice initiative addresses an important issue, and it has
triggered considerable outside literature and commentary in addition
to the lengthy discussion within the institution.[60] But to repeat the
immortal words of one director: '[T]he acoustics are so bad that in reality
no one has a voice'. The prior concern is whether the basic system of
governance is adding or subtracting value. The role of governance in the
operational effectiveness of the Bank remains the Cinderella issue, that
is, the one that has not been invited to the annual meetings! This we
consider further in the conclusion of this study.

---

[60] Notably in Buira, Ariel, ed., *Reforming the Governance of the IMF and the World Bank*,
Anthem Press, 2005. The voluminous literature is probably not a good sign for those
hoping for action, and indeed the discussion on voting representation has so far
continued for five years.

11

The Leadership

THE LEADER AND HIS LIEUTENANTS

The Strategic Compact was an agreement between the executive directors and the president. The president was not only the key figure during the reorganization but also, of course, as chief executive, important to the institution in the longer run. The president's character, style, and capacities would normally be critical to the direction and effectiveness of an institution even if the institutional persona changed only slowly. However, since the chief executive was signatory to the Strategic Compact, the characteristics of the chief executive's position – its style, qualifications, responsibilities, fiduciary duties, reporting, performance, and selection – were, unsurprisingly, not part of the Compact or the subsequent reform process. Yet one particular aspect of leadership, the selection process, was increasingly in question.

Whereas in performing their role several of the past presidents, such as Clausen and Preston, had been relatively distant figures, and had shaped the culture and functioning of the Bank rather by default, Wolfensohn took an aggressive and proactive stance. His demeanor reflected an unusual background. While he had strong Wall Street connections, he also regarded himself as having capacities beyond Wall Street. He was a lawyer and Harvard MBA and had excelled in the corporate finance world, where he led the first Chrysler rescue, and latterly he set up his own boutique investment firm that had attracted the participation of world-class individuals such as Paul Volcker. In addition, he had fenced for Australia at the 1956 Olympic Games, and had reached concert standard as a cellist after having only apparently taken up the instrument when he was forty. He had a gift for high-level networking and he became president of the Kennedy Center, where he used his prodigious fundraising talents and expanded his network into the civil society arena. However, he had never been head of a large-scale organization and had no noteworthy experience in the area of development assistance. Thus he brought to the Bank an array of talents and experience that did not necessarily have much to do with traditional Bank needs but were thought to have the potential to create a transforming kind of leadership.[1]

Running the Bank also required a cadre of effective top managers. Presidents have, in the course of the Bank's history, tried a number of approaches. McNamara created a president's council consisting of all the vice presidents but found it too unwieldy and replaced it with an executive committee of two senior vice presidents, a general counsel, and a secretary. In 1981 Clausen formed a formal management committee on a collective management model, as a type of substitute for a corporate management board. In 1986 Conable used the management committee as an advisory council, and in 1991 Preston created the managing director's office, replacing the senior vice presidents with three managing directors to help him run the Bank. All three were long-term insiders who were to act as advisers to the vice presidents without line responsibilities, intended to eliminate of a layer of decision-making. Wolfensohn maintained the managing director's position, and recast it later, once again, as a management committee.

Just as he had arrived with his own set of talents that were outside traditional Bank experience, Wolfensohn's instinct seemed to be to replace the long-serving incumbent managing directors (as well as nearly all the vice presidents) with outsiders from more colorful, and perhaps better politically connected, backgrounds. A large number of the Bank's top managers rapidly left, either fired or of their own accord. These included Messrs Ernest Stern, Gautam Kaji, Kim Jaycox, Shahid Husain,

---

[1] Sebastian Mallaby provides a detailed portrait of Wolfensohn's personal background in *The World's Banker*, Penguin, 2004.

and, after only one year, even his personal appointee, Rachel Lomax, a star performer from the British civil service, left the organization[2].

Wolfensohn instead hired four managing directors. As mentioned, these were Ramphela Mamphele, an African who had been the first female vice chancellor of the University of Capetown; Jeffrey Goldstein, who came in from Bankers Trust and BT-Wolfensohn; Peter Woicke, who came from JP Morgan; and Shengman Zhang, who had been the executive director for China in 1994–1995 and was previously at the Chinese Ministry of Finance. The only remaining insider managing director was Sven Sandstrom, but he announced his retirement in October 2001.

It had long been argued that outside expertise was needed at the helm of the Bank to provide a balance to the insider domination and sup-posed lack of innovative initiatives that resulted. By the end of 2001 there was *only* outside expertise. The Bank entered a period when a top management lacking in institutional knowledge reported to a CEO uninterested in operational details who reported to a board lacking in both experience and inside knowledge, which was in turn under the oversight of governors who were not able to pay attention. What impact did this have on the effectiveness of the institution?

TOP MANAGEMENT GAMES

After the departure of Sandstrom in 2001, the new top layer of management was reallocated to a mixture of responsibilities. Zhang became the operations chief, which he now combined with a number of other responsibilities such as Board relations; Goldstein became the finance chief with a few other things like macroeconomics, and pov-erty, of which he presumably had not acquired great insight at Bankers Trust. These two posts had been once held (without the extra baggage) by a legendary duo of Ernie Stern and Moeen Qureshi. Another man-aging director was now given responsibility for a mixed group of three operational regions, two thematic groups, and the chief information

---

[2] Lomax was reportedly unsure whether she had been appointed as his chief adviser or his chief office assistant.

office. Another one was responsible for the other three operating regions, external affairs and corporate strategy. Woicke ran the IFC and a thematic group. In April 2003 their responsibilities were reshuffled again purportedly to strengthen implementation and out-reach. Zhang now took charge of nearly all operations plus most of the networks.

Here was a top management team that was selected under unusual criteria and managed in an unusual way. The top management structure of 1987 was in effect recreated in 2003, but now with confused roles and without the people who had intimate knowledge of how the Bank worked. While, doubtless, able people in their own right, none had operational knowledge. One reflection of this was Woicke's determina-tion, on arrival from JP Morgan, to forge a synergy between IFC's investment bankers and the World Bank's development specialists. Wolfensohn's own recent top management experience had been in running a boutique investment firm where personal relations no doubt worked better than bureaucratic ones.

The role of the managing directors nevertheless became more impor-tant when, in 2002, Wolfensohn, responding to charges that he was out of touch, formed them into a management committee. After the stra-tegic forum in 2002, an action plan allocated an even more complex and intertwined set of strategic responsibilities between the Management Committee members. The following shows one part of the new respon-sibilities of the management committee.

Under just one of the strategic areas, called '*global positioning*', Zhang and Goldstein handled the impact of '9/11'; all committee members were responsible for the Millennium Development Goals; most were responsible for the financing of development (post the Monterrey conference of 2002); most were responsible for the Banks role in the provision of Global Public Goods, divided into communicable diseases, the environment, ICT/knowledge, trade and integration, and the international financial architecture. The 'communicable diseases' responsibility went to Goldstein (with Ramphele) – thus the investment banker took responsibility for malaria, AIDS, and the pharmaceutical industry, as well as poverty and macroeconomic development. Zhang took responsibility for the environment. Ramphele and Woicke took the development gateway and distance learning. Goldstein/Ramphele and Zhang took Agriculture and textile liberalization. Goldstein looked after the International Financial Architecture. Zhang and Goldstein were to harmonize the Bank's development approach with its partners. This complex set of inter-linked responsibilities ensured a continued hands-off, ceremonial top management with little focus on practical matters, continuing the approach that had been present during the reorganization.

The complexities were such that the Bank's standard organization chart was only elaborated as far down the hierarchy as the vice-presidential level – that is, two levels below the president. But the inter-linked responsibilities of the MDs seem to confuse the system even at the top level. There can be little doubt that if one of the Bank's own governance specialist teams was sent to carry out one of its 'diagnostic functional analyses' of such a structure in a client country implementing public sector reform, it would recommend urgent and drastic changes. The difficulty in simply charting the Bank's reporting relationships was in itself a signal of such a need.

By past experience, the managing directors did not stay for very long. Following Sandstrom, the first to leave was Mamphele, who as a political appointee never seemed to find a role in the intricate and perplexing Bank world. By 2005 all the MDs had left, the last being Zhang, who, after quite successfully taking the reins for a couple of years, followed Wolfensohn to CitiGroup.

The assumption of office by Paul Wolfowitz in 2005 did not seem to improve the selection of top management. He seemed to treat the Bank to some extent as though it was a type of federal agency, staffed at senior levels by Republican political appointees.[3] As Wolfensohn's own lieutenants either left or were obliged to leave,[4] he appointed two managing directors. The first was generally considered to be a reasonable appointment, that of Graeme Wheeler, a New Zealander and a well-reputed former treasurer of the Bank. His second appointment, from outside, was less successful – Juan Jose Darboub – the former

---

[3]   These were Suzanne Rich Folsom, Robyn Cleveland, Kevin Kellems, and Karl Jackson.
[4]   Of these, Christiaan Poortman reportedly resigned rather than open a Bank office in Iraq, partly influenced by the death of the previous UN representative in a bomb explosion.

minister of finance of El Salvador, whose proactive conservative views were not always welcomed. Although Wolfowitz initiated a search for top talent outside the Bank, his focus during his short time in the post was not on the structure of his top management but more on the supposed inadequacies of his staff, that is, the usual target. Within two years of his departure all his own outside appointees had also left.

WHAT KIND OF LEADERSHIP?

The character of the presidents of the Bank impacted in different ways on how the institution worked, and Wolfensohn's relatively aggressive and proactive leadership posture forced many changes that might not have occurred under other leaders. Whereas the board that appointed him expected that his atypical background and proactive posture would somehow galvanize the institution to improvements, in the end, however, as we have shown, his leadership was not consistent with institutional effectiveness. What kind of leader in fact would work best for an organization like the Bank?

Leadership has been for a long time a favorite topic in business schools and in management texts. One leadership typology that was influential in the 1990s, attributable to Bass, among others[5] used the dichotomy of transactional and transformational leader. Studies showed that transformational leadership as defined significantly increased organizational performance. While more traditional transactional leadership is centralized, control-oriented, and rule-based, transformational leaders are hands-off and base their leadership on trust of subordinates. They are visionaries, good communicators, and convey a strong sense of mission, instilling pride and drawing out innovative thinking. They coach and pay attention to individual needs. Organizational transformation would be most consistent with a transformational leader.

---

[5]   Bernard Bass was a leading contemporary author on transformational leadership. See, for example, Bass, B. and B. Avolio, eds., *Improving Organizational Effectiveness Through Transformational Leadership*, Sage, 1993.

Table 11. *Mintzberg's leadership types*

Category	Leadership type	Cultural type	Working method
1	Entrepreneurial	Power culture	Central/personal
2	Machine	Role culture	Logical, rational, rule-bound
3	Professional	Role culture plus	Highly logical, rational
4	Innovative	Task culture	Teams, flexible, partnerships
5	Missionary	Person culture	Unstructured, specialist idealist

Another possible way of characterizing leadership that might be usable in this discussion relates leadership type to the type of organization led, to determine the best fit. Henry Mintzberg, another leading thinker on the subject, compiled the typology, shown in Table 11.[6]

The World Bank's presidents in the past would usually have been characterized as transactional, and type 2, the 'machine', or type 3, the 'professional'. One exception was possibly Robert McNamara, who was transformational but appeared to combine several Mintzberg types. Leadership effectiveness, according to Mintzberg, needs a fit between leadership type, cultural type, and working method. Leadership and organizational change need to observe limits imposed by these. Thus, whereas a type 3, professional, leader fits in well with a role culture and a rational working method, a type 4 innovative, task culture, built up around a highly rational and rule-bound system, may not fit well with a missionary leader, type 5. Nor might a type 4 culture fit in with a machine leadership, type 2.

McNamara is generally thought to have been the most successful president in terms of building organizational effectiveness. He combined a keen mind with rigorous attention to detail, type 3 on the Mintzberg scale, and a sense of wider purpose – the vision of the Bank as an advocate for the poor, which also placed him as type 4 or 5. Despite his high-level background as U.S. Defense Secretary and head of the Ford motor company, McNamara was also

---

[6] Henry Mintzberg is a leading author on corporate leadership. See his *Mintzberg on Management: Inside Our Strange World of Organizations*, Free Press, 1989.

quite ascetic – he traveled economy class and tended to maintain a relatively low profile in his dealings with staff and with the outside world, which built respect and trust, conditions also needed in a transformational leader.

WOLFENSOHN AS LEADER

Wolfensohn's leadership style was, as he himself saw it, transformational and innovative. He would probably not have seen himself as fitting in with the type 2 or 3, rule-bound system. He wanted to move people, and he wanted idealistic partners. Unlike McNamara, he was not ascetic, nor was he detail-oriented. The way he exercised leadership was also polarizing. Unlike the transformational model of a leader, he did not instil pride, or draw out innovative thinking, and he was not interested in the individual needs of his staff. On the whole, he was derivative of type 1 or 5. This could be said to have been one of the less well-fitting personalities in relation to the organization he led, and the struggle over the reorganization was partly about whether he could change such an the organization in his own image.

On first entering the Bank, when he seemed to view its employees as still in a sense his clients, Wolfensohn was in effect concerned to win over partners to a deal. He gave a reception on his arrival on June 2, 2005 for randomly chosen staff. A report by a very impressed writer for the internal newspaper *Bank's World Today* who attended spoke of how caring, concerned, and gentle he was, and how lucky the Bank was to get him. 'He has given up quite a lot to become the ninth President of the World Bank – and he's given it up willingly because he sees the job as a privilege', she wrote. In fact, however, the job was one that he had been campaigning for intermittently since 1980, when he became a U.S. citizen in order to qualify for it.[7] While his caring and concern were initially consistent with his transformational pretensions, it seemed that later on, when he perceived his

---

[7] Sebastian Mallaby recounts that Wolfensohn changed his citizenship in 1980 to qualify for the job when it was suggested by Robert McNamara that he could be a candidate. When it was finally in sight, he lobbied aggressively and got round the initial opposition of such a person as Bob Rubin, Treasury Secretary. As Mallaby puts it, the Bank's top management took exception to the 'showboating newcomer' who thought he was doing the institution a favor by taking the job.

'clients' as having reverted to their real identity of paid employees, the charm offensive ended and the treatment became less accommodating.

Wolfensohn's familiarization trips, notably in Africa, just after he had entered office, showed him quick to identify problems but also equally quick to attribute blame for them among his top staff, and to create difficult personal relationships that could not help him achieve his overall mission.[8] A tenuous relationship with his employees continued throughout his tenure, but it was not confined to the employees. In 1997, the French executive director, in his parting speech, was bold enough to use a metaphor about narcissus and his reflection to describe Wolfensohn's attitude.[9] His transformational qualities were apparently mixed with an element of insecurity. Even after achieving reappointment by the board for a second five-year term he told one meeting of middle managers in early 2001 that he had succeeded in 'outlasting you when you expected to outlast me'.[10]

The news spread of the president's demeanor. Stephen Fidler wrote in *Foreign Policy*[11]: '[O]bservers blame the World Bank's troubles on Wolfensohn's personal failings – his phenomenal temper, constant need for approval, and inability to resist the latest development fad'. Wolfensohn, he claimed, 'had precipitated a crisis because of his personal idiosyncrasies – his inability to stand criticism and unwillingness to accept the presence of other powerful personalities near him'. But, he also had strong supporters. Executive Director Terrie O'Leary, from Ireland, for example, said in a 2002 farewell address: '[W]hat a fine man you are. What an inspired leader you have been for this institution'. Claire Short, Britain's minister for international development at the time, was another staunch supporter.

In an interview on the tenth anniversary of his term of office, Wolfensohn was asked, '[W]hat in your view was your major accomplishment?' He replied, characteristically: '[W]ell, I think my greatest accomplishment is that ten thousand people in this institution and I

---

[8] For an illustration, see Mallaby's account of Wolfensohn's public face-off with Kim Jaycox, who was vice president for Africa, in Mallaby, op cit., 2004. Kim Jaycox himself was a transformational figure who had been an architect of the 1987 reorganization.
[9] This is recounted in Mallaby, op cit.
[10] Personal communication.
[11] Fidler, Steven, 'Who Is Minding the Bank', *Foreign Policy*, September 2001.

now see eye to eye on where we are going, and I think I have been greatly
influenced by my colleagues and I think I have probably had some
influence on them'. Yet the opposite case applied in some views. One
of his main goals for the Bank had in effect been to get others to agree
with and promote his personal vision.

In 2003 the psychoanalyst Michael Maccoby attempted a further
enrichment of the literature on leadership by introducing three new
categories – the 'erotic', the 'obsessive', and the 'narcissistic'.[12] While
Mintzberg and Bass provided insights into the functional characteristics of leaders, Maccoby provided insights into their personalities.
The 1990s, he wrote, was the era of narcissistic enterprise leadership.
Bill Gates, Jack Welch, and George Soros were, says Maccoby, productive narcissists, gifted, creative, charming risk-takers who aim to leave
behind a legacy and are less interested in the details than the vision. But
narcissists could also be disruptive and dysfunctional for an organization.
Whatever the case, it was especially important for the Bank to have a
board strong enough to manage the personality of this chief executive.

At the end of his tenure, when things were looking better for both
the Bank and Wolfensohn, a reminder of the past came in the form of
another book, that of Sebastian Mallaby of the *Washington Post*, which
portrayed the president as equally a builder and a destroyer. The author
accordingly found after his book's publication that he no longer had
an open door to the president's office or to the Bank. Reputedly,
Wolfensohn's top managers were afraid to admit that they had read
the book.

WOLFOWITZ AS LEADER

The 2005 appointment by George W. Bush of Wolfowitz to replace
Wolfensohn was vigorously, but fleetingly, opposed despite the fact that
he had a background that was in principle quite acceptable to the Bank.
He was from the same quasi-academic Ivy League skill pool as many of
the Bank's staff and with a reflective and cerebral manner.

---

[12] Maccoby, Michael, *The Productive Narcissist, the Promise and Peril of Visionary Leadership*, Broadway Books, 2003.

While having sound academic and diplomatic credentials, Wolfowitz subscribed to a controversial ideology. This may have originated at the University of Chicago, where, along with others of the Neo-Conservative movement, he came under the influence of the hegemonic ideas of Leo Strauss.[13] He was a member of the lobby group PNAC (the Project for the New American Century), together with other luminaries of the Right, including Cheney, Rumsfeld, Kristol, Perle, Quayle, Bolton, Libby, and Abrams. PNAC wanted to use U.S. military power to reshape the world. A letter of June 3, 1997, signed by Wolfowitz and others, asked, '[D]oes the United States have the resolve to shape a new century favorable to American interests and principles?' Another, better known, letter to President Clinton in 1998, read: 'American Policy cannot continue to be crippled by a misguided insistence on unanimity in the UN Security Council'.

As such, this was by no means an obvious candidate to head up the world's leading international development assistance organization. When Wolfowitz' candidacy was announced Jeffery Sachs made a statement to the ECOSOC in New York: 'I]t's time for other candidates to come forward that have experience in development . . .. This is a position on which hundreds of millions of people depend for their lives'. 'Let's have a proper leadership of professionalism', he said. A courageous Bank staff member attempted to start a campaign to prevent his selection.

Like all presidents past, Wolfowitz also brought with him personality issues, but at first sight they seemed manageable. He came across as earnest, rational, and eager to understand other opinions, on which he took copious notes. But, as Thomas Ricks wrote,[14] 'Wolfowitz's low-key manner cloaked a tough-minded determination that ran far deeper than is common in compromise-minded Washington'.

Despite first impressions, like his predecessor, his apparent belief that he was going to personally facilitate the development of the world

[13] Leo Strauss's ideas centered on, among other things, the 'natural order' of leadership, and the need for the elites of powerful nations to assume national and world leadership to preserve traditional social values against the dilutions caused by mass empowerment. Such philosophies were preconditions of the aggressive neo-conservative Middle-Eastern policy, and the interest in a 'Pax Americana'. See Drury, Shadia, *Leo Strauss and the American Right*, St. Martins Press, 1999.
[14] Ricks, Thomas E., *Fiasco: The American Military Adventure in Iraq*, Penguin, 2006.

resulted in his coming to treat the organization adversarially, as though it was a barrier to the achievement of his unique personal insights, rather than the material with which he had to fulfill them. His copious note-taking turned out to be more a feint than a genuine interest in others' opinions. Wolfowitz did not move to create alliances but aggravated his initial credibility problem by deploying his small inner circle, who held the ritual Republican disdain for 'bureaucracies', especially ones suspected of harboring political liberals and even socialists. His lack of interest in alliances apparently stemmed from an assumption of ideological certitude common to members of the Bush administration. He had the missionary and transformational instincts of Wolfensohn, strengthened by his conscious philosophical leanings, and he had the same lack of interest in detail, especially regarding the management of the organization. But he also apparently did not have the political antenna that had seen Wolfensohn through ten years of office.

Wolfowitz looked like a Mintzberg type 5. He did not conform to the type 3 individual who could run the Bank well as an organization. He did not have the liberal-internationalist perspective typical of World Bank staff, but apparently believed more in a mission to combat evil forces. Here was a political appointee who seemed to see the Bank as a platform for a political and philosophical agenda rather than for the grueling and pragmatic negotiations required to bring about development, combined with the detail-orientation needed to improve the Bank's performance. The lingering resentment at how an unlikely U.S.-nominated candidate had once more been maneuvered past the board meant that he had little political capital and few allies on which to depend when he came up against opposition in terms of his development policies, and none when it came to his personal activities.

THE SELECTION OF LEADER

The World Bank's Articles of Agreement (Article V, Section 5(a)) state that 'the Executive Directors shall elect the President . . .'. This function has never been seriously fulfilled, but instead the American president has nominated the Bank's president and the nomination has always been accepted. The Italian Executive Director, Bossone, in his farewell speech on October 31, 2006, went so far as to describe this provision of the Articles as a 'joke at the expense of the Board'.

The 'free pass' for U.S. selection of the Bank's leader has, however, been under increasing pressure. In a 2003 interchange in the British Parliament, Ann Clwyd, the Welsh MP, challenged Clare Short, who was then Minister for International Development. *Clwyd:* 'I wonder how you are supporting the introduction of an open process for selecting the next President of the World Bank'. *Short:* 'The US gets the World Bank and Europe gets the IMF and it cannot go on, surely. What about the rest of the world? The geographical carve up is intolerable and the system for selecting is a kind of political fix system. It is an outrage the present system and it needs continuing pressure to make it transparent'.

From the point of view of corporate effectiveness, what matters is not the nationality of the president but his expertise. While it was not on the table for discussion during the time of the reorganization, it emerged as an issue, triggered by Wolfensohn's management style and the rejection of Caio Koch-Weser as IMF chief; and it was accentuated by the Wolfowitz affair. A joint working group of Fund and Bank executive directors was formed as early as 2001 to prepare shortlists of future presidents for Board consideration. Nevertheless, Wolfowitz's appointment in 2005 was under the traditional system of U.S. presidential patronage, as was his successor, Robert Zoellick in 2007.

What are the characteristics that would be appropriate for a president of the leading global financial institution, with a worldwide mandate for guiding economic development policy? They might reasonably include: 1) experience running a world class public or private organization specializing in economic development and/or finance, and 2) high-level professional experience and top qualifications in disciplines related to economics or finance with a development slant.

As shown in Table 12, the principal academic training of the eleven presidents, all exclusively U.S.-based, breaks down as six law graduates, two liberal arts graduates, one scientist, one with no formal

Table 12. *Presidential resumes*

Name (age on arrival)	Academic level, specialization	Prior professional experience
1. Meyer (70)	Yale AB Law	Industry/Wall St./ U.S. Administration/ Federal Reserve/ Reconstr. Finance Corp.
2. McCloy (52)	Amherst, Harvard Law LLB	U.S. Administration/ Wall St./Council on Foreign Relations/ Rockefeller Foundation
3. Black (51)	Univ. Georgia Latin AB	Wall St. finance
4. Woods (62)	None (night school)	Wall St. finance
5. McNamara (52)	UCal Berkeley Economics BSc Harvard MBA	Industry/U.S. Administration
6. Clausen (58)	Carthage, Minnesota Law LLB	Wall St./Commercial Banking
7. Conable (64)	Cornell Law LLB	Politics/Congress
8. Preston (65)	Harvard History BA	Wall St.
9. Wolfensohn (61)	Sydney Law LLB, Harvard MBA	Law/Wall St./ Rockefeller foundation
10. Wolfowitz (61)	Cornell Maths/chemistry BSc Chicago Political Science PhD	Academia/diplomat/ U.S. Administration
11. Zoellick (53)	Swarthmore, Harvard Law, MPP Kennedy School	U.S. Administration/ diplomat/Wall St.

academic training, and one economist. Economics training is not at all a *sine qua non* for Bank leadership, but it is a dominant discipline. An economist's caste of mind is important to issues such as economic reform and development strategy and policy, the positioning of the Bank within the development assistance agenda, the evolution of development products, decisions about individual new loans, and evaluations of the effects of past loans and programs, as well as the range of corporate issues relevant to an international financial institution. A score of three out of eleven might be defensible but one out of eleven just does not seem so. It is also notable that, despite the 2,000 or so PhD holders in the Bank, only one president has held such a qualification.

At the professional level, seven out of eleven leaders, including Wolfensohn, have had primarily Wall Street banking careers, most with some government experience. Of those with government experience, three were political appointees at the Pentagon. Two have had primarily U.S. administration backgrounds. One was an industrialist as well as a member of the administration, and one was a politician. Of the eleven, only four have had enough normal pre-retirement years ahead of them to complete one tour of duty.

Of the eleven presidents of the World Bank appointed by the U.S. president, a few have had relevant public interest–oriented experience. The first, Meyer, was briefly chief of the Reconstruction Finance Corporation, and of the Federal Reserve; McCloy and Wolfensohn were both directors of the Rockefeller Foundation, and Wolfowitz was dean of the School of Advanced International Studies at John Hopkins University. Zoellick has served on boards such as the Overseas Development Council, the World Wildlife Fund, and the Institute of International Economics. But not a single one has had a formal background in development economics or development finance, and not a single one has had any experience working in an international assistance agency.

Without such experience it is not easy to comprehend the practical difficulties of designing, implementing, and managing effective assistance in developing country environments, and it is too easy to make the standard assumption that ineffectiveness is somehow due to 'bureaucrats' who have to be 'shaken up' from time to time. Substantial international experience in a developing country seems to have been confined to Wolfowitz, who was ambassador to Indonesia for three years, while the international experience of others has been based on intermittent diplomatic, business, or military missions. The Wall Street background that applies to the majority was quite appropriate in the early phase of the Bank's life, when it was largely an investment finance institution, but that phase came to an end with Robert McNamara.

The broad experience pattern of the eleven choices for president is not only inconsistent with, but surprisingly far removed from, what would be expected if the selection had been made on a systematic merit basis. That none of the eleven has previously held a job in a development assistance agency at any level seems particularly incomprehensible.

TAKE US TO ANOTHER LEADER

After the Wolfowitz affair, the selection of the eleventh president was quickly finalized by the White House and approved by the board. Robert Zoellick took over on July 1, 2007. Zoellick is the sixth lawyer-president out of the eleven, continuing the tradition of non-economists and non-leaders in the development field. He is, however, a detailed-oriented internationalist with serious international trade credentials as Bush's trade secretary, who brought China into the World Trade Organization (WTO). He was most recently at Goldman Sachs. At the start of his tenure the signs were that he retains an important element of 'Mintzberg type 3'.

Despite the more positive signs, Zoellick was still a partisan choice. He was a long-time Bush ally and a signatory to the 1998 PNAC letter to President Clinton. The selection of an individual who was not linked to the Bush team, even a non-American, with wide international recognition would have answered to international concerns and could have preserved the U.S. selection tradition. But rather than recognize a reasonable international interest, George W. Bush instead raised U.S. presidential patronage to a higher level. Only one other Bank chief had been appointed from the U.S. president's top-level administration, and that was McNamara in 1969. Bush appointed two (though Zoellick had left the administration briefly for Goldman Sachs before being appointed). The failure, once again, to give due weight to a simple point, echoing on a micro-scale the foreign policy miscalculations of the Bush era, has surely precipitated an end to the informal agreement on the U.S. role in leadership selection.

From the corporate effectiveness point of view, it is widely accepted that future appointments of the president of the Bank should be based on criteria of broadly agreed merit and expertise, and should not be within the political patronage of any particular country's president or prime minister. The selection of a broadly internationally acceptable, highly regarded figure with world-class professional qualifications has to be the aim. Academic background is secondary, but the Bank's president has to be able to advocate global economic policies credibly at world fora and needs to be able to offer intellectual leadership in that role while also effectively managing the institution that he or she leads. The leader has to have the patience to negotiate small gains across a broad spectrum, find the right alignments of resources and objectives, and persuade the many stakeholders to support his or her actions. While all the presidents have been able and successful men in their own way, no doubt, they have as a general rule not fulfilled the requirements of this job. Yet the selection of an outstanding and capable individual as president is as, or more, important as the selection of an outstanding and capable board of directors. If the opening up of the World Bank presidency will be at a 'cost' to the Europe member nations of the opening up of the IMF chief's position, then, from the global point of view, it is difficult to see why that need pose an issue.

12

Looking Back and Looking Forward: What Is to Be Done?

GAINS, QUALIFIED GAINS, AND LOSSES

Over twenty years of reorganization the Bank has struggled to find a formula for organizational effectiveness. Despite continual claims of progress, it has not found it. At the beginning of this study the question was asked: Who, or what, was responsible for the debacle of the Bank reorganization? Was it poor leadership? Was it inappropriate governance? Was it the incompetence of managers and employees? Was it external pressures? Perhaps lack of skills? Did it mean that the Bank is inherently unmanageable, or did it mean that it was simply badly led? The hope is that this critique is one that will help to answer these questions and highlight the urgency of maintaining the legitimacy of a global economic development leader.

This look at twenty years of reform has mainly been about the latter half, the late 1990s and beyond, because that is when the major effort was made. The problems that James Wolfensohn undertook to solve were numerous. According to his understanding, the Bank's projects were often of doubtful quality; their impact on development was ambiguous; it was very expensive to do business with; it was increasingly bureaucratic and complex; it failed to innovate; it was too fragmented internally, too arrogant and distant from its clients; and it needed re-skilling. He had ten years in which to do something about these problems.

This book has looked at changes in organizational structure, processes, skills, and types and qualities of products and services that could be traced to the reorganization of the Bank. Despite the overall poor results, there were some areas that could be pointed to as showing improvement within these categories, but they were few. Here is a summing up of the main initiatives, in terms of organization structure, product, and inputs.

Switching resources to the front line. Organizationally, one of the key aims was an attempt to switch resources from back-line overheads to front-line operations. This initiative was intended to facilitate or complement increased organizational efficiency, decentralization, and country responsiveness.

On some measures such a shift to the front line was achieved. However, on more realistic measures of what constituted the front line, a shift did not take place, except in reverse. The budget cuts of the Strategic Compact damaged the Bank's core capacity and its operations for several years. The Bank became less operationally focused as overheads rose, and the front-line effort ratio has remained at substantially below 50% since then. The ratio of administrative costs to lending has risen as bureaucratic complexity has increased, reflecting the shift away from the front line, while internal fragmentation remains an unresolved problem reducing efficiency in front-line work.

The knowledge bank. Organizationally, this was the other key change. The Bank was a knowledge producer before the reorganization, but following Wolfensohn's 1996 Annual Meeting address this role was reinforced. Either to achieve this shift, or in parallel with it, the networks were created to provide advisory inputs directly and to manage the greatly expanded information system. Reorganization of professional staff into regional skill pools was also complementary to the knowledge initiative, considerably enlarging the skill pools that had existed before.

The networks have in practice been of questionable value to the organization. Initially within the reduced budget they diverted resources from operations in return for a doubtful gain in usable knowledge compared to what could have been provided without them. In the longer term, they have tended to bureaucratize the knowledge generation and management sphere and to set up 'information silos' operating alongside 'operational silos'. The enlarged skill pools that accompanied the networks have not necessarily achieved the knowledge 'critical mass' that they were aimed at. The triple reform consisting of: a) skills pooling in a matrix, b) skills pooling within a network, and c) skills pooling through the intranet/Internet was excessive to the institution's requirements. The intranet system alone may have improved access to usable information without the reorganization of the 'boxes'. The skill pools were a product of the matrix system, but the skill synergy sought through the matrix was in any case offset by a loss in country continuity that existed in the previous system. The matrix, combined with the internal market in its initial form, is unlikely to have enhanced usable knowledge.

Information systems. The information system was part of the creation of the knowledge bank, as well as an instrument to increase operating efficiency. An organizational gain arose through the establishment of the system, both in terms of technology platforms and content. There were information and advisory centers, expanded videoconferencing, and distance learning. Internal and external information availability improved through development of inter- and intranet systems and investment in communication facilities. Some information technology advances would no doubt have occurred in the absence of this initiative, but the Strategic Compact particularly concentrated resources on it.

But the major investment in a unified information system by the Bank was not matched by its investment in implementation. There was a delay of several years to get near its proclaimed productivity levels, often requiring ad hoc amendments to make it usable, and it was over budget. It had serious launch problems. Initially the unified system was unable to provide accurate expenditure data, resulting in cycles of over- and underspending that probably exacerbated the redundancy missteps. The level of integration of the information system into operations is still inadequate. The system has possibly succeeded in finally approaching its potential capability, but only after major corrections and at considerable cost – financial to the institution and psychological to those who attempted to manage it.

Decentralization. An organizational gain came in the form of decentralization. Although decentralization had been taking place for decades, in the 1990s there was a clear acceleration designed to make the

Bank more answerable to its country clients. By 2003, three-quarters of the newly created country director posts were located out of Washington, DC. Decentralization in a practical way has strengthened outreach and the Bank's client relationships and capacity in-country, improving the responsiveness to actual problems on the ground. Supporting this, there is considerably increased provision of information about the Bank's activities with a much extended external relations function in the country offices, and a more open attitude as a whole.

However, the decentralization was limited because of its cost, and there has since been a partial re-merging of offices, so that on average one director now manages three countries. In Africa, some of the country groupings under single management are now as large as under the previous system. The reorganization also tried to decentralize at the same time as the establishment of the advisory networks required centralization. This contrary reallocation of resources occurred as budgets were cut, so that the HQ operational units were severely restricted in their ability to back up the in-country units. Additionally, although in a better position to monitor events, people sitting in comfortable offices in Jakarta or Dacca and monitoring neighboring countries are physically but not spiritually really closer to the circumstances and interests of the poor. The pre-1997 system of individual country representatives under Washington-based directors could have been strengthened at lower cost and with the same benefit by raising their profile and resources under proactive and credible leadership from the top.

Pro-poor projects. Pro-poor lending was a key product initiative. The lending and advisory strategies of the Bank were intended to become increasingly pro-poor, and it was advertised as such, with the Bank's principal mission statement announcing the fight against poverty.

However, during the reorganization period the profile was not pro-poor, for two main reasons. First, even without the Asian economic crisis lending, structural adjustment lending to middle income countries was stepped up to unprecedented levels, to countries such as Turkey. Second, the sectors containing the greatest poverty, agriculture and rural, received record low levels of Bank assistance, paralleled by a reduction in Bank expertise. Instead there were major increases in lending to reform banking systems and government administrations.

The lending strategy became less, not more, selective and lost focus while, contrary to a pro-poor objective, much Bank assistance continued to be allocated on implicit, if not explicit, political criteria.

Knowledge products. This was the other key product change. There was a significant shift to new capacity- and institution-building projects, in accordance with the knowledge bank initiative. This shift from loans to knowledge products involved both the Bank's direct knowledge services and the new knowledge-intensive projects.

Despite the overt change in emphasis, however, the reorganization period in fact saw a precipitous decline in the production of direct knowledge services because the restricted budget was transferred to networks and other back-line functions, while the front-line products, including the Bank's basic economic and sector reports for each country, were starved of resources for several years. Furthermore, while knowledge-intensive projects expanded, their performance was often moderate because of the difficulties in delivering institutional change from outside. Many projects that were highly rated for their institution-building impact may in fact have had little impact when their counterfactual is considered. Institution-building projects are also often small, labor-intensive, and loss-making, and a broad shift to such products carries risks for the Bank's financial sustainability, unless combined with large loans. The Bank has thus not established that institution-building projects are within its comparative advantage.

Participatory projects. This approach was strongly promoted during the reorganization in order to increase local ownership, by governments, civil society, and other stakeholders, getting away from the intrusive conditions previously attached to loans largely prepared outside the recipient country. Credit for promoting the participatory process with stronger partnerships between the donors and extended outreach to the world, whether through the so-called Comprehensive Development Framework or through other avenues, goes to Wolfensohn.

Nevertheless, the participatory process is highly labor-intensive and requires expensive nurturing, thus begging the same question about financial sustainability as does institution-building. Furthermore, the Comprehensive Development Framework and its successor

Poverty Reduction Strategies have an extra-parliamentary political dynamic and aid-driven timeframe, and have started to resemble the discredited former externally driven initiatives. The Bank is not well positioned to conduct participatory projects, and it cannot enter the political arena. Neither is it positioned as a 'first responder' (which seems to have been Wolfensohn's ideal[1]). It is questionable whether in the long run it has the mandate, the capacity, or the incentives to get involved in intricate, labor-intensive, time-consuming, and often politically charged participatory initiatives with uncertain and slowly arriving results. If it cannot do it, in keeping with the spirit of aid cooperation initiated under the Comprehensive Development Framework it should be selective and pass responsibility to other agencies.

Development advocacy. The Bank under Wolfensohn fulfilled increasingly a role as a development advocate – in causes such as corruption, debt forgiveness, trade fairness, and the removal of rich country production subsidies. Advocacy also extended to the energy needs of poor countries, HIV/AIDS, education for girls, and climate change. The use of the Bank as a platform for development advocacy was important and quite consistent with its public goods role.

However, adequate organizational resources must underpin such advocacy work, that is, development research capability. Despite the growth of advocacy, the budget for development research declined during the reorganization to an inadequate level, to be exceeded by the budget for external relations, implying that the latter took precedence over substantive development thinking.

The quality of products. A major expansion of the quality control infrastructure occurred during the reorganization, and the quality of both the Bank's projects and its knowledge products, both at initiation and at completion, were found to have improved steadily during the reorganization period and to have largely met the Strategic Compact

---

[1] Wolfensohn was particularly keen on the 'Bosnia model', where a group of Bank staff went above and beyond the call of normal duty to broker deals in difficult personal circumstances in the midst of a war. See Mallaby's description of this. This ideal, however, is not necessarily one that would be compatible with effective organizational performance.

targets set for them of near 100% satisfactory design quality and about 80% satisfactory project outcome.

There are, however, reasons to question both the value of the expanded infrastructure and the claimed large improvements. Quality is very difficult to measure, and only in the last four years has a major effort been made to measure impact properly, considering the counter-factuals, while the changing character of the projects implemented has probably made the overall performance increasingly prone to overvaluation. The overall impact of the reorganization itself on project performance is not yet clear because of the time lag between project preparation and completion, but the significant dip in quality in the early 1990s can be most simply traced back to the disruption of the 1987–1988 reorganization, rather than to the skills or the dress habits of the project officers. A similar relationship between organizational disruption in the late 1990s and reduced quality may now be showing up in the results. It was organizational disruption, not lack of skills, that reduced project quality.

An organization that devotes large proportions of its resources to 'looking over its shoulder' will tend to be top heavy and dysfunctional, and ineffective in defining and taking on challenges. The Bank should be interested in its operational efficiency and the costs and benefits of its projects and services, but the international donor community should be interested in the broad evaluation lessons from global experience, and should probably pay for such lessons separately.

Skill restructuring. The restructuring of skills was the main input change, intended to complement the changes in product, and central to the reforms. More than 4,000 employees, nearly half of the 1997 workforce, had left by 2002, to be replaced by close to 4,000 new hires.[2]

While in terms of turnover numbers reform objectives were probably achieved, the process by which this occurred was highly flawed. Since the product quality declines as cited in the Wapenhans Report

---

[2] Out of the 4,500 who left the Bank over five years from 1997, about half would have been over and above the normal attrition rate of 4 to 5% per annum. Allowing for greater than normal rates of voluntary departure, either because of monetary incentives or dissatisfaction, it may be reasonably concluded that close to 2,000 employees left the Bank involuntarily over the period.

were already being reversed well before the reorganization started, it was unclear exactly what was the rationale for skill restructuring, what were the appropriate skills, and what was the right way to renew them. It was difficult to see what different outside skill pools or attitudes could be tapped than already existed in the institution, and the stringencies of the working environment in the Bank themselves de-skilled the employees. Much important institutional memory based on country knowledge was lost. Strategic staffing failed to anticipate skill demands, and by 2002, at the end of the reorganization, top management was asking for strengthening of non-specialist areas like project management, where capacity had just been shed. De-layering and re-grading did not achieve their objectives either of increasing teamwork and effectiveness, and were put into reverse. Restructuring was compromised by a stop-go process under budgetary pressure, precisely what the Strategic Compact had undertaken to avoid.

WHY DID THE REFORMS GO WRONG?

In Chapter 9 six possible causal factors were reviewed for why the reforms generally failed. The first was a fundamental one – that an institution such as the Bank was simply the wrong concept for development assistance. But this was set aside. At the more practical organizational level, five other possible causes were weak and obstructionist management and staff, the prevalence of new and untested reform ideas, the inherent difficulties of managing multilateral public organizations, weak leadership, and poor governance. Ideas and organizational systems are not agents of change, however, without actors ready to use them, so here let us revisit just the role of the three agents of change.

Staff and middle management could be faulted. Turnover was traditionally slow and the managers had been in the organization on average for twenty years, a situation that might be blamed for inertia or lack of innovation. Some individuals may have taken advantage of the new management system to play line managers off against staff managers. The implementation of the matrix system, including the initial manager-as-coach concept, the inconsistent and dysfunctional span of management control, and measures such as re-grading, were within management discretion. The eccentricities of the skill restructuring program and the excesses of evaluation scoring were also the result of management decisions. Good management is not regarded as a priority in knowledge-driven organizations, including many development assistance organizations. Thus some of the problem could be traced to the management and rank-and-file employees of the organization.

Top management could be faulted. Top management organization appeared dysfunctional. There was a disconnect between reform vision and implementation, and too little engagement by top management with the latter. The ill-judged introduction of the matrix system combined with the internal market simultaneously with budget cuts were the results of top management decisions. A more cautious, phased approach to introducing new information systems within the Bank could have preempted the expenditure errors and numerous other problems of the system when it was launched. Clear leadership and phased reform might have achieved better results by retaining the focused country team organization plus central advisory and research functions of the previous organizational regime boosted by the unprecedented access to information through the intranet/Internet. The mechanics of the reorganization involved rushed, simultaneous initiatives whereas the institution's problems needed proper diagnosis and targeted changes. Thus part of the problem lies with the leadership and top management.

The governance system could be faulted. The exigencies of the Strategic Compact, along with the board's lack of awareness or expertise and the chief executive's inattention, created an environment in which careful planning and execution was expendable, while it also created time pressures for the introduction of an inadequately tested management system, a complex information system, significant employee turnover, and pressure to claim good performance throughout this process. The assumption that the central problem centered on deficient skills rather than deficient oversight apparently led to costly, largely misdirected, and often pointless reforms. The misdiagnosis was partly wilful because an element on the board seemed to consider a 'shakeout' as an all-purpose cure for organizational problems. Cutting workforces was nothing unusual in the business climate of the late 1990s, and even professional employees got used to the end of tenured jobs. But the frequency of such actions did not provide a justification for any particular one of them.[3]

The institution's governance, despite its critical importance, has never been reformed except marginally and by internal consensus. This meant that a key, problematic, and very costly part of the organization was held sacrosanct while it presided over changes in the rest of the organization. To the extent that momentum was maintained without adequate direction is more testament to the strength rather than the deficiencies of the management and employees. But, basic to effective corporate governance, in the end no organization can police itself.

The reasons for the poor results could also be placed beyond board governance, to the Bank's multiple and conflicting objectives and the pressure of outside interest groups and constituencies. In this environment the board may be unable to act in the best interests of the organization. Pressure, for example from the U.S. administration, may have tended to undermine the very improvement that the United States wanted, because it significantly increased complexity, obscured direction, and led to poor decisions. But effective governance should also have the ability to insulate an organization from external pressure.

Board accommodation of top management decisions may have been exacerbated by a public organization culture that encourages employees to 'hunker down' in the face of hostile pressure. Accordingly, the Bank has absorbed many organizational blows and kept working, while still claiming relentless increases in effectiveness. 'Industrial action' by Bank staff has been extremely rare, the last example being in 1985. This might have made it difficult for the directors and shareholders to gauge or interpret the cost to the organization of the pressure put on it. Indeed, the major shareholders incur less and less financial cost in making demands on the institution as their paid-in capital proportion decreases. This de-linking of power from accountability may have created a form of moral hazard.[4] As the cost of wielding power falls, the

---

[3] Many of the layoffs meant not just unemployment but also a change of country because the Bank's non-U.S. employees only hold temporary residence permits.

[4] See Woods, Ngaire, *The Globalizers; the IMF, the World Bank and their Borrowers*, Cornell Studies in Money, Cornell University Press, March 2006.

appetite for driving the institution to new responsibilities has grown. 'To whatever extent that the Bank has "failed" ', says Devesh Kapur, 'it is the wider bank, its management, Board and above all, major shareholders, that bear the brunt of the responsibility. Power must come with responsibility and there can be no doubt about where the location of power lies'.[5]

In the end, whatever small reform gains were made could almost certainly have been better achieved by a committed and informed leadership executing phased, moderate, and targeted organizational reforms following a rational plan in cooperation with the employees. To achieve this required strong governance, and it is to this that attention needs to be turned if similar future failures are to be avoided.

THE REFORM OF GOVERNANCE

Good governance of the Bank will not of itself resolve the problems either of world development or even, on its own, the problems of the Bank's organization or strategy. Good governance is a necessary, not a sufficient, condition for solving these problems. But if the waste of resources that is associated with the current governance structure could be avoided, then the institution's management would at least be better able to focus on the important issues, increasing the chances that solutions could be found. It is important at least to have a system in place whereby the big issues can be faced squarely and expertly without outside distraction, but with outside guidance.

The board has been subject to nine formal effectiveness reviews over the years, averaging recently about one every three years. The same issues re-emerge with each cohort of directors who ask the same questions about the role, power, and relevance of the board. Almost all reforms actually carried out have been of process. For the past four years the main non-process concern has been with equal board representation ('enhancing the voice of the poor') but not with the efficiency of governance.

[5] Kapur, Devesh, 'From Shareholders to Stakeholders: The Changing Anatomy of Governance at the World Bank', in Pincus, Jonathan and Jeffery Winters, *Reinventing the World Bank*, Cornell University Press, 2002.

There have been a number of outside proposals for the design of a new governance structure[6] and the following points are not a substitute but complementary to those. The basic requirement of an efficient board of executive directors is that it: a) copes with the full range of issues, across both development policy and corporate strategy; b) has freedom to address corporate interests without political or policy interference; c) has the capacity to add value professionally; d) is sufficiently in touch with operations to be able to add that value; and e) is not too expensive. To deal with two major deficiencies, inadequate expertise and inappropriate information, there appear to be two key elements of effective governance that need to be considered in redesigning the system. The first is private sector representation, and the second is inside representation.

The bank has a two-tier governance system, but it has not functioned properly. The first tier, the board of governors, makes high-level policy at a distance, with largely ceremonial meetings twice a year supported by its own staff in home ministries and its Development Committee. It has delegated most of its responsibilities to the second tier, the board of executive directors, which is resident, has its own staff, its standing committees, a large secretariat, and an evaluation department reporting to it. But the inside executive directors are not effectively 'inside', and they do not execute, while the governors are outside but do not supervise. In practice this is a system of two ineffective policy boards.

Board models vary between regions of the world, and within each region they have evolved according to local conditions such as shareholder structures, banking systems, and legal tradition.[7] For example, in the United States, recent change has focused on fiduciary responsibility.[8] In the UK and France, recent changes have sought independent and non-executive directors, and separation of the role of CEO and

[6] E.g., recent studies have been conducted by Ngaire Woods, op cit., and Buira, Ariel, ed., *Reforming the Governance of the IMF and the World Bank*, Anthem, 2005.
[7] See Hopt, Klaus J. and Leyens, Patrick C., 'Board Models in Europe – Recent Developments of Internal Corporate Governance Structures in Germany, the United Kingdom, France, and Italy', ECGI – Law Working Paper No. 18, 2004.
[8] As under the Sarbanes-Oxley Act of 2002 that followed the collapse of Enron and other companies, which establishes new or enhanced reporting standards for all U.S. *public company* boards, management, and public accounting firms.

chairman. In Germany, where governance functions are separated into oversight/supervision and corporate direction, the positions of the CEO and board chairman have been separated and the strategic role of the supervisory board has been strengthened.

While the factors influencing board models internationally have been complex and further affirmation of the solution is called for, the case for a two-tier board of the Bank remains compelling, to cover, on the one hand, development policy and major corporate decisions (such as the appointment of the president or changes in shareholding) and, on the other hand, ongoing development assistance management and corporate strategy decisions.[9] The continental two-tier model has been subject to criticism for allowing management to gain leverage when there are opposing views on the two boards. However, this has not been a determining factor in the Bank, where managerial leverage has been affected by other means. Bearing in mind possible deficiencies in any arrangement, for an institution with the complexity and broad range of activities and issues that the World Bank faces, a formal separation seems to make sense.

The relationship between the two reconstructed boards would need to be carefully worked out. Conflicts between policy and corporate strategy would be expected to arise. However, these conflicts would be more transparent and the reasons for trade-offs and compromises would be public knowledge. Political interference is also unavoidable, but it should be applied transparently through an explicit forum.

The membership of the boards would be critical. One approach would be to create: a) a policy, or supervisory, board of governors consisting nominally of ministers or central bank heads, with 'executive directors' as their alternates; and b) a management board composed of internal and external directors.

Based on this model, the representation of countries on the policy/ supervisory board could be similar to the current structure of the board

---

[9]   Similar ideas for board structure at the IMF have been aired. One proposal, by Peter Kenen at Princeton, is for a combination of a managing board that would replace the present executive board, and a council. The managing board would consist of about sixteen individuals nominated by the managing director. The council would comprise ministers of finance or equivalents, appoint the managing director, ratify appointments to the managing board, adopt the Fund's budget, and deal with funding approvals beyond the norm.

of governors. However, because it would not make operational decisions, its size may not be as critical. This would allow it possibly to expand in numbers beyond the current twenty-four to improve the distribution of votes. The management board of directors would be both 'internal' and 'external'. External directors would be appointed on the basis of experience both in development and development finance, and in corporate leadership. The representation of countries on the management board would be restricted through an appropriate formula since the size of a functionally efficient management board should be about fifteen.

Subject to an appropriate selection formula, member country governments could submit a slate of nominations for approximately eleven available external directorships of the management board. This slate of nominees would be from both the public and the private sectors. They would include active or former top-level corporate, development, and financial sector executives as well as senior development ministry and treasury officials.

The second group of about four directors on the management board would be the inside group. These would be likely to include the president and the (senior) vice presidents for operations, finance, and human resources.

The president could chair this board and may sit on the supervisory board. In accordance with current thinking, top management may however be split into a) a chairman and b) a CEO. This arrangement could allow a compromise, if indeed a compromise was the only practical way forward, whereby the chairman could continue as a U.S. appointee, purely in recognition of the United States as the host nation, while the CEO was appointed on merit. Each could chair one board.

The term of office of a supervisory board director should be adequate to permit meaningful contributions to the work of the board, subject possibly to a minimum rather than a maximum, and to renewal for successive terms. The term of office of a director on the management board would be set according to efficiency standards, not pressure for rotation, and would generally be expected to exceed three years.

The management board would be permitted a large degree of independence that would allow it to make operational decisions, including all lending decisions, with the possible exception of a category of extra-ordinary loans that require policy changes. It would operate in a framework of 'constrained discretion' that would provide the guidance within which it is able to focus on ensuring that policies are well delivered. Such a regime enables the leadership, within the constraint of clear overall, longer term, objectives, to exercise decision-making power in the shorter run. The management board would need three main conditions for it to be effective. First, it would need freedom of action within broad policy guidelines. This requires that it is trusted, which in turn requires that its activities are transparent. Second, it would need to be held visibly accountable for its task, in a credible accountability-enforcing process. Third, and crucially, accountability enforcement would be free of inappropriate political interference.[10]

THE WORK OF THE NEW GOVERNANCE STRUCTURE

Along with its direction of existing activities, the new governance structure would have the task of rationalizing the changes made during the reorganization, and reshaping the Bank for the future.

Critical decisions would be needed on the evolution of the matrix and internal market systems, and the role, scale, and positioning of the networks vis-à-vis operational units. There would need to be an investigation of the financing–knowledge product split from the point of view of the Bank's product strategy and financial sustainability. Product strategy would need to address the Bank's pro-poor focus, middle income country focus and its selectivity, and the centrality of global public goods. Process concerns would need to review the way in which fiduciary and safeguard responsibilities are integrated into operational work and assess the level of functionality of the complex quality control, evaluation, and anti-corruption structures, to allow management to focus on operational efficiency and development effectiveness.

The reformed governance structure would be charged with expertly tackling the long-term Bank strategy, and how it should be configured

---

[10] These suggestions are partly based on a communication from David Vines.

for it. This may require a clean slate, returning to essentials and examining the end-to-end business process and objectives, to draw up a blueprint of how the organization should be configured in the long run and then developing a strategy of moving toward that configuration in phases over time – perhaps a '2020 project'.

In this task the governors would be able to consider the proposals of several outside observers. For example, Gilbert and Vines[11] considered the optimal allocation of effort relative to development impact between lending (the 'conditionality bank') and knowledge (the 'knowledge bank'). In 'Reinventing the World Bank'[12] Pincus and Winters add a third option – the knowledge bank, a development bank, and a 'niche bank'. The knowledge bank would be similar to the Gilbert and Vines' version; the lending bank would focus on mobilizing international resources for large infrastructure loans that the private sector cannot initiate, rather than lending for macro-economic reforms. Their third option would be that of the Meltzer Commission, that is, an institution that is significantly reduced in size, cutting out loans to investment grade countries, focusing on certain regions, and shifting to grants. Ngaire Woods proposes four options: the knowledge bank, the listening bank, the dams and irrigation (infrastructure) bank, and the 'big, expensive bank'.[13] The infrastructure bank and the knowledge bank would be similar to the Pincus and Winters' options. The listening bank would specialize in participatory development programs, derivative of the Wolfensohnian CDF and the PRSP. The big, expensive Bank is in essence the current configuration, with little control over its objectives and an expanding budget to fulfill them.

Whatever the configuration adopted, a key direction in which the new Bank would need to go is to strengthen its role as the supplier of global public goods while correspondingly de-emphasizing areas where the public goods role is inherently problematic. The problematic areas might include aspects of its 'private sector development' mandate such

[11] Gilbert, Christopher L. and David Vines, *The World Bank: Structure and Policies*, Cambridge University Press, 2000.
[12] Pincus, Jonathan R. and Jeffery A. Winters, *Reinventing the World Bank*, Cornell University Press, 2002.
[13] In Birdsall, Nancy, ed., *Rescuing the World Bank: A CGD Working Group Report and Selected Essays*, Center for Global Development, 2006.

as improving the financing and growth of private enterprise. This is not, of course, because private enterprise development is unimportant, but because it is inherently difficult for the Bank to design interventions in this area that cost-effectively create additionality over and above what the private sector would be doing anyway.

There is a vast array of possible interventions that could be included under the global public goods heading, and which could provide a full agenda of business to the Bank, to be addressed through both project assistance and advocacy. These range through the areas of global health, climate change (including the creation of new global markets such as carbon trading), environmental protection, new seed varieties, new energy sources, certain key international information (such as may be needed for economic and financial stability or civil order), and also more traditional areas such as the development of international waterways and other major cross-border infrastructures that cannot be coordinated and/or financed by single governments or private investors. After his arrival in 2007, Robert Zoellick started to move the institution more in the direction of global health, climate change, and the environment.

The production of a blueprint is more urgent and at the same time more difficult because the major shareholders in the Bank have treated it increasingly as a *platform* for broad development initiatives and wide-ranging public mandates, and not as a *corporation*. One of the best illustrations of this is the enormous trust fund responsibility that it has steadily assumed, managing other donor funds of more than $10 billion. The all-encompassing *platform* approach has also allowed the proliferation of small, expensive projects and capacity-building assistance that cannot be covered by revenue.

Most recently, as the costs of the development assistance platform approach have started to become apparent, the Bank is turning back to infrastructure projects and is considering new forms of profitable, large budget-support lending. So a dualism is being entrenched whereby very large money-making projects will subsidize very small money-losing projects, including money-losing trust fund management, on the same development assistance platform. But this is not part of a coherent strategy; instead, it is more an ad hoc response to evolving circumstances.

The Bank cannot operate efficiently as a 'development assistance platform'. A corporation cannot pursue efficiency objectives internally if it is subject to proliferating mandates from outside, none of which have been thought through from a cost-effectiveness point of view. Apart from the lack of attention to financial sustainability, the 'development assistance platform', with or without big projects, creates organizational confusion and management disarray that are not only dysfunctional for the institution itself but dysfunctional for the development process, and reduces the quality of development thinking and project design and implementation. Efficient organization leads to efficient development assistance, and the obverse.

Only if the organization rationalizes its profile and narrows down its responsibilities can it be called to account for its efficiency, especially by those very outside interests that are piling on the responsibilities, the shareholders. For these reasons there is a presumption that the corporate model should be preferred, and it follows that there should be an effort by the international donor community and the Bank's governors to rationalize development assistance under the responsibility of separate coherent corporate entities.

A clean slate blueprint toward which the institution evolves over time is one that will allow thinking unfettered by vested interests in current organizational structures and products. Expert governance will not be able to resolve it in any automatic way, but it will at least bring to bear on the issue without continual distractions the best resources available.

SHOULD THE OVERSEERS REMAIN IN-HOUSE?

The introductory chapter referred to the disagreement between Britain and the United States at the foundation of the Bank about whether the executive directors should be located in Washington or in their home countries. The U.S. view prevailed then, but the time is overdue for the original British view to be adopted. Despite the fact that they walk the corridors and have access to large secretariats, the executive directors have not been able to adequately penetrate the inner workings of the Bank because, *inter alia*, they do not have legitimacy as inside directors, they have too short a tenure even after reforms, and they are not able to acquire information in an appropriate form. In-organization location, combined with diplomatic status, seems, perversely, to have obscured the vision of the overseers, while at the same time creating the potential for collusive relationships and a lack of systematic oversight, not because of intent but because of the organizational facts of life. The age of videoconferencing and instant communication, however, makes distance oversight quite feasible combined with on-location board meetings at agreed intervals, which would reduce the potential for and the appearance of collusion. The era of the quasi-ambassadors should be ended, with board members being stationed in their home countries while retaining, if necessary, a liaison office on the Bank premises.[14] The management board would be located in their primary places of work outside the Bank, but would have access to research staff located in the Bank – a reduced and restructured version of the existing corporate secretariat.

THE ORGANIZATIONAL GAINS OF GOVERNANCE REFORM

Beyond the improved effectiveness of governance itself, there would be other important spin-off benefits from reform that would enable the Bank to operate more efficiently. These can be divided into three.

First, the heavy service infrastructure of board support (the directors' staff and the corporate secretariat) could be partly dismantled if a newly constructed management board does a professionally expert, value-adding job on specialist rather than country constituency lines, reducing duplication, and if some of the management board directors are insiders. The management board research staff would be divided by specialization, not as currently by country constituency, and operational information would not be duplicated many times in the service of country constituencies, thus saving significant staff costs. The policy/

---

[14] Mervyn King, Governor of the Bank of England, speaking about the IMF, also suggested a non-resident board that meets some six to eight times a year. Directors would comprise senior finance ministry or central bank officials, subject to a clearly defined remit and guidelines on accountability.

supervisory board members would use their own home civil service staff resources, as is the current case.

The dismantling of the current dysfunctional relationship between management and board and the reduction in the time and cost burden of presenting unchallengeable documents to the board would help the management to assume direct responsibility for the quality of its work rather than spending its time discussing how to improve quality and pre-empting challenges from the board. With a working specialist board, directors might also be able, subject to limits, to reach down into the organization to summon up responses on particular questions and management could save time by presenting draft papers for preliminary board feedback. Returning quality responsibility to the producers of the actual services would reduce transactions costs and clean up the business process, in line again with the advice of Messrs Hammer and Champy.

Second, with a regular and transparent governance system and a functioning, expert board with a clearly defined independent role and a mandate to mediate and channel outside criticism, from the U.S. Congress or elsewhere, the outside demands for transparency would be more likely to subside and the Bank would be in a more secure position to get off its performance treadmill, substituting its score-cards by realistic assessments for the world at large of what can and cannot be achieved for poor people, and advocating appropriate change.

Third, the internal advisory functions, fiduciary functions, and skill pools, along with the burgeoning evaluation capacity, which have inflated overhead costs and reduced front-line efforts, could be significantly cut or redeployed. If expert board, and top management, direction is able to focus on aligning resources and objectives, identifying and rationalizing the redundant parts of the institution over a period of time, then the savings could be used to better fund the core operational work. This would then allow the operations staff to a) focus attention where it should be – on how to make development effective, and b) cut the amount of time spent in raising outside funds to support development work. Related to this, the spinning off of development impact evaluation to an outside international body would help concentrate the institution's resources on improving the design quality and cost-benefit ratios of its products.

If these changes occurred, several hundred professional jobs could be released from back-line functions to refocus on operations and the design of development. The Bank could have a truly front-line posture that is better positioned to help the poor, deliver global public goods, or carry out other mandates. It is likely that the potential transfer of resources to direct development efforts would amount to several hundred million dollars a year, or up to 30% of the administrative budget.

GOVERNANCE: OTHER PERSPECTIVES

The political nature of the organization and its continued multiple objectives, it could be argued, results in inevitable inefficiencies that have to be tolerated in the interests of multi-country consensus, and radical changes based on private sector practice are not relevant when that system was never intended to emulate the private sector. As long as the institution is in the long run able to make reasonably sound decisions, oversight is not a critical issue, and the governance somehow works.

However, even if political interference and sub-optimal governance are inevitable, there are several major reasons why this argument is unacceptable. First, the institution's governance is not insignificant in terms of the organizational resources that it uses up – on the contrary, it is enormously costly in direct cash terms, in terms of its indirect costs and its incentive effects, costing directly and indirectly as much as $400 million a year. Second, the existing quid pro quo relationship of the board and management is collusive. The lack of a clear space between the overseers and the overseen, or a precise clarification of their respective de facto roles, involves a conflict of interest and creates a *potential* for continuing ineffectiveness. Third, there are bound to be hidden efficiency and incentive costs to supporting (often cynically) the continuation of a system that does not work properly and protects vested interests. Fourth, and obviously, the governance system as it is currently cannot deal effectively with complex organizational or policy problems.

The often ill-informed and self-interested attitude of some shareholding countries has bordered on irresponsibility. If a global governance institution is to continue to be a conscious vehicle for rich country foreign policy, then that should be a transparent feature of the organization, just as bilateral aid agencies may well be instruments of their own countries' foreign policies. But in that case the Bank's 170 or so other members would also have the option of and indeed probably the interest in opting out. And with the rise in economic power of the Asian industrial nations and energy producers, this is a viable option. Nations whose views are currently underrepresented would have a greater incentive to establish their own institutions, sovereign wealth funds, regional banks, and regional monetary funds, as they have started to do.

For the future, the key to the reform of the World Bank has to be *shareholder accountability* rather than management accountability. In addition, contrary to the perception in conservative circles of a 'public bureaucracy' that is inherently inefficient, wasteful, and tainted with unproductive socialist thoughts, it should be appreciated that ill-informed and misplaced outside pressure to improve performance has itself probably been a main reason for deficiencies in performance.

LESSONS OF REORGANIZATION

At the start of this study I asked the question about whether twenty years of reorganization (including $500 million of reengineering investment over 1997 to 2001) was justified. The answer has been 'no'. The principal good things that happened during the reorganization could have been achieved by moderate reforms at relatively low cost under strong, committed, professional leadership without a bias for world fame. In many ways, the useful changes were already taking place. Strong and committed leadership alone could have created a stronger country focus, improved processes and information and better management within this system, and also strengthened the Bank as an advocate, without collateral damage. There are indications that the current regime might do better in this regard.

The 1990s was a heady era for the corporate world – first the re-engineering revolution and then the technology boom. But Michael Hammer and others came to revisit their prescriptions. To reiterate, Hammer said: '[P]erhaps predictably, re-engineering quickly became a bandwagon that everyone tried to jump on; but, problematically not everyone knew precisely what it was he or she was getting involved in. . . .. Give me re-engineering and give it to me fast' was the command from many uninformed chief executives. This was a situation ripe for disaster. Re-engineering came to be viewed as an easy panacea that the CEO can simply delegate. The reorganization of the Bank was one of these cases. It is now more bureaucratic, more enmeshed in confusing objectives, more hostage to outside pressure, and more subject to over-complex projects. The claim that it is 'better positioned to fight poverty' just does not stand up.

On his arrival at the Bank in 1995, Wolfensohn said that he found 'enormous cynicism' and lack of commitment. He seemed to assume that the problem lay with his newly acquired pool of employees rather than a poorly run organization. The reason for the situation as he found it was not so much cynicism as frustration at working in a difficult environment under weak top-level direction for a long period of time. The employees were, for the most part, ready to make changes but, as in all organizations, needed to believe that the new leader, despite his neophyte ideas about development and his reluctance to listen to other people's views, was able to lead change effectively. Had he been able to understand and respond constructively to such a dynamic, he might indeed have led meaningful change.

The lessons from the generally mishandled change process are to have a reasonably long-term plan that has been properly thought through – not based on impulsive reactions to events, or the pressure of fashion, or to a political constituency; to do it carefully and to take one major step at a time and assess the results; and to make simple changes rather than com-plex ones, including supporting worthwhile existing processes of change. For the future, a clean slate approach may provide the long-term blueprint that the Bank could move toward on a phased basis, say a '2020 project'.

This approach is not the one that was recommended in the corporate revolution literature, but it is the one increasingly recommended since then, and certainly by one author who wrote: '[T]he degree of radical change called for and often implemented was in reality disastrous to the long-term interest of the organizations involved ... a few years later companies are beginning to understand the price of their decisions. They had sacrificed many of their best people'.[15]

Ten years after the start of the reorganization, the pattern of the World Bank's lending operations is returning to where it was a long time ago. From 2005 IBRD lending recovered a little, partly as a result of new infrastructure loans to India and other Asian countries. Infrastructure loans to India were among the first the Bank ever gave to a developing country. The unexpected return to its roots is perhaps an epitaph for the years of re-engineering. It was, for the most part, not worth it. It would be best to leave behind that heroic era and simply work on the serious problems that have to be dealt with in the interests of world economic development, without fanfare, under leadership that wants to work on the details, with rational corporate management, and without poorly conceived doctrinaire pressure from outside, or inside.

Effective organization of the World Bank has taken second priority throughout its history behind the special interests and objectives of its constituencies. Yet effective organization is a key to effective practice and, by extension, a determinant of developmental effectiveness. The reorganization of governance is a key to organizational effectiveness, and therefore must also impact development effectiveness. Reform of governance will not of itself improve the quality of development assistance. But it is a necessary condition. It is equally necessary to remove the dead weight of reviewing and checking, reintegrate knowledge with practice, and restore the judgment of individuals in doing the best that can be done.

A LAST THOUGHT ON FOREIGN AID

As well as having an ambiguous effect on economic growth, foreign aid is at best quite marginal to the world's economic activities. Its resource

---

[15] MacDonald, John, *Calling a Halt to Mindless Change; a Plea for Commonsense Management*, American Management Association, 1998.

flows are dwarfed by the impact of import tariffs and controls, agricultural and industrial subsidies within the rich nations, indebtedness, and even by the level of personal remittances by migrant workers, while its qualitative contribution is overwhelmed by the institutional and cultural issues that affect the possibilities of development. It is sobering that the amount of money spent in Iraq up to 2008 exceeded the real value of the non-military U.S. foreign aid budget for the entire world over about the last thirty years, and far exceeded the total U.S. taxpayers' contribution to the IDA and IBRD combined since their foundation. The total value of annual subsidies to rich country farmers alone would pay for clean water and sewage for all; pay off the debt of the most heavily indebted countries; provide access to energy for all for twenty years; provide basic health and nutrition for the entire world, including the fight against AIDS, TB, and Malaria; and pay for universal education.[16]

In addition to its relatively small size, foreign aid is limited by its own internal anomalies, which go along with its grant-based, publicly subsidized, and politicized nature. It also consumes to dubious effect an enormous amount of human resources worldwide, remarkably and disproportionately highly educated, devoted to teaching, research, writing, governance, administration, consultancy, implementation, management, monitoring, and evaluation.[17]

But even so, much specific assistance is helpful, both at the micro-level, and when it addresses global problems that neither individual governments nor individual businesses are willing to address on their own. Given that properly conceived, designed, and delivered assistance can be worthwhile and cost-effective, the enhanced performance of existing organizations becomes an important concern, and the World Bank is an integral part of that.

---

[16] Estimate by Friends of the Earth at the Johannesburg Development Summit of September 2002.

[17] Riddell, Roger, *Does Foreign Aid Really Work?*, Oxford, 2007, is a recent, serious part of the enormous human resource pool dedicated to the aid industry. The voluminous writing on aid effectiveness does not, however, seem to adequately address its rapidly decreasing importance as foreign private investment flows and personal wage remittances overwhelm it. The marginalization of aid might be more likely explained by the sociology of post-colonial societies than by earnest attempts to evaluate its development impact.

A globally responsible economic development institution, transcending national interests, is increasingly needed that has the professional authority and legitimacy, and the financial muscle, to address and influence global economic development problems and provide global public goods. The balance of power in development finance is shifting away from the Bank's donor shareholders. In April 2008, President Zoellick asked Sovereign Wealth Funds to channel $30 billion to Africa, a mere 1% of their holdings but more than the total of the previous seven years' Bank lending in Africa.[18] Unless the rich countries take seriously the requirements for sustaining the integrity of an effective world organization through both increased effectiveness and equitable treatment of its members, there is a good chance, indeed a near certainty, that global economic governance will be hurt and initiatives for economic development will split regionally and geopolitically as the energy producers and the new industrial powers of Asia assume a world role.

[18] Zoellick spoke at the Center for Global Development, Washington, DC, on April 2, 2008. Reported in *World Bank Press Review*, April 3, 2008.

Index

academics
as Bank managers, 68
qualifications of, 101–102,
275–277
activist groups/interests. *See also*
advocacy/advocated positions;
Bretton Woods Project;
Mobilization for Global Justice;
Structural Adjustment
Participatory Review Initiative
(SAPRI)
broad opposition, 31–33
NGOs, 13–14, 232, 241
Adams, Jim, 94
additionality, 174–177
adjustment lending
and loan conditionality, 121–124
opposition to, 25, 27–31
and product reorganization, 152–
153, 283–284
PRSCs, 133–136, 160–161
SAPRI, 124–126
shift from, 9
administrative costs. *See* costs
advisory services/income, 149
advocacy/advocated positions
actions vs. politics, 217–218
and board papers, 254
development advocacy, 147–148,
285
and leadership qualifications, 278–
279, 301
and organizational resources, 153

African countries
aid to, xii
capacity building, 129, 130, 183
delinquent borrowers, 201
loss provisions, 203
RIDPs, 156–157
structural adjustment lending to, 29–30
African Development Bank, 21–23
aid/economic growth relationship, xii–
xiii
aid-for-development, x–xi, 212
aid-for-reform, 28, 125–126, 136, 152–
153
aid-optimism, xiv–xv
aid-pessimism, xiv
Albania, 29–30
anti-corruption/corruption issues
bureaucracy, 186
country selectivity, 131
Department of Institutional Integrity
(DII), 56–57, 105–106
evaluation infrastructure, 184–185
and institution/capacity building, 153
and Iraq reconstruction, 56
and poor societies, 130–131
'Wolfowitz Affair', 250–252
Argentina, 176, 183, 201–203
Armenia, 179, 180–181
Articles of Agreement, 4, 17, 274–275
Arun 111 project, 27
Asian crisis loans/lending
and Bank profits, 195–196
contradictory fiscal policies, 30